CAN ONLY ONE RELIGION BE TRUE?

PAUL KNITTER AND HAROLD NETLAND IN DIALOGUE

ROBERT B. STEWART, EDITOR

Fortress Press
Minneapolis

CAN ONLY ONE RELIGION BE TRUE?

Paul Knitter and Harold Netland in Dialogue

Cover image: Religious symbols © iStockphoto.com / pop_jop; Medieval World Map ©iStockphoto.com / Classix

Cover design: Tory Herman

Library of Congress Cataloging-in-Publication Data is available

ISBN: 978-0-8006-9928-4

Manufactured in the U.S.A.

In piam memoriam
John Paul Newport
(1917–2000)

CONTENTS

Contributors

Paul Copan (Ph.D., Marquette University) is the Pledger Family Chair of Philosophy and Ethics at Palm Beach Atlantic University in West Palm Beach, Florida. He is the author of several books, including *Loving Wisdom: Christian Philosophy of Religion* (Chalice, 2007) and *"True for You, but Not for Me"* (Bethany House, 2007), and he is coauthor of *Creation out of Nothing: A Biblical, Philosophical, and Scientific Exploration* (Baker Academic, 2004). He has coedited a number of books, including *The Rationality of Theism* (Routledge, 2003), *The Routledge Companion to the Philosophy of Religion* (Routledge, 2012), and *Philosophy of Religion: Classic and Contemporary Issues* (Blackwell, 2007). In addition, he has written many articles in professional philosophical and theological journals. He has served as president of the Evangelical Philosophical Society, and he lives with his wife, Jacqueline, and their six children in West Palm Beach.

Paul Rhodes Eddy (Ph.D., Marquette University) is Professor of Biblical and Theological Studies at Bethel University in St. Paul, Minnesota, and Teaching Pastor at Woodland Hills Church in St. Paul. He has authored, coauthored and coedited several books, including *John Hick's Pluralist Philosophy of World Religions* (Ashgate, 2002), *The Jesus Legend: A Case for the Historical Reliability of the Synoptic Jesus Tradition* (Baker, 2007), *The Historical Jesus: Five Views* (InterVarsity, 2009), *Across the Spectrum: Understanding Issues in Evangelical Theology* (Baker, 2009), and *Justification: Five Views* (InterVarsity, 2011). He has also authored a number of articles and essays related to the theology of religions and the historical study of Jesus.

Millard J. Erickson (Ph.D., Northwestern University) has taught at Southwestern Baptist Theological Seminary, Western Seminary (Portland and San Jose), and Truett Seminary, Baylor University. He has authored numerous books, including *Christian Theology* (Baker, 1986, 1998, 2013), *The Word Became Flesh: A Contemporary Incarnational Christology* (Baker, 1991), *Truth or Consequences: The Promise and Perils of Postmodernism* (InterVarsity, 2001), and

How Shall They Be Saved? The Destiny of Those Who Do Not Hear of Jesus (Baker, 1996).

R. Douglas Geivett (Ph.D., University of Southern California) is Professor of Philosophy at the Talbot Department of Philosophy, Biola University in La Mirada, California. In addition to contributing numerous articles to various philosophical and theological journals, as well as writing numerous chapters in books, he has written *Evil and the Evidence for God* and is coeditor of *Being Good: Christian Virtues for Everyday Life* (Eerdmans, 2011), *In Defense of Miracles: A Comprehensive Case for God's Action in History* (InterVarsity, 1997), and *Contemporary Perspectives on Religious Epistemology* (Oxford University Press, 1993). His interests range over the philosophy of religion, epistemology, and the history of modern philosophy.

S. Mark Heim (Ph.D., Boston College–Andover Newton joint doctoral program) is the Samuel Abbot Professor of Christian Theology at Andover Newton Theological School. He has been deeply involved in issues of religious pluralism and Christian ecumenism. He is the author of *Is Christ the Only Way?* (Judson, 1985), *Salvations: Truth and Difference in Religion* (Orbis, 1995), *The Depth of the Riches: A Trinitarian Theology of Religious Ends* (Eerdmans, 2001), and *Saved from Sacrifice: A Theology of the Cross* (Eerdmans, 2006). He has also edited several volumes, including *Faith to Creed: Ecumenical Perspectives on the Affirmation of the Apostolic Faith in the Fourth Century* (Eerdmans, 1991) and *Grounds for Understanding: Ecumenical Resources for Responses to Religious Pluralism* (Eerdmans, 1998). An ordained American Baptist minister, Heim represents his denomination on the Faith and Order Commissions of the National Council and World Council of Churches. He has served on numerous ecumenical commissions and interfaith groups, including the Christian-Muslim relations committee of the National Council of Churches and the planning team for the current Muslim-Baptist dialogue in North America. He has served as a member of the Christian Scholars of Judaism group and has been elected to the American Theological Society. He was awarded a Henry Luce fellowship in 2009–2010 for a comparative theology project on atonement in Christianity, Buddhism, and Islam.

John Hick (D.Phil., University of Oxford; D.Litt., University of Edinburgh) taught at Cornell University, Princeton Theological Seminary, Cambridge University, and Claremont Graduate University. A seminal thinker in the field of theology of religions, he wrote many books on the subject, including *God and the Universe of Faith* (Macmillan, 1973), *God Has Many Names* (Westminster John Knox, 1982), *The Myth of Christian Uniqueness*, edited with Paul Knitter (Orbis, 1987), *A Christian Theology of Religions: The Rainbow of Faiths* (SCM/Westminster John Knox, 1995), *The Metaphor of God Incarnate*, (2nd ed., SCM, 2005), and *An Interpretation of Religion: Human Responses to the Transcendent* (Palgrave, 2004), for which he received the Grawemeyer Award for new religious thinking.

Paul F. Knitter (L.Th., Pontifical Gregorian University; D.Th., University of Marburg) is the Paul Tillich Professor of Theology, World Religions, and Culture at Union Theological Seminary, New York. He received a Licentiate in theology from the Pontifical Gregorian University in Rome (1966) and a doctorate from the University of Marburg, Germany (1972). His many books include *No Other Name? A Critical Survey of Christian Attitudes toward the World Religions* (Orbis, 1985), *One Earth Many Religions: Multifaith Dialogue and Global Responsibility* (Orbis, 1995), *Introducing Theologies of Religions* (Orbis, 2002), and *Without Buddha I Could Not Be a Christian* (Oneworld, 2009). From 1986 to 2004, he served on the board of directors for CRISPAZ (Christians for Peace in El Salvador). He is also on the board of trustees for the International, Interreligious Peace Council, formed after the 1993 World Parliament of Religions to promote interreligious peacemaking projects.

Nancy Fuchs Kreimer (Ph.D., Temple University) serves as Director of the Department of Multifaith Studies and Initiatives at the Reconstructionist Rabbinical College, where she is also Associate Professor of Religious Studies. She holds a master of religion degree from Yale Divinity School and Ph.D. from Temple University in Jewish-Christian relations. She serves on the boards of Clergy Beyond Borders and the Islamic Society of North America's Shoulder-to-Shoulder. Recent publications include "Trouble Praying," in *My Neighbor's Faith: Stories of Interreligious Encounter, Growth and Transformation* (Orbis, 2012). She is currently coediting a book of Jewish spiritual essays, *Chapters of the Heart* (Wipf & Stock, 2013).

Harold A. Netland (Ph.D., Claremont Graduate University) is professor of philosophy of religion and intercultural studies at Trinity Evangelical Divinity School in Deerfield, Illinois. He completed his doctoral studies under

John Hick at Claremont Graduate University in 1983. He has lived much of his life in Japan and taught at Tokyo Christian University from 1990 to 1993, at which time he began teaching at Trinity. Among his publications are *Dissonant Voices: Religious Pluralism and the Question of Truth* (Eerdmans, 1991), *Encountering Religious Pluralism* (InterVarsity, 2001), and with Keith Yandell, *Buddhism: A Christian Exploration and Appraisal* (InterVarsity/Paternoster, 2009).

Robert B. Stewart (Ph.D., Southwestern Baptist Theological Seminary) is Professor of Philosophy and Theology, and Greer-Heard Professor of Faith and Culture at New Orleans Baptist Theological Seminary. He is also pastor of Ames Blvd. Baptist Church in Marrero, Louisiana. He is editor of *The Resurrection of Jesus: John Dominic Crossan and N. T. Wright in Dialogue* (Fortress, 2006), *Intelligent Design: William A. Dembski and Michael Ruse in Dialogue* (Fortress, 2007), *The Future of Atheism: Alister McGrath and Daniel Dennett in Dialogue* (Fortress, 2008), and *The Reliability of the New Testament: Bart D. Ehrman and Daniel B. Wallace in Dialogue* (Fortress, 2011). A contributor to the *Cambridge Dictionary of Christianity*, he has published articles and book reviews in numerous journals.

Terrence W. Tilley (Ph.D., Graduate Theological Union, Berkeley) is the Avery Cardinal Dulles, S.J., Professor of Catholic Theology and Chair of the Theology Department at Fordham University in New York. He has previously taught at Georgetown University, St. Michael's College (Vermont), the Florida State University, and the University of Dayton. He has written reviews of over a hundred books and scores of scholarly articles, edited or coedited three books, and authored ten books, most recently *Faith: What It Is and What It Isn't* (Orbis, 2010). He has been elected and served as president of the College Theology Society, the Catholic Theological Society of America, and the Society for Philosophy of Religion.

Keith E. Yandell (Ph.D., Ohio State University) was Julius R. Weinberg Professor of Philosophy at the University of Wisconsin, Madison, until his retirement. His many books include *The Epistemology of Religious Experience* (Cambridge University Press, 1994); *Philosophy of Religion: A Contemporary Introduction* (Routledge, 1999); with Harold Netland, *Buddhism: A Christian Exploration and Appraisal* (InterVarsity/Paternoster, 2009); *Christianity and Philosophy* (Eerdmans, 1984); *Basic Issues in the Philosophy of Religion* (Allyn and

Bacon, 1971). He also served as editor for *Faith and Narrative* (Oxford University Press, 2001).

PREFACE

The purpose of the Greer-Heard Point-Counterpoint Forum in Faith and Culture is to provide a venue for fair-minded dialogue to take place on subjects of importance in religion or culture. The intention is to have a respected Evangelical scholar dialogue with a respected non-Evangelical or non-Christian scholar. The forum is intended to be a dialogue rather than a debate. As such, it is a bit more freewheeling than a traditional debate, and it is not scored. The goal is a respectful exchange of ideas, without compromise. So often in our contemporary culture, the sorts of issues that the forum addresses stoke the emotions, and consequently the rhetoric is of such a nature as to ensure that communication does *not* take place. There may be a place and time for such preaching to the choir, but minds are rarely changed as a result of such activity—nor are better arguments forthcoming. The result often is that what passes for argument is really nothing more than a prolonged example of the straw-man fallacy.

The subject of the 2009 Greer-Heard Point-Counterpoint Forum in Faith and Culture was "Pluralism: Can Only One Religion Be True?" In our post-9/11 culture, this is a hugely important question for all persons, whether they are religious or not. The dialogue partners were Paul F. Knitter of Union Theological Seminary in New York City and Harold A. Netland of Trinity Evangelical Divinity School in Deerfield, Illinois.

The dialogue took place March 27–28, 2009, in the Leavell Chapel on the campus of the host institution, New Orleans Baptist Theological Seminary. On a stormy March evening, the chapel was filled with an enthusiastic and appreciative crowd of approximately seven hundred people who had come to hear the exchange. The discussion between Knitter and Netland was spirited but extremely civil and frequently punctuated with good-natured humor. Knitter and Netland are passionately committed to their positions but also good friends with deep respect for the other's scholarship. Such was obvious. One of the consistent fruits of the forum has been the realization that disagreement does not have to be shrill or heated, and that one does not have to check one's convictions at the door in order for respectful dialogue to take place.

Along with my introductory chapter, this book includes a transcript of the March 27–28, 2009, dialogue between Knitter and Netland (including audience Q&A), as well as the papers presented the following day by S. Mark Heim, R. Douglas Geivett, and Terrence W. Tilley. In addition to the papers that were presented at the Greer-Heard Forum, other essays are included. Keith Yandell was scheduled to speak, but illness at the last moment kept him from being able to attend. Nevertheless, his paper was read at the conference and is part of this book. In addition, there are essays by Millard J. Erickson, Paul Copan, and Paul Rhodes Eddy, who were present and read these papers for the EPS event. Nancy Fuchs Kreimer and the late John Hick also were willing to contribute chapters for the book.

While one could easily note issues that are still not addressed in this volume or think of significant scholars who are not included, we believe these chapters make for a rich treatment of the issue. No doubt readers will have to judge for themselves whether this is, in fact, the case.

I am grateful that Fortress Press has seen fit to allow us to present the fruit of the 2009 Greer-Heard Forum. I trust that you will read it with an open mind and carefully consider what each author has to say. If you will, I have no doubt that you will be the richer for having done so.

Robert Stewart
March 1, 2012
New Orleans Baptist Theological Seminary

Acknowledgments

Thanking others in print always causes me a bit of anxiety because I fear I will fail to recognize someone who truly deserves a word of appreciation. But many deserve to be publicly thanked—and even praised—so I must go on. First of all, I must thank Bill and Carolyn Heard for their passion to have a forum where leading scholars can dialogue about important issues in faith and culture in a civilized manner and on a balanced playing field—and their willingness to fund such a project! Without them, the Greer-Heard Point-Counterpoint Forum in Faith and Culture would be a dream rather than a reality. As always, I thank Dr. Chuck Kelley, NOBTS president, for his support and encouragement.

I must thank my former assistant, Rhyne Putman. He did everything he was asked to do and more—and all of it with a cheerful attitude. As in past years, he maintained the Greer-Heard website. He also oversaw any number of other things that didn't fall under somebody else's job description..

The forum would never have come off successfully without the efforts of J. P. Cox and his staff at the Providence Learning Center. J. P. is a true professional. I also am grateful to Vanee Daure and her team for the work they did in media support. Sheila Taylor and the NOBTS cafeteria staff must be applauded for serving numerous meals of all varieties to large numbers. Without the high-quality graphic art and public relations work of Boyd Guy and Gary Myers, the task would have proven too great. Lisa Joyner of Johnson Ferry Baptist Church in Marietta, Georgia, deserves a word of recognition for her work in producing the conference programs and CD case covers.

I am appreciative of the Evangelical Philosophical Society (EPS) for sponsoring a "special event" that took place in conjunction with the Greer-Heard Forum. I also thank Scott Smith for his efforts in publicizing the event and Joe Gorra for providing EPS support materials.

I am grateful to NOBTS provost Steve Lemke for making it possible for several university groups to attend the event. His efforts, along with those of Archie England and Page Brooks and their respective staffs, were much appreciated.

Our contributors, Paul Knitter and Harold Netland, along with Terry Tilley, Doug Geivett, and Mark Heim, must all be thanked. Keith Yandell was scheduled to speak, but illness at the last moment kept him from being able to attend. Nevertheless, his paper was read at the conference, and I am very pleased to have it as part of this book. In addition, Millard Erickson, Paul Copan, and Paul Eddy were all present and read papers for the EPS event, which are included in this book. Furthermore, I must thank Nancy Fuchs Kreimer and the late John Hick for being willing to contribute chapters for the book.

Brantley Scott and the staff at the NOBTS campus LifeWay bookstore deserve a word of thanks for working so hard at the book signing and for going the extra mile to ensure that all the books ordered actually arrived on time. This was a massive undertaking, but they never complained.

Michael West, past editor-in-chief of Fortress Press, must be thanked for his enthusiasm for fair-minded, respectful dialogue on important issues and his interest in publishing the fruit of the Greer-Heard Forum. I am especially grateful for Michael's successor, Will Bergkamp. Though we have not known each other very long, I sense that he too has the same passion for dialogue that Michael and I share. Without his support and encouragement, this project would never have been completed. I look forward to more fruitful work together on such projects. Susan Johnson of Fortress Press also deserves a word of thanks. Her cheerful attitude, eagerness to help in any way possible, and consummate professionalism are much appreciated.

As always, my wife, Marilyn, and my children must be thanked. I suspect they enjoy the rush that accompanies an event like the forum, but they still make numerous sacrifices.

I mentioned earlier the passing of Professor John Hick. In a very real sense, this book would not exist without the pioneering work of John Hick. I never met him personally. All of our interaction was via e-mail. When I invited him to contribute a chapter, he initially declined. In response, I told him that "reading a book on pluralism without John Hick is like playing chess without the queen." I then asked if he had by chance an unpublished work or a published article on which he held the copyright that he would be willing to let us include. He then suggested that we include his article "Is Christianity the Only True Religion, or One among Others?" I am very pleased to be able to do so. In a way, this book and the conference out of which it arises are a result of Professor Hick's scholarship.

I first encountered John Hick's work in a seminar taught by John P. Newport. In this two-semester course, every student read Paul Knitter's *No Other Name? A Critical Survey of Christian Attitudes toward the World Religions* and John Hick's *Death and Eternal Life*. Newport passed away in August 2000. In John Newport, one encountered both a critical mind and a charitable spirit. He was able to interact critically with those with whom he disagreed without feeling the need to caricature their positions or resort to ad hominem arguments. In his classes, students breathed in an atmosphere of unrelenting clarity and contagious curiosity that was both challenging and refreshing. I was privileged to sit under his tutelage. John modeled Christian scholarship for all his students. I owe him for many things, among them introducing me to the work of scholars representing a wide variety of ideological and theological perspectives. I dedicate this book to the memory of John Paul Newport.

Can Only One Religion Be True? Considering This Question

Robert B. Stewart

Of any ethnic religion, therefore, can it be said that it is a true religion, only not perfect? Christianity says, No. The attitude of Christianity, therefore, towards religions other than itself is an attitude of universal, absolute, eternal, unappeasable hostility.

—William C. Wilkinson, at 1893 World's Parliament of Religions[1]

Howsoever men may approach me, even so do I accept them; for, on all sides, whatever path they may choose is mine.
—John Hick[2]

I am now, you might say, a card-carrying Buddhist. In 1939 I was baptized. In 2008 I took refuge. I can truly call myself what I think I've been over these past decades: a Buddhist Christian.
—Paul Knitter[3]

The church bus was dark that night as our youth group made its way back home. I don't remember where we had been, but I do remember the subject of the conversation. A friend of mine asked what happens to people who die without ever hearing of Jesus. I had never considered that question prior to that night. Our youth minister declared authoritatively that nobody would be saved apart from knowing Jesus as Lord and Savior. The implication was that people who had never heard of Jesus were still in their sins and faced eternal torment in hell when they died. It seemed unjust.

A little more than a year later, I was a student at a state university, living on campus with members of other world religions. I was struck by their sincerity and their moral way of life. In very many ways, they seemed just like me. Yet I believed them to be lost. There was a definite tension in my beliefs. On the one hand, I believed the Bible, and in the Bible, Jesus says, "I am the way, and the truth, and the life; no one comes to the Father but through Me" (John 14:6). The apostle Peter also declares, "And there is salvation in no one else; for there is no other name under heaven that has been given among men by which we must be saved" (Acts 4:12 NASB). On the other hand, I was seeing with my own eyes young people who did not claim Christ as their personal Savior and were as serious about their religions as I was about mine. They seemed as moral and spiritual as I. How was I to make sense of these seeming contradictions?

I don't want to make it appear as though I was existentially undone or troubled about these issues every moment of every day; I confess I was not. Most nights, I did not lose sleep pondering these questions. I just told myself that God was God and he could work it all out even if I didn't know how he would do so. But at times, I pondered these issues with great seriousness. Would I be a Christian if I had not been born into a Christian family? What if I had been born in Asia or the Middle East? Though I would never have put it this way, the philosopher Rousseau expressed my feelings:

> You announce to me God, born and dying, two thousand years ago, on the far side of the world, in some small town I know not where, and you tell me that all those who have not believed in this mystery will be damned. These are strange things to be believed so quickly on the authority of an unknown person. Why did your God make these things happen so far off, if he would compel me to know about them? Is it a crime to be unaware what is happening half a world away? Could I guess that in another hemisphere there was a Hebrew nation and a town called Jerusalem? You might as well hold me responsible for knowing what is happening on the moon. You have come, you tell me, to teach me of it; but why did you not come to teach my father? Or why do you damn that good old man for never having known anything about it? Must he be punished throughout eternity for your laziness, he who was so kind and helpful, and who sought only for truth? Be honest and put yourself in my place; see if I ought to believe, on your word alone, all these incredible things

which you have told me, and reconcile all this injustice with the just God you proclaim to me.[4]

The idea that God, who is morally perfect, could unjustly condemn people for not believing what they never had the chance to believe seemed absurd. What was I to do? Though I knew nothing about it at this point in my life, much ink has been spilled seeking to show that God is not, after all is said and done, unjust. So apparently I was not alone in feeling this way. Unbeknownst to me, I was wrestling with questions that arise in what theologians refer to as the theology of religions.

THEOLOGY OF RELIGIONS

At the risk of oversimplifying the matter, theology of religions is the branch of Christian theology[5] that formally addresses issues related to the phenomena of religions. I had come face-to-face with the two primary questions that the Christian theologian of religions seeks to answer: (1) What is the fate of the unevangelized? and (2) Is Christianity the only true religion, i.e., the only religion in which one can be saved? These are important questions indeed.

As far back as our historical records go, we find religious diversity. The Christian religion was born into a world filled with religions, just as was Judaism, the parent-religion of Christianity. Religious diversity is nothing new. Yet it *feels* like there is something new about interreligious encounters in today's multicultural, postmodern world. I suspect that the reason our contemporary situation feels new is due to access. Two hundred years ago, the average Christian in Europe or North America knew that there were Hindus, Buddhists, Muslims, etc. but rarely if ever met a faithful member of another world religion. That experience was largely reserved for explorers, sailors, and missionaries. Today, I have Facebook friends from every continent on earth, and I can place a call over the Internet to virtually any place on this planet. Additionally, I can fly in hours to places that two hundred years ago would have taken months or longer to reach. In this sense, then, the world today is much smaller than it used to be. Religious diversity is nothing new—but widespread recognition of it certainly is.

The upshot of all this is that we live not only in a religiously diverse world, but also in a world that has been religiously desegregated. As long as those other religions were "over there," we could live happily in our homogeneous environment. Out of sight, out of mind. Our theological and religious lives were all neat and clean. But in today's world, thinking about Christianity and other religions is complicated. Complicated does not mean the worse for, but certainly it does mean more difficult. So where are we? We live in a world that is aware of the fact of great religious diversity and is in one way or another obliged to react to it, difficult though that may be.

Ever since Alan Race coined the terms *exclusivism*, *inclusivism*, and *pluralism* in his 1982 book, *Christians and Religious Pluralism*,[6] his threefold typology has become the standard terminology for theologians working in the theology of religions.[7] Exclusivism is the position that holds that salvation is available only through personal knowledge of and commitment to Jesus Christ. Concerning exclusivism, Race states, "Undoubtedly, the predominant attitude of the church through Christian history has been to regard the outsider as in error or darkness, beyond the realms of truth and light. More than simply an expression of popular piety, it was institutionalized and enshrined, for instance, in the axiom of the Catholic Church, '*Extra Ecclesiam nulla salus.*'"[8] Exclusivism, therefore, "counts the revelation in Jesus Christ as the sole criterion by which all religions, including Christianity, can be understood and evaluated."[9]

Concerning inclusivism, Race states, "Inclusivism in the Christian theology of religions is both an acceptance and a rejection of the other faiths, a dialectical 'yes' and 'no'. On the one hand it accepts the spiritual power and depth manifest in them, so that they can properly be called a locus of divine presence. On the other hand, it rejects them as not being sufficient for salvation apart from Christ and the way of discipleship which springs from him."[10]

Race does not explicitly define pluralism but writes, "The pluralism of this chapter refers therefore to a range of other possible options in the reconciliation of a 'truly Christian charity and perceptivity with doctrinal adequacy.'"[11] John Hick supplies a prime example of religious pluralism: "The great world faiths embody different perceptions and conceptions of, and correspondingly different responses to, the Real from within the major variant ways of being human, and that within each of them the transformation of human existence from self-centredness to Reality–centredness is taking place. These traditions are accordingly to be regarded as alternative soteriological 'spaces' within which, or 'ways' along which, men and women can find salvation/liberation/ultimate fulfillment."[12] Harold Netland helpfully summarizes Hick's statement of pluralism: "In other words, all religions (or at least the 'major' ones) are in their own ways complex historically and culturally conditioned human responses to the one ultimate Reality."[13]

There is an increasing awareness that Race's typology, though helpful, needs to be expanded. In answering the question "Is there any basis for hope that those who do not hear of Christ in this life will be saved?" Christopher Morgan expands the typology from three to nine:

1. **Church exclusivism:** No, outside the church there is no salvation.
2. **Gospel exclusivism:** No, they must hear the gospel and trust Christ to be saved.
3. **Special revelation exclusivism:** No, they must hear the gospel and trust Christ to be saved, unless God chooses to send them special revelation in an extraordinary way—by dream, vision, miracle, or angelic message.
4. **Agnosticism:** We cannot know.
5. **General revelation inclusivism:** Yes, they can respond to God in saving faith through seeing him in general revelation.
6. **World religions inclusivism:** Yes, they can respond to God through general revelation or their religion.
7. **Postmortem evangelism:** Yes, they will have an opportunity to trust Christ after death.
8. **Universalism:** Yes, everyone will ultimately be saved.
9. **Pluralism:** Yes, many will experience "salvation" as they understand it because they embrace their version of the real, though the question is erroneous because it assumes that Christianity is ultimate.[14]

A fuller explication is in order. *Church exclusivism* is the traditional position of the pre–Vatican II Roman Catholic Church. Accordingly, membership in the church was required for salvation. Cyprian of Carthage (d. 258) stated it thus: "Extra Ecclesiam nulla salus" (Outside the church there is no salvation).[15] Pope Boniface I (d. 422) declared, "It is clear that this Roman Church is to all churches throughout the world as the head is to the members, and that whoever separates himself from it becomes an exile from the Christian religion, since he ceases to belong to its fellowship."[16] In 1215, the Fourth Lateran Council affirmed, "There is one Universal Church of the faithful, outside of which there is absolutely no salvation."[17]

Gospel exclusivism is a common Evangelical position. James Borland succinctly states it thus: "Everyone must hear and believe the gospel to be saved."[18] The emphasis here is that salvation is made possible by hearing the propositional content of the New Testament message of salvation through Jesus Christ. Since the coming of Christ, one cannot be saved simply by trusting in a merciful Creator to be gracious. John Piper concurs:

The question we have been trying to answer . . . is whether some people are quickened by the Holy Spirit and saved by grace through faith in a merciful Creator even though they never hear of Jesus in this life. . . . The answer of the New Testament is a clear and earnest No. . . . But now the focus of faith has narrowed down to one Man, Jesus Christ, the fulfillment and guarantee of all redemption and all sacrifices and all prophecies. It is to his honor now that henceforth all saving faith shall be directed to him.[19]

Special-revelation exclusivism insists that none can be saved without hearing the gospel in this life unless God sends them special revelation in an extraordinary way, such as through a vision, dream, angelic encounter, etc. The emphasis here is that general revelation is not sufficient to save. The Second Helvetic Confession stresses that God commands evangelistic activity but stresses that he is also able to illuminate individuals apart from human proclamation: "At the same time we recognize that God can illuminate whom and when he will, even without the external ministry, for that is in his power; but we speak of the usual way of instructing men, delivered unto us from God, both by commandment and examples."[20] The Westminster Confession of Faith also states, "God, in his ordinary providence, maketh use of means, yet is free to work without, above, and against them, at his pleasure."[21] Two contemporary proponents of this position, Bruce Demarest and Timothy George, stress that special-revelation exclusivism does not differ from gospel exclusivism as far as the *content* of the message is concerned. The difference is in the *means* by which the gospel is made known—God himself may reveal the message, whereas the gospel exclusivist insists that the only means by which one can hear the gospel is through human proclamation.[22]

General-revelation inclusivism maintains that general revelation is sufficient to lead someone to salvation but denies that salvation comes through any religion other than Christianity. All types of exclusivism and inclusivism agree that salvation is only through Jesus, but inclusivists deny that ignorance disqualifies one from God's grace.[23] Essentially, inclusivists say that one can be saved *by* Christ without ever hearing *of* Christ. John Sanders puts it this way: "Inclusivists concede that in an ontological sense their salvation ultimately depended on the atonement of Jesus, since no one is saved apart from the redemptive work of Christ. . . . But inclusivists hold that while the source of salvific water is the same for all people, it comes to various people through different channels."[24] This may have been the position of Justin Martyr. In his first *Apology*, he states, "Those who lived reasonably are Christians, even though they have been thought atheists; as, among the Greeks, Socrates and Heraclitus."[25] Note that he speaks of them being regarded as "atheists," i.e., they rejected Greek religions. It appears then that Justin would not be a world religions inclusivist.[26]

World religions inclusivism affirms not only that general revelation is sufficient to lead to salvation but also that the world religions are *means by which* someone could be saved. Without doubt, the two best-known proponents of this view are the Roman Catholic theologian Karl Rahner and the Anglican layman C. S. Lewis. Rahner championed the idea of the "anonymous Christian": "Therefore no matter what a man states in his conceptual, theoretical and religious reflection, anyone who does not say in his heart, 'there is no God' (like the 'fool' in the psalm) but testifies to him by the radical acceptance of his being, is a believer. . . . And anyone who has let himself be taken hold of by this grace can be called with every right an 'anonymous Christian.'"[27] In *Mere Christianity*, Lewis declares something quite similar: "There are people in other religions who are being led by God's secret influence to concentrate on those parts of their religion which are in agreement with Christianity, and who thus belong to Christ without knowing it."[28] Perhaps most famously, though, Lewis pictures world religions inclusivism in a fictional work, *The Last Battle,* the concluding volume in his Narnia series, when Emeth, a faithful and virtuous Calormen, who has worshiped the god Tash all his life, relates his startling conversation with Aslan, Lewis's Christ figure in the Chronicles:

> He answered, Child, all the service thou has done to Tash, I account as service done to me. Then by reason of my great desire for wisdom and understanding, I overcame my fear and questioned the Glorious One and said, Lord, is it then true, as the Ape said, that thou and Tash are one? The Lion growled so that the earth shook (but his wrath was not against me) and said, It is false. Not because he and I are one, but because we are opposites, I take to me the services which thou hast done to him, for I and he are of such different kinds that no service which is vile can be done to me, and none which is not vile can be done to him. Therefore, if any man swear by Tash and keep his oath for the oath's sake, it is by me that he has truly sworn, though he know it not, and it is I who reward him. And if any man do a cruelty in my name, then though he says the name of Aslan, it is Tash whom he serves and by Tash his deed is accepted. Dost thou understand, Child? I said, Lord, thou knowest how much I understand. But I said

also (for the truth constrained me), Yet I have been seeking Tash all my days. Beloved, said the Glorious One, unless thy desire had been for me thou wouldst not have sought so long and so truly. For all find what they truly seek.[29]

Between exclusivism and inclusivism, Morgan lists *agnosticism* as an option. Essentially, those who hold to this position grant either that God might give extraordinary special revelation to select individuals and then they could respond in an appropriate way, or they might respond to the light of general revelation that they have and then God would respond by granting them salvation—but we can never know for certain that either is the case, because we have no clear biblical examples of this ever happening.[30]

Postmortem evangelism maintains that those who never heard the gospel in their earthly lives will have the chance to respond to it after death. Concerning this position, Morgan states, "It concurs with exclusivism when it stresses that faith is a conscious and explicit trust in Christ but sides with inclusivism when it contends that the love and justice of God require that everyone be given an opportunity to trust Christ."[31] Though preferring the terminology of "divine perseverance," Gabriel Fackre holds this opinion. Based in part upon his reading of 1 Peter 4, he states, "But the graciousness of God is such that *even these* failing to live up to the rainbow light they are given (sinners 'judged in the flesh as everyone is judged'), will not be denied the good news proclaimed to all sinners—'for this is the reason the gospel was proclaimed even to the dead' (1 Pet 4:6). Sinners who die outside the knowledge of the gospel will not be denied the hearing of the Word."[32]

Universalism is the position that God will eventually save everyone on the basis of Christ's atoning sacrifice. This is an ancient position that was held at least as early as Origen.[33] In the eighteenth century, it was vigorously argued by Charles Chauncy in his book *The Mystery Hid from Ages and Generations*.[34] The most outspoken contemporary advocate of universalism is Thomas Talbott. Talbott argues for universalism both on a biblical basis and on a theological/ philosophical basis. Arguing from the nature of an essential property he puts the matter thus: "This follows from the very nature of an essential property. If omniscience is an essential property of God, then it is logically impossible for God to hold to a mistaken belief; if justice is an essential property of God, then it is logically impossible for him to act in an unjust way, and similarly, if loving-kindness is an essential property of God, then it is logically impossible for him to act in an unloving way."[35]

Others, such as Ted Peters,[36] writing from a Lutheran perspective, and Kallistos Ware, from an Orthodox perspective, make less dogmatic assertions. Peters prefers universalism to the alternative positions but stresses, "Now let me repeat a methodological caution mentioned earlier. The hypothesis regarding universal salvation is just that, a hypothesis. It is not dogma. It is an attempt to explicate evangelically the New Testament symbols. But in pursuing this line of theological reasoning I have never ceased to be aware that some other biblical texts seem to lead in another direction, in the direction of an everlasting double destiny."[37] Ware, a bishop in the Orthodox Church, writes what he considers to be acceptable belief and practice for Orthodoxy—in making a qualified case that Christians should hope and pray for universalism:

> How far can we go in our affirmation of the all-embracing character of salvation? "God desires for everyone to be saved" (1 Tim. 2:4): are we to believe that God's plan will ultimately be frustrated? Or may we hope for an ultimate *apokatastasis* or "restoration" of things, in which every rational creature will be saved, including even the devil himself? Origen (d. c. 254) did not hesitate to affirm such a doctrine of universal salvation, but for this he was condemned by the Fifth Ecumenical Council. St. Gregory of Nyssa also entertained the hope that the devil might eventually be saved, but he expressed himself in a more guarded way than Origen had done, and so he escaped condemnation; a qualified version of *apokatastasis* has therefore a legitimate place within Orthodoxy. Certainly, God's ultimate plans for his creation remain a mystery which none of us at this present moment can begin to fathom, and we must be careful not to assert too much. But at least we know two things. First, God has given us free will, and he will never withdraw that gift from us; it is therefore possible for us to choose for all eternity to say "No" to him. Second, divine love is inexhaustible. Beyond this we cannot go; but, obedient to the words of St. Silouan the Athonite (1866–1938), "We must pray for all."[38]

Finally, Karl Barth is somewhat ambivalent in his position:

> If we are to respect the freedom of divine grace, we cannot venture the statement that it must and will finally be coincident with the world of man as such (as in the doctrine of the so-called *apokatastasis*). No such right or necessity can legitimately be

deduced. Just as the gracious God does not need to elect or call any single man, so He does not need to elect or call all mankind. His election and calling do not give rise to any historical metaphysics, but only to the necessity of attesting them on the ground that they have taken place in Jesus Christ and His community. But, again, in grateful recognition of the grace of the divine freedom we cannot venture the opposite statement that there cannot and will not be this final opening up and enlargement of the circle of election and calling.[39]

The categories in this typology are not cut-and-dried. Nor are they distinct and airtight. Sometimes a theologian will hold to more than one position. For instance, Clark Pinnock held to both world religions inclusivism and postmortem evangelism.[40] Therefore, it is probably best to think of these categories as positions along a continuum.

All of the positions are *particular* in nature. They all agree in affirming that salvation is available on the basis of the atonement of Jesus Christ. Furthermore, they all assume that humanity needs atonement for sin and that this need constitutes the ultimate religious problem. They disagree, however, as to how God makes salvation possible and to how many. But most significantly for our purposes, we must recognize that none of these positions affirms religious pluralism.

Unlike all forms of particularism, *pluralism* denies the necessity of faith in Jesus. In other words, pluralism belongs to an entirely different family and as such represents a radically new school of thought in the Christian theology of religions. This becomes clear in the preface to *The Myth of Christian Uniqueness* when one reads, "We wanted to gather theologians who were exploring the possibilities of a *pluralist* position—a move away from insistence on the superiority or finality of Christ and Christianity toward a recognition of the independent validity of other ways. Such a move came to be described by participants in our project as the crossing of a theological Rubicon. In the words of Langdon Gilkey, it represents 'a monstrous shift indeed . . . a position quite new to the churches, even to the liberal churches.'"[41]

Pluralism is not universalism. It is not asserting that, in the end, all will be saved by Christ. Neither is pluralism as simple as saying that all religions are really saying the same thing. Not all roads lead to God. Nor is it insisting that there are different roads up the religious mountain; there are different mountains. The great religions of the world diagnose the human predicament differently and as a result really do disagree and therefore offer different solutions to humanity's predicament.

Harold Netland writes this concerning pluralism:

> Pluralism, then, holds that salvation (or enlightenment or liberation) should be acknowledged as present and effective in its own way in each religion. No single religion can claim to be somehow normative and superior to all others, for all religions are in their own way complex historically and culturally conditioned human responses to the one divine reality. Thus, although Christians can hold that Jesus is unique and normative for them, they cannot claim that Jesus is unique or normative in an objective or universal sense. Jesus may be the savior for Christians, but he is not the one Savior for all peoples.[42]

Without a doubt, the late John Hick was the foremost and best-known proponent of religious pluralism. His mature pluralist position is most fully stated in *An Interpretation of Religion* (see note 10, page 5).

But Hick has not published and will not publish the final word on this matter. In his recent book *Without Buddha I Could Not Be a Christian*, Paul Knitter has moved beyond granting that all religions (or at least the "great" or major world religions) are legitimate responses to the real, and has begun to speak of the religions as complementing and completing one another. In particular, he records his personal investigation of and participation in Buddhism. Knitter is clear that he still considers himself a Christian. He conceives of himself as having sort of a dual religious citizenship and "dually belonging" to both Christianity and Buddhism.[43] And he has made his dual citizenship official by becoming a Buddhist:

> And so I made a big, but also an easy, decision during the summer of 2008 when I was doing the final revisions of this book. It was at the end of a ten-day Dzogchen Buddhist retreat at the Garrison Institute on the Hudson river. After careful consultation with my teacher, Lama John Makransky (who is also Professor of Buddhist Studies and Comparative Theology at Boston College), I decided to "Take Refuge" and to pronounce the "Bodhisattva Vows" as part of the Dzogchen community in the United States. I was given the *Dharma* name of *Urgyen Menla*—Lotus Healer.

So it's official. I am now, you might say, a card-carrying Buddhist. In 1939 I was baptized. In 2008 I took refuge. I can truly call myself what I think I've been over these past decades: a Buddhist Christian.[44]

Knitter grants that it is legitimate to question whether he is still a Christian or not—indeed he asks this himself, though, clearly, he seems to believe that he is.[45]

One obvious implication of Knitter's insistence that Buddhism completes his Christianity (and also that Christianity completes his Buddhism) is that both Christianity and Buddhism are incomplete in and of themselves. This seems to imply that all religions are incomplete in and of themselves. So the question then is this: is dual citizenship enough? This leads to the question of whether or not pluralism—at least Knitter's pluralism—is headed in the direction of *pantheologiae*. (I think I'm creating a neologism. *Pantheologiae* is not to be confused with metaphysical pantheism. It is an attempt to say "all theologies," not "all is god.") In other words, only in all religions taken together does one find the full answer to the human problem. At first glance, this appears to be syncretism on steroids. Knitter might say that Christianity and Buddhism have a unique and singular relationship and that one only needs dual citizenship rather than to be citizens of all world religions. But if this is the case, he needs to explain how and why this is so. And if no religion is complete in and of itself, and if we thus need to embrace and practice all religions, does he not run the risk of undermining pluralism's affirmation that all religions are valid *independent* responses to the real?

Possibly he might say that, for him, Buddhism completes Christianity (as Christianity completes Buddhism) but that such may not be the case for all. But then he seems faced with having to explain how his position does not disintegrate into relativism. Of course, he may be OK with relativism at this point, but I don't get that feeling from reading him.

Knitter desires to hear from his fellow theologians. No doubt he already has and will continue to do so.

CONCLUDING QUESTIONS

I have tried in this essay to lay out some of the answers that theologians of religions give to questions such as those I wrestled with as a young Christian (and still wrestle with today). I have made little attempt to critique them at any length or to state my own position. Space simply does not permit me to do so, and such is not the purpose of this introduction. Even then, though, the range of issues that come to mind and deserve attention is so immense that unavoidably, important questions are left out altogether.

In seeking to answer the question "Can only one religion be true?" certain obviously important issues arise that can only be mentioned in this introductory essay. Questions about the nature of truth are vitally important. Is truth that which corresponds to reality or something else—perhaps that which makes life meaningful? Can contradictory propositions both be true? Different scholars give various answers to these sorts of questions. What about the authority of Scripture? What role do sacred texts play in theology? What about hermeneutics? What of the efficacy of general revelation? What of conscience? What of original sin, if there is such a thing? What of hell? Does it exist? Is it forever? What of divine love and divine justice? What about the holiness of God—and his mercy? And unavoidably, one set of questions is invariably raised when Christian theologians of religion come to this question: What about Jesus? Is he unique? Is he necessary? If so, how and why? I could go on.

The question "Can only one religion be true?" is an extremely important question. If any single religion alone is true, then the nonreligious and those of other religions need to learn this. Similarly, if all religions are true, then those who think that only one religion is true need to learn this as well. How these questions are answered will necessarily have huge implications for missions and evangelism. It will also affect religious ethics and politics in a significant way. If more than one religion is true but not all religions are true, then obviously we need to know which religions are true and which are not. Furthermore, if more than one religion is true but one is more true than the others (or has more truth than the others), then we need to know that as well.

Evangelicals like me insist that the truly important question is not simply one of truth but one of salvation. Is salvation found in more than one religion? Logically speaking, it may be the case that salvation is not needed, that religious people are actually deluded, or that religions that hold that salvation is needed are simply mistaken. But what if salvation is needed? And what if salvation is not possible through all religions? Then it would seem to be vitally important to make certain that one's religion was one that offered salvation. And if salvation is possible through only one religion, then it seems even more important to do so. In other words, this would then be a question of life and death—eternal life and death!

Unavoidably, sincere men and women from all religious groups and traditions will reach different conclusions as to whether or not only one religion is true. Serious thinkers will want to examine the evidence and hear the arguments from all sides on this issue. Doing so will necessarily involve interacting with those who have different opinions. Emotions can run high when religion is the topic. Conflict is possible. Indeed, nobody living in our post-9/11 world could deny this. But reasonable people of good will can agree to disagree reasonably and also to continue to dialogue for the sake of all involved.

Not all of our authors agree. In fact, there is some serious disagreement on very important issues, but all agree that persons of good will can and should discuss these matters. We hope that you will carefully read the dialogue between Paul Knitter and Harold Netland and read each essay. Then make up your mind on this question. And after you've done that, study this issue some more—we intend to—because it's that important. Regardless of your religious background or persuasion, I pray that you—and I—will know the truth on this issue and then respectfully share it with others who need to know it as well. Grace and peace!

Notes

1. William C. Wilkinson, "The Attitude of Christianity to Other Religions," in *The Dawn of Religious Pluralism: Voices from the World's Parliament of Religions, 1893*, ed. Richard Hughes Seager (La Salle, IL: Open Court, 1993), 321–22. Wilkinson ends this sentence by adding "by no means excepted, its attitude is an attitude of grace, mercy, and peace, for whosoever will." Ibid., 322.

2. John Hick, *God Has Many Names* (Philadelphia: Westminster, 1982), 78.

3. Paul Knitter, *Without Buddha I Could Not Be a Christian* (Oxford: One World, 2009), 216.

4. Jean-Jacques Rousseau, *Emile*, trans. Barbara Foxley (New York: Dutton, 1969), 269.

5. Philosophy of religion also addresses these questions but in a more controlled way, along the lines of what is typically called natural theology, whereas a theologian of religions will also seek to synthesize his or her convictions with systematic and biblical theology. Theology of religions also relates to the study of world religions. The focus of world religions typically is on understanding the main tenets and practices of the major world religions. Theology of religions will also relate to missiology.

6. Alan Race, *Christians and Religious Pluralism: Patterns in the Christian Theology of Religions* (Maryknoll, NY: Orbis, 1982).

7. Despite their widespread usage, there is a growing recognition that the threefold criteria are not nearly as useful as they are intended to be. In fact, numerous recent authors have criticized this threefold paradigm. To see only a few, see Ian Markham, "Creating Options: Shattering the 'Exclusivist, Inclusivist, Pluralist' Paradigm," *New Blackfriars* 74, no. 867 (January 1993): 33; Tim Perry, "Beyond the Threefold Typology: The End of Exclusivism, Inclusivism, and Pluralism?" *Canadian Evangelical Theological Review* 14 (Spring 1997): 1–8.

8. "Outside the Church there is no salvation." Race, *Christians and Religious Pluralism*, 10. Hendrik Kraemer is frequently mentioned as the paradigmatic modern exclusivist. See Hendrik Kraemer, *Religion and the Christian Faith* (Philadelphia: Westminster, 1956).

9. Race, *Christians and Religious Pluralism*, 11.

10. Ibid., 38.

11. Ibid., 71. Race does state that he will be studying especially Paul Tillich, John Hick, and Wilfred Cantwell Smith. Ibid.

12. John Hick, *An Interpretation of Religion: Human Responses to the Transcendent*, 2nd ed. (New Haven: Yale University Press, 2004), 240.

13. Harold Netland, *Encountering Religious Pluralism: The Challenge to Christian Faith and Mission* (Downers Grove, IL: InterVarsity, 2001), 54.

14. Christopher W. Morgan, "Inclusivisms and Exclusivisms," in *Faith Comes by Hearing: A Response to Inclusivism*, ed. Christopher W. Morgan and Robert A. Peterson, 25–36 (Downers Grove, IL: InterVarsity, 2008).

15. Cyprian, *De Unitate Ecclesiae* 6.

16. Pope Boniface I, *Epistle* 14.1.

17. Canon 1.

18. James Borland, "A Theologian Looks at the Gospel and World Religions," *Journal of the Evangelical Theological Society* 33 (March 1990): 3–11.

19. John Piper, *Let the Nations Be Glad! The Supremacy of God in Missions* (Grand Rapids: Baker, 1993), 163. Cf. Robertson McQuilken, *The Great Omission* (Grand Rapids: Baker, 1984), 42–53.

20. The Second Helvetic Confession, 1.7.

21. "The Westminster Confession of Faith, a.d. 1647," 5.3 in *The Creeds of Christendom*, 6th ed., ed. Philip Schaff (Grand Rapids: Baker, 1996), 3:612–13.

22. Bruce A. Demarest, *The Cross and Salvation* (Wheaton, IL: Crossway, 1997), 90; Timothy George in "Forum Discussion on Inclusivism," in *Who Will Be Saved? Defending the Biblical Understanding of God, Salvation, and Evangelism*, ed. Paul R. House and Gregory A. Thornbury, 145–48 (Wheaton, IL: Crossway, 2000).

23. J. N. D. Anderson, *Christianity and Comparative Religion* (Downers Grove, IL: InterVarsity, 1977), 99.

24. John Sanders, *No Other Name: An Investigation into the Destiny of the Unevangelized* (Grand Rapids: Eerdmans, 1992), 226.

25. Justin, *First Apology* 46.

26. James Sigountos questions whether Justin was an inclusivist. See James G. Sigountos, "Did Early Christians Believe Pagan Religions Could Save?," in *Through No Fault of Their Own? The Fate of Those Who Have Never Heard*, ed. William V. Crockett and James G. Sigountos (Grand Rapids: Baker, 1991), 241.

27. Karl Rahner, *Theological Investigations*, trans. Karl Kruger and Boniface Kruger (Baltimore: Helicon, 1969), 6:395.

28. C. S. Lewis, *Mere Christianity* (San Francisco: HarperCollins, 2001), 209.

29. C. S. Lewis, *The Last Battle* (New York: Collier, 1970), 164–65.

30. Morgan, "Inclusivisms and Exclusivisms," 26–32. Those advocating agnosticism include J. I. Packer, "Evangelicals and the Way of Salvation," in *Evangelical Affirmations*, ed. Kenneth S. Kantzer and Carl F. H. Henry (Grand Rapids: Zondervan, 1990), 121–23; and Millard J. Erickson, *How Shall They Be Saved? The Destiny of Those Who Do Not Hear of Jesus* (Grand Rapids: Baker, 1996), 130–39, 147–58.

31. Morgan, "Inclusivisms and Exclusivisms," 34.

32. Gabriel Fackre, "Divine Perseverance," in *What about Those Who Have Never Heard? Three Views on the Destiny of the Unevangelized*, ed. John Sanders (Downers Grove, IL: InterVarsity, 1995), 84.

33. Origen, *De Prinicipiis* 1.6.1–2, 3.6.3, 6.

34. Charles Chauncy, *The Mystery Hid from Ages and Generations, Made Manifest by the Gospel—Revelation; or, The Salvation of All Men the Grand Thing Aimed at in the Scheme of God, as Opened in the New Testament Writings, and Entrusted with Jesus Christ to Bring into Effect* (New York: Arno, 1969). This is the most vigorous argument for Christian universalism until Thomas Talbott.

35. Thomas Talbott, "On Predestination, Reprobation, and the Love of God: A Polemic," *Reformed Journal* 33, no. 2 (February 1983): 13. For a book-length treatment of his position, see Thomas Talbott, *The Inescapable Love of God* (Boca Raton, FL: Universal, 1999). For critical interaction with Talbott's position, see Robin A. Parry and Christopher H. Partridge, *Universal Salvation: The Current Debate* (Grand Rapids: Eerdmans, 2004).

36. Ted Peters, *God—the World's Future: Systematic Theology for a New Era*, 2nd ed. (Minneapolis: Fortress Press, 2000), 366–71.

37. Ibid., 370.

38. Kallistos Ware, *How Are We Saved? The Understanding of Salvation in the Orthodox Tradition* (Minneapolis: Light and Life, 1996), 84–85. For Saint Silouan, see Archimandrite Sophrony (Sakharov), *Saint Silouan the Athonite* (Yonkers, NY: St. Vladimir's Seminary Press, 1999), 48.

39. Karl Barth, *Church Dogmatics*, ed. G. W. Bromiley and T. F. Torrance, trans. G. W. Bromiley, J. C. Campbell, Iain Wilson, J. Strathearn NcNab, Harold Knight, and R. A. Stewart (Peabody, MA: Hendrickson, 2010): 2/2:417–18. Interestingly enough, Race sees Barth as the paradigmatic exclusivist. Race, *Christians and Religious Pluralism*, 11.

40. Clark H. Pinnock, *A Wideness in God's Mercy: The Finality of Jesus Christ in a World of Religions* (Grand Rapids: Zondervan, 1992), 168–72. In fact, Pinnock argues not only that those who never heard the gospel would have a postmortem opportunity to hear the gospel but also that some who did hear of Christ would have additional postmortem opportunities. Ibid., 173–75. Further complicating matters are the facts that there are competing typologies and that different scholars are assessed differently by differing critics and thus placed in different categories depending on who is assigning the categories. So the problem is not only terminological but also one of perspective.

41. John Hick and Paul Knitter, preface to *The Myth of Christian Uniqueness: Toward a Pluralistic Theology of Religions*, Faith Meets Faith Series, ed. John Hick and Paul Knitter (Maryknoll, NY: Orbis, 1987), viii.

42. Harold Netland, *Encountering Religious Pluralism: The Challenge to Christian Faith and Mission* (Downers Grove, IL: InterVarsity, 2001), 53.

43. Paul Knitter, *Without Buddha I Could Not Be a Christian* (Oxford: Oneworld, 2009).

44. Ibid., 216.

45. Ibid., xiii. I must add here that, given what I know of Paul Knitter (I know him but not yet as well as I would like), it is inconceivable to me that he would have taken such a step unless he deeply believed he could remain a Christian. Failing that, he would not have become a Buddhist or would have left Christianity and would today profess to be only a Buddhist. We have many theological differences, but I have never questioned his honesty, forthrightness, or sincerity. Still, this is one of the points at which he and I disagree.

1

Can Only One Religion Be True?: A Dialogue

Paul F. Knitter and Harold A. Netland

OPENING REMARKS

Harold A. Netland

Given the bewildering degree of religious diversity in our world, the assertion that Christianity is the one true religion for all people strikes many today as hopelessly out of touch with current realities. The claim seems to display generous amounts of both intellectual naïveté and arrogance. Nevertheless, with proper qualification, I do believe that the Christian faith, as defined by the Christian Scriptures, is true and that this sets it apart from other religious traditions. But tonight I will not be arguing that Christianity *is* in fact the only true religion. Rather, I will be exploring what is involved in making such a claim, clarifying what is and what is not included in it, and considering in a very preliminary way how one might defend such a thesis.

But first, some preliminary remarks. Like many people today, I would very much like for all religions to be true and for all morally good and sincere religious believers, of whatever faith, to be correct in their beliefs and practices. Life would certainly be much simpler if this were the case. But, as I have discovered in other areas, reality frequently has a stubborn way of not conforming to my desires. I suspect the same is true here. Given the very different, at times mutually incompatible, claims advanced by the major religions, I simply do not see how we can affirm them all as somehow being true.[1]

Let me clarify at the outset what is *not* included in the assertion that Christianity is the one true religion. Affirming Christian faith as the true religion does not mean that there is no truth or goodness or beauty in other religions. If the Christian faith is true, then any teachings from other religions which are incompatible with essential teachings of Christianity must be rejected. But this does not mean that there are no truths embraced by other religions. Indeed, I think that the Christian faith shares some significant common beliefs with other religions, with some more so than with others. And surely we can and must acknowledge that there is goodness and beauty in other religious traditions as well.

Nor, in claiming that the Christian faith is true, am I suggesting that Christians are necessarily morally better people than, say, Muslims or Hindus or Sikhs. Nor am I defending everything that the institutional church has done or represented over the past two millennia. Sadly, there is much in the history of the Christian church that betrays the teachings of our Lord.

Furthermore, in claiming that Christianity is the true religion, I am not saying that Christians should not cooperate with other religious communities in a variety of ways to further the common good. Given the very real religious tensions in our world, I think that leaders of the major religions need to be especially vigilant in working to reduce conflict between religious communities and to cooperate together in addressing our many global problems. Nothing that I say tonight should be taken as in any way detracting from the urgency of such interreligious understanding and cooperation.

In speaking of the truth of Christianity, we must also distinguish the issue of truth from the question of salvation. To affirm that Christianity is the true religion does not, by itself, commit one to any particular view about the extent of salvation. Christians, including Evangelicals, disagree over important questions concerning the extent of salvation.[2] But this issue needs to be settled on the basis of criteria internal to the Christian faith itself, including questions of the proper interpretation of Scripture and the historical understandings of the church. There is no logical connection between the claim that Christianity is the true religion and any particular view of the extent of salvation.

For example, it is no doubt the case that most who believe that Christianity is the true religion also believe that not everyone will be saved. Yet there certainly are those who believe that Christianity is uniquely true but who also embrace soteriological universalism (e.g., Origen, John Scotus Erigena, Jacques Ellul, and perhaps Karl Barth). Conversely, while it might be the case that many religious pluralists are also universalists, in the sense that they hold that ultimately all people will attain the desired soteriological state, there is nothing about religious pluralism as such that requires universalism. Religious pluralism maintains that the major religions are roughly equal with respect to truth and soteriological efficacy,[3] and thus it affirms "equal soteriological access" among the religions. But it is compatible with this to maintain that, despite such equality, in fact relatively few people will actually attain the soteriological goal, however this is understood. Thus, questions about the extent of salvation must be addressed separately from the issue of the truth of Christian theism itself.

RELIGION AND TRUTH

Our world today is deeply religious. According to *The Atlas of Religion*, from the University of California, Berkeley, 80 percent of people worldwide profess some religious affiliation.[4] There are today roughly 2.1 billion Christians, 1.3 billion Muslims, 860 million Hindus, 380 million Buddhists, 25 million Sikhs, and 15 million Jews. To these numbers must be added the many millions who follow indigenous religious traditions or one of the thousands of new religious movements.

But what do we mean by the term *religion*, and how is truth to be understood in religion? The concept of religion is notoriously difficult to define, but we might adopt Roger Schmidt's definition of religions as "systems of meaning embodied in a pattern of life, a community of faith, and a worldview that articulate a view of the sacred and of what ultimately matters."[5] Religions are thus multifaceted phenomena, and there is some overlap between the concepts of religion and culture, although neither concept can be reduced to the other. Ninian Smart has helpfully suggested that we think in terms of seven dimensions of religion.[6] These include the ritual dimension, the mythological or narrative dimension, the experiential, the doctrinal, the ethical, the social, and the material dimensions of religion. A complete discussion of religion would also include what is called folk religion—the religious expression of the common people in ordinary life—as well as the high religion of the intellectuals and the authoritative structures of a given religion.

Religions, then, include much more than just beliefs or doctrines. Nevertheless, beliefs are central to religion. A religious community is expected to live in a certain way and to regard all of life from a particular perspective. A religious tradition expresses a distinctive worldview, or way of understanding reality. At the heart of a religious worldview are some basic beliefs about the nature of the cosmos, the religious ultimate, and the relation of humankind to this ultimate. Religious beliefs are significant, for as Ninian Smart observes, "The world religions owe some of their living power to their success in presenting a total picture of reality, through a coherent system of doctrines."[7] Thus, religious believers are expected to accept the authoritative teachings of their tradition and to pattern their lives in accordance with such beliefs. Religions make claims, and adherents of a given religion are expected to accept and to act upon the claims as true. As Paul Griffiths puts it, "A religious claim . . . is a claim about the way things are, acceptance of or assent to which is required or strongly suggested by the fact of belonging to a particular form of religious life."[8]

How should we understand the concept of truth in religion? There are many issues here, but let me say simply that I think that the major religions do intend to make truth claims and that these claims can and should be understood in terms of a realist and propositionalist understanding of truth. Following William Alston, then, "a statement (proposition, belief . . .) is true if and only if what the statement says to be the case actually is the case."[9] For our purposes, statements, beliefs, and propositions are interchangeable.

Now, understanding religious truth as propositional truth is strongly resisted by many today, especially by those in religious studies. Much more popular are pragmatic or subjective views which regard religious truth as a function of the dynamic, personal relation between a religious believer and his or her religious tradition. Wilfred Cantwell Smith, for example, argued that religious truth should be understood as personal truth, or the faithfulness and authenticity of life that accompanies the existential appropriation by the religious believer of a particular religious way of living. Applying this to religions, Smith states, "Christianity, I would suggest, is not true absolutely, impersonally, statically; rather, it can *become* true, if and as you or I appropriate it to ourselves and interiorize it, insofar as we live it out from day to day. It becomes true as we take it off the shelf and personalize it, in actual existence."[10] Similarly, John Hick, who was influenced by Smith, speaks of religious truth as mythological truth: "A statement or set of propositions about X is mythologically true if it is not literally true but nevertheless tends to evoke an appropriate dispositional attitude toward X."[11] Claims about God being incarnate in Jesus of Nazareth, or about the Qur'an being dictated by the angel Gabriel to Muhammad, or about the essential identity between atman and Brahman, while not literally true nevertheless can be mythologically true to the extent that they tend to evoke in Christians, Muslims, and Hindus appropriate dispositional responses to what is religiously ultimate.

But there are at least two significant problems with these views.[12] First, it seems clear that the great religious leaders, and many ordinary believers as well, do not think of their religious beliefs as true merely in the sense of personal or mythological truth. For them, the beliefs *do* actually reflect the way reality is, whether one existentially appropriates such beliefs or not. And the religions characteristically maintain that a proper understanding of the way things are is essential to attaining the soteriological goal. Second, personal or mythological truth cannot be an alternative to propositional truth in religion. For one can only existentially appropriate religious beliefs in the sense of personal truth, or adopt an appropriate dispositional response to the religious ultimate, as in mythological truth, if one first accepts certain beliefs about the religious ultimate and our relation to this ultimate as being true in a nonpersonal or nonmythological sense. Thus, the statement "Allah is a righteous judge" can become true for a Muslim in the sense of either personal truth or mythological truth only if the Muslim accepts certain beliefs about Allah and judgment in a propositional sense—that is, if the Muslim actually believes that Allah is a righteous judge and then responds appropriately to this belief.[13]

Conflicting Truth Claims

Applying the seven dimensions of religion to the major religions will reveal both similarities and differences across the religions. And this is what produces such rich diversity in religious expression. Now, differences in dress, food, architecture, or rituals are not particularly problematic. But what does create difficulty is the fact that the religions advance very different teachings, and thus difference often turns into disagreement. Each religion regards its own assertions as correct or superior to those of its rivals.

To be sure, there are significant areas of agreement in beliefs among the religions. Such similarities are perhaps most apparent in the ethical teachings of the religions. The ethical principle behind the Golden Rule, for example, is reflected in the teachings of many religions.[14] Without minimizing this, however, it is clear that when we consider carefully what the religions have to say about the religious ultimate, the human predicament, and the nature of and conditions for salvation/enlightenment/liberation, there is significant disagreement among them.

Christians and Muslims, for example, believe that the universe was created by an eternal Creator; Buddhists deny this. Christians traditionally have insisted that Jesus Christ is the incarnate Word of God, fully God and fully man. Muslims reject this as blasphemous. While Hindus, Buddhists, and Jains all agree that there is rebirth, they disagree vigorously over whether there is an enduring, substantial person or soul that is reborn. All of the religions acknowledge that the present state of the world is not as it should be, but they disagree over the cause of this unsatisfactory state and its proper remedy. For Christians, the root cause is sin against a holy God, and the cure consists in repentance and reconciliation with God through the person and work of Jesus Christ on the cross. For many Buddhists, Hindus, and Jains, by contrast, the cause lies in a fundamentally mistaken view of reality, and the remedy involves overcoming the limitations of such false views. But Hindus, Buddhists, and Jains disagree among themselves over the nature of the error and how it is to be overcome. Early Indian philosophical literature contains vigorous disputes among them over just which view is correct and thus how liberation is to be attained.[15]

Disagreements over beliefs result in differences over how we are to pattern our lives. Differences between Christianity and Theravada Buddhism, for example, over what one ought to do—whether one should repent of one's sins and follow Jesus Christ as Lord and Savior or follow the Noble Eightfold Path—reflect not so much diverse *means* toward a common goal but rather very different *ends* that are to be pursued. And such differences grow out of more basic disagreements over what is religiously ultimate, the nature of the problem plaguing the universe, and the proper remedy for this predicament.

Now, some teachings in the religions which seem different might actually be compatible with each other.[16] Others, however, seem not to be mutually compatible. Here it is important to distinguish two kinds of incompatible teachings.[17] Two religious claims are *contradictory* if each makes a claim to truth, both cannot be true, but one claim must be true. The statements "There is an eternal creator God" and "There is not an eternal creator God" are contradictories. On the other hand, two religious claims are *contraries* if each makes a claim to truth, both cannot be true, but neither claim need be true. The statements "The ultimate reality is *sunyata*" and "The ultimate reality is Allah" are contraries. They cannot both be true, although they might both be false. Most religious disagreements that seem incompatible are examples of contraries, not contradictories. And yet there are cases in which Christianity and Islam or Buddhism do put forward contradictory claims.

WHAT IS IT FOR A RELIGION TO BE TRUE?

What does it mean for a religion to be true? Keith Ward has remarked that, given the diverse and multidimensional nature of religions, we should avoid speaking of religious traditions themselves as being true but rather focus upon the truth or falsity of particular truth claims.[18] But while agreeing with his emphasis upon particular claims, I do not see how we can avoid completely assessing religions in terms of truth. The religious traditions themselves advance certain claims and reject others. Thus, for example, focusing upon the truth value of the claim that God was incarnate in Jesus of Nazareth has enormous implications for other religions which have very different views on God and Jesus.

The ancient Indian philosophical and religious traditions sometimes used a medical analogy to speak of religious issues. Religions typically identify something as a pervasive problem or illness, then seek to identify the cause of this problem and finally to prescribe the cure for this malady. Keith Yandell captures this well when he states, "A religion proposes a diagnosis of a deep, crippling spiritual disease universal to non-divine sentience and offers a cure. A particular religion is true if its diagnosis is correct and its cure efficacious. The diagnosis and cure occur in the setting of an account of what there is—an account whose truth is assumed by the content of the diagnosis and cure."[19]

Does this mean that every claim made by a religion must be true if the religion is to be true? Here we must distinguish between beliefs or doctrines which are essential to a religion and those which are not. Not all beliefs in a religion are equally important. Some are relatively insignificant, and adherents of a religion might disagree among themselves over the truth of such beliefs. Protestant Christians, for example, disagree over the proper form of baptism. Buddhist traditions disagree over whether monks should be celibate. But in neither case are these disagreements over essentials.

Other beliefs are much more significant for a religion, and some beliefs are so important that one cannot be an adherent of that religion in good standing while simultaneously rejecting these beliefs. William Christian speaks of these as primary beliefs.[20] We might also think of them as defining beliefs, for they define what is essential to the worldview of the religion in question. Determining just which beliefs are defining beliefs can be a controversial matter, as adherents of a religion sometimes disagree among themselves over the question. But that there are defining beliefs for the major religions and that we can identify at least some such beliefs seems clear. For example, belief that Allah has revealed his will for humankind in the Qur'an would seem to be a defining belief of Islam. Similarly, belief in an eternal God who created the universe is generally accepted as a defining belief of Christianity. Belief that the Buddha attained enlightenment and thereby became aware of the causes of suffering is usually taken as a defining belief of Buddhism. And so on.

More specifically, we might think of the defining beliefs of Christianity as including certain beliefs about God, Jesus Christ, sin, and salvation. The apostle Paul's statement in 2 Cor. 5:19 (NIV) that "God was reconciling the world to himself in Christ" is a concise expression of a dominant theme in the New Testament, and it is difficult to imagine a tradition that is identifiably Christian while flatly rejecting this theme. Paul's statement in turn draws upon at least three related beliefs or teachings which find ample expression throughout the New Testament: (1) There is an eternal, righteous God; (2) Sin has separated humankind from God and is the root cause of the human predicament; (3) In the life, death, and resurrection of Jesus Christ, God has made possible forgiveness and reconciliation. In this sense, then, we might speak of these three statements as defining beliefs of Christianity while also acknowledging that there can be a measure of disagreement among Christians over just how we are to understand the implications of these statements.

In light of these points, I suggest that we speak of a religion as true if and only if its defining beliefs are true. For Christianity to be true, then, the defining beliefs of Christianity—certain affirmations about God, Jesus of Nazareth, sin, and salvation—must be true. If they are true, then Christianity is true.

But can there be more than one religion with true defining beliefs? Could there be other religions apart from Christianity true in this sense? The answer depends in part upon how broadly or narrowly one understands the notion of a religion. Suppose that we think of Protestant Methodism and Greek Orthodoxy as different religions. The issue then is whether Methodism and Greek Orthodoxy have mutually compatible defining beliefs. If so, it makes sense to speak of both as true religions.

More broadly, then, the question is whether it makes sense to say that the defining beliefs of religions such as Christianity, Buddhism, Islam, and Shinto are all compatible. If the central teachings of these religions are taken as they are understood within their own traditions, then it is implausible to hold that there are two or more of these religions with defining beliefs which are true. For as noted earlier, some religions affirm an eternal creator God while others deny this, and no other religion that I am aware of accepts the central beliefs concerning Jesus Christ that have been at the heart of Christianity through the centuries.

CAN WE KNOW THAT CHRISTIANITY IS THE ONE TRUE RELIGION?

It is one thing to argue that there can be one true religion and to claim that Christianity is the true religion. But can we know that Christian theism is the true religion? Are there good reasons for accepting Christianity as true? Since the defining beliefs of Christianity concern the nature of God and the person of Jesus Christ, there are two critical questions to be addressed here: (1) Does God, as understood by Christians, exist? (2) Who is Jesus Christ? There are, of course, many complex and controversial issues stemming from each question. But a few general comments are appropriate.

I do not think we should expect here a demonstrative, knockdown argument for the truth of Christian theism which settles all questions and which all reasonable persons will find persuasive. That is the wrong way to approach these issues. But I do think there are good reasons for accepting the defining beliefs of Christian theism as true. Although I will not argue for it here, I think there are good reasons for accepting both that God exists and that, in an admittedly mysterious manner, God was present and active in Jesus of Nazareth so that we can say Jesus Christ was God incarnate, both God and man.[21]

The endeavor to show that there are good reasons for accepting Christian theism is usually identified with natural theology.[22] Natural theology can take many forms, and some of the most creative and rigorous work in philosophy of religion today deals with questions associated with it. Now, the agenda of natural theology calls into question what is sometimes called the "epistemic parity thesis." This is the view that evidential and rational considerations relevant to religious belief are such that no particular religious tradition can be said to be rationally superior to others; the data are sufficiently ambiguous that the major religions all enjoy epistemic parity.[23] The claims of no single religion can be shown to be more likely to be true than those of any other. This assumption is widespread today, and it is often taken as providing support for the perspective of religious pluralism.

But suppose that there were good reason to accept the epistemic parity thesis. The proper conclusion would then be not religious pluralism but rather religious agnosticism. For if there are no good reasons for accepting any single religious tradition as true, why should we suppose that all of them collectively are equally true? Could we not just as well conclude that, although they all have various attractive features, they are all equally false? Religious pluralism thus requires a further argument to support the conclusion that, despite the fact that no single religion is true, the various religions taken together can nevertheless all be regarded as somehow "true." This is a very difficult argument to make.

But why should we accept the epistemic parity thesis in the first place? Is it really the case that the proposition "God exists" has no greater evidential or rational support than its denial? Or is it really true that the central claims of Theravada Buddhism or Jainism or Shinto have the same degree of rational support as those of orthodox Christianity? I think not.

Those engaging in natural theology should be appropriately modest in expectations.[24] There is no reason to expect that an appropriate natural theology in contexts of religious diversity requires a simple algorithmic procedure for testing worldviews or even that it should seek a conclusive knockdown argument for Christian theism. There will, of course, be vigorous debate over particular beliefs, as indeed there has been among adherents of the religions for many centuries. We should not suppose that all reasonable persons, when presented with the relevant evidence and arguments, will be readily convinced. Few issues of any real significance meet these expectations. I do think, however, that there are strong reasons for accepting Christian theism as true rather than other religious alternatives.

It is tempting at this point to sketch in broad strokes what I think an appropriate natural theology in contexts of religious diversity might look like. But rather than do this, I would like to conclude on a different note. Suppose that we are fully justified in accepting the defining beliefs of Christian theism as true. What follows from this for the way we are to think about and relate to other religious traditions? Answering this question involves us in the exciting but challenging field of theology of religions.[25] I would like to conclude tonight by quoting from the Manila Declaration, a statement made by a group of eighty-five Evangelical theologians from twenty-eight countries who met in 1992 at Manila under the auspices of the World Evangelical Fellowship. The theologians, many of whom came from Asia, met together to address the theme "The Unique Christ in Our Pluralistic World":

> We evangelicals need a more adequate theology of religions. . . . The term "religion" refers to a complex phenomenon and it is important to distinguish between its various aspects. In many societies, religion forms an important part of their identity. As such, a diversity of religions—or, more accurately, a diversity of certain aspects of the religions—may be affirmed as part of the richness of God's good creation, although it must be immediately added that people have often sinfully used these religions, including Christianity, to create a false ultimacy and superiority for their own cultures and religious groups.
>
> Religions may also be understood as expressions of the longing for communion with God, which is an essential human characteristic since we are created in the image of God for the purpose of service to him, fellowship with him, and praise for him. Here also, while always corrupted by sin in practice, we may affirm in principle the goodness of a diversity of some aspects of the religions.
>
> We are not able, however, to affirm the diversity of religions without qualification because religions teach a path to salvation, or a concept of salvation, that is not consistent with God's saving action in Jesus Christ as recorded in the Bible. To the extent that a religion points away from Jesus Christ, we deny the validity of that religion. We would also deny the validity of the Christian religion should it

fail to proclaim Jesus as the Christ, the Lord of all creation, and the sole savior of the world.

We wish to explore the Trinitarian basis of a Christian theology of religions. Remembering that the Father and Spirit created the world through the Word, and remembering also that the Holy Spirit is the Spirit of Jesus and always points to him, it is possible to affirm that God draws people who live far beyond the religious boundaries of Christianity towards salvation while at the same time denying that God saves any one [sic] "beyond" or "apart from" Jesus Christ. Thus the true aspects of the world's religions stem from God's creative power or from the work of the Holy Spirit as he prepares individuals, people groups, and even whole cultures to hear about Jesus Christ. Moreover, this same Trinitarian basis undergirds the decisive, normative, and unique work and person of the historical Jesus Christ.[26]

In this carefully articulated and balanced statement, I think we have the broad contours for an Evangelical theology of religions, one which is rooted in the conviction that the central claims of the Christian faith are distinctively true and yet is also open to the presence and work of the Triune God throughout the world.

CAN CHRISTIANITY BE THE ONLY TRUE RELIGION?

Paul F. Knitter

PRELIMINARY REMARKS

The answer to the question of whether Christianity can be the only true religion depends on the context. Ours is not a free-floating question. But it is a recurring question. It arises out of particular contexts. It is felt differently in different contexts. And it will be answered differently in different contexts. If "the medium is the message," I think we can say the context is the question—and the answer.

Today we are in a very different context than that in which our Christian ancestors formulated their first confessions of faith, which became our New Testament. Yes, there was religious pluralism at the time. But I believe it was felt, perceived, reacted to in a very different way than is the case for us today. At that time, for the minority Christian community, the other religions were primarily a threat. Today, as I will contend, the others are our fellow citizens, our fellow collaborators in promoting the well-being of this world (or what we Christians would call the reign of God).

There are also epistemological issues to consider. I do believe that in order to take our question seriously and in order to have a productive conversation, all of us—that means me as well as Harold—have to be open to the opposite answer from the one we now hold. We have to be truly open to whatever is the true, the correct answer to our question. That means that Harold has to be genuinely ready to acknowledge, if the evidence moves him in that direction, to recognize that Christianity is *not* the only true religion. And I—despite all my liberal baggage and history—have to be truly ready to affirm that Christianity *is* the only true religion. There has to be this openness, this readiness to listen and to be convinced otherwise. There cannot be any preestablished or unconscious obstacles to our ability to change our minds. I say this much more for myself than for Harold.

This leads to a convergence of reasons urging a negative response to the question "Can Christianity be the only true religion?" So let me now lay out as clearly, but also as cautiously, as I can what I truly believe is a convergence of reasons why I, as a professed Christian and struggling disciple of Jesus, can and must insist that Christianity is *not* the only true religion. Those reasons come under the categories of history, of philosophy, of ethics, of theology, and finally of sacred scripture.

HISTORY: A CHANGE IN CHRISTIAN BELIEFS

There has been a change of Christian beliefs. If we look at the history of our churches, we cannot deny that although at one time just about all the churches held firmly that Christianity is the only true religion, today many churches do not. My Roman Catholic community is an example of a major Christian denomination that, as it were, has changed its mind (although, when my church changes its mind or teachings, it never admits of doing so). Simply stated, at one time, all Christians, before the Reformation and after, held that "Extra ecclesiam nulla salus"—outside the church, no salvation. (The Protestant version might read, "Extra verbum"—outside the preached Word, no salvation.) Today, all Catholics and most mainline Christians don't hold such beliefs. And from the data of the recent Pew research project, as stated on the Greer-Heard website, "A majority of American Christians (52%) believe that at least some non-Christian faiths can lead to eternal life." And the website adds, "At least

37% [of these Christians] are members of evangelical churches that teach that salvation comes only through faith in Jesus Christ."[27]

Our question has already been answered by a broad swath of Christians. And as theologians, we have to take the faith of the faithful seriously. We Catholic theologians call that the "sensus fidelium," and it must play a major role in guiding our theological deliberations.

This change in no way has diminished our commitment and discipleship. I want to point out that, as far as I can measure the fervor of my fellow Catholics at Sunday Mass or of my fellow Christians at daily chapel at Union Theological Seminary, this change of belief has in no way diminished their commitment to Christian living and witness.

This means that more change can come. One further observation from this historical perspective: what has changed can continue to change. Many of us so-called progressive theologians within the mainline churches are suggesting and trying to pave the way for a further change: if the church has shifted from exclusivism to inclusivism (I would call my friend Harold a "fuzzy inclusivist"!), a further shift from inclusivism to pluralism would seem to be possible—again, without in any way diminishing the fervor of faith and discipleship. (If such fervor is diminished by a new theological proposal, the proposal is most likely heretical.)

ETHICS: THE DANGER OF ONLY ONE TRUE RELIGION

The claim that there is only one true religion is dangerous, for two reasons: it prevents the necessary dialogue of civilizations, and it fosters the clash of civilizations.

First, holding that there is only one true religion prevents dialogue. What I'm arguing here is based on the well-known and broadly affirmed dictum of Hans Küng: "There will be no peace among nations without peace among religions. And there will be no peace among religions without a greater dialogue between them."[28] Küng's admonition is based on an ethical imperative: The religions of the world have the moral obligation to engage each other in a peacemaking dialogue. It is here, in this moral imperative of dialogue, that I find the danger of exclusive truth claims. The danger, I think is evident: If we understand dialogue in its most simple and succinct description as "a mutual exchange through which all sides seek to help each other grow in knowing and doing what is true and right," then how can any of the partners really be open to growing in the truth when they believe that they have the fullness of God's truth? The game of dialogue is not possible when one religion enters the game claiming that God has dealt them all the aces. What impedes a moral imperative can be considered, I believe, immoral.

If we are really serious and sincere about wanting to promote a dialogue of civilizations and religions (as, for example, Pope Benedict XVI claims), then we have to question our own assertions that God has given the only or the final revelation to our religion (which the pope refuses to do). You can't have it both ways.

Second, holding that there is only one true religion promotes violence. Claiming that my religion is the only true religion is dangerous not only because it prevents true dialogue but also because it fosters violence. I deliberately chose my words in that last sentence: exclusive claims *foster* violence between religious groups or civilizations. They do not necessarily *cause* such violence, but they can condone it, encourage it, and strengthen it. In general, the root cause of religious violence is, I believe, *not* religious. If I may indulge in an extravagant generalization, I would argue that the usual cause of religious violence is, as it is for most international (or national) violence, conflict over power, often economic power. Violence becomes a necessary tool either to carry out and defend, or to resist and change, forms of economic exploitation. But if you are a president or a king seeking to advance your cause, or if you are a political or popular leader seeking to defend your cause, it sure helps to have at your disposal a religion that holds itself up as God's privileged faith and plan for the world. If you can tell your followers that they are advancing or defending not only their own cause but God's cause, God's ultimate vision for the world, God's privileged people, then you will be able to swell your ranks not only with *more* soldiers but with *better* soldiers. Fighters in state armies or resistance movements who believe that "Gott ist mit uns" (God is with us), that they are struggling for God's truth and doing God's will, not only will be braver, they also can be more brutal—ready to give their lives as they pilot planes that crash into buildings or drop bombs on villages. As Charles Kimball has argued in his fine little book *When Religion Becomes Evil*,[29] one of the principal reasons (though certainly not the only) why religion can so easily be enlisted to justify and intensify violence, or why religion can so easily be used to declare that the others—terrorists or imperialists—are the evildoers while we are the good-doers, is the way religions have claimed to deliver the absolute or final or superior truth over all others. Absolute religious truth so easily becomes violent religious truth.[30]

I believe Sharon Welch has it right: "The logic of religiously sanctioned violence is straightforward. Whether it be the Buddhist defenders of imperial Japan, the abolitionist John Brown, or the Muslim leader Osama bin Laden, the justifications for terror and violence are the same: they and their followers are the bearers of unassailable truth and harbingers of ultimate good, commanded by the absolute to destroy their enemies and bring about a reign of peace and justice for all of humankind."[31]

THEOLOGY: TO BE A CHRISTIAN IS TO BE A PLURALIST

For all our Christian communities, the most compelling reasons for recognizing that there is truth—and I would add *salvific* truth—in other religions are to be found not outside our own "cultural-linguistic" system, but from within our own beliefs, our own guidelines for being disciples of Christ. Let me offer three theological considerations why I believe this to be so.

First, the God that Jesus experienced and incarnated was a not just the Creator God, not just the God of history; the God of Jesus was also, and especially, the Abba God, a God best symbolized as a loving parent. Yes, this God was a God who makes demands, who insists on justice, who is intent on freeing slaves and the oppressed. But in all that, before all that, supporting all that is the first and fundamental truth about this God: the God of Jesus is a Power of pure, unbounded love. To say this is to say, further, that this God wants to embrace all of God's children, all of God's creation. As Saint Paul states it, this God "wants all people to be saved and to come to a knowledge of the truth" (1 Tim. 2:4 NIV).

As my teacher Karl Rahner insisted, if God wants to save all people, then God will act in such a way as to make this a real possibility for all people. In other words, if as Christians we believe that God's grace is necessary for salvation, then God will find ways of offering God's grace to all people. To deny or question this is not to believe in a God of love. Rahner, as you know, went on to claim that the religions are among the most available and readily-at-hand ways in which God will make this offer of grace. (This piece of Rahner's case is based on his conviction that God's grace and action in our lives requires some form of concrete—or incarnational—mediation.) I must admit that after all these years, I find that Rahner's theological case for the presence of truth and grace in other religions continues to be compelling: a God who loves all will offer that love to all, and one of the most likely ways to do that is the religions.

My question for Harold would be this: It seems to me that the belief in a God of universal love is incompatible with the belief that Christianity is the only true religion. The only way to hold together these two assertions (God is love, and Christianity is the only true religion), I believe, is either to fabricate a theological deus ex machina and hold the God provides a special revelation of Christ at the moment of death, or to affirm (with Karl Barth) an *apokatastasis*—everyone will be saved at the very end.

Second, the kenotic Christ is the Way that is open to other Ways. One of the richest resources for retrieving and elaborating a Christian theology of religions that recognizes the value and potential truth of other traditions is to be found in the way theologians are exploring the depths and implications of a truly kenotic Christology. If we take Paul in Phil. 2:5-11 seriously, we will have to recognize and allow ourselves to be challenged by what for Paul and the early community was an essential ingredient in proclaiming the divinity of Jesus: God incarnates God's self—and Jesus becomes the incarnation of God—through a process of self-emptying. No self-emptying, no incarnation.

So incarnation requires kenosis. But we must ask why. Self-emptying in itself is not a value (as feminists remind us). It is always a means to an end. God empties God's self, Jesus empties himself, in order to make room for the other—in order to embrace the other, in order to enter into a reciprocal relationship with the other. In other words, the purpose of kenosis is dialogue. And relationship and dialogue require that we affirm the value, the dignity—and that means the potential truth—of the other. A dialogue which insists that one side has the truth and the other does not is not based on the kenosis, or self-emptying, that we find in Jesus.

David Jensen makes this point beautifully and powerfully: "The movement of kenosis is to de-center the 'self'—and anything else—from a privileged place of permanence. . . . The confession of the kenotic Christ cannot rest in pointing to the *figura* of Jesus Christ alone, above all others. . . . Christomonism—the proclamation of Jesus Christ at the expense of everything else—is a distortion of the life of discipleship and not its faithful execution. Indeed, conformity to Christ involves being claimed by others, and not claiming others as our own."[32] A kenotic, dialogical Christology leads us to a dialogical understanding of the uniqueness of Jesus. John B. Cobb Jr. formulates it as "Jesus is the Way that is open to other Ways."[33] The truth of Jesus' way is open to the truth of other ways.

This means that the particularity of Jesus is a strange kind of particularity: its role is to make known the universality of God. The God whom Jesus reveals is a God who reaches beyond the revelation that Jesus offers. In knowing and understanding the truth that Jesus makes known to us, we are opened to the truth that the Spirit of Jesus makes known beyond Jesus. Douglas John Hall describes this in his efforts to follow this Jesus: "What is so fascinating about the 'necessary,' if 'scandalous,' *particular* named Jesus is that, being person, he puts us in touch with a *universal*, God, who as living Person transcends our ideas and images of the divine *in the very act of coming close to us.* . . . Contrary to later (and usually heretical) Christologies, Jesus as he is depicted in the Gospels and epistles of the newer Testament, does not wish to be considered (as it were) all the God of God there is."[34] And on the basis of such theological analysis, Hall makes a personal confession of faith that epitomizes a kenotic-dialogical Christology: "I can say without any doubt at all that I am far more open to Jews and Muslims and Sikhs and humanists and all kinds of other human beings, including self-declared atheists, *because* of Jesus than I should ever have been *apart* from him."[35]

Third, the Spirit of Christ is universal. Such a kenotic Christology views the particularity of Jesus as essentially linked to the universality of God, as emptying itself in order to make room for the universality of the Divine. Such a Christology clamors for help from pneumatology. We cannot truly understand and take seriously the particularity of Jesus unless we link it to the universality of the Holy Spirit.

Here I see what I believe is the richest resource that contemporary theologians are drawing on—especially Pentecostal theologians—in order to lay the foundations for a Christian recognition of the truth and value of other religions. Some of these theologians, such as Amos Yong, are suggesting that pneumatology is the way around the impasse that Christology has become for Christian dialogue with other believers.[36] The universal God that Jesus points to can best be understood as the universal Spirit who moves as she will, often as unnoticed as wind, throughout all creation.[37] The activity of this Spirit is essentially the same as, but reaching beyond, the work of the incarnate Word in Jesus. The Spirit, like the Incarnate Word, is at work in communicating the presence and power and love of God, drawing all of creation to an awareness of its source and true being in the Divine.

AN EGALITARIAN TRINITY

This pneumatological path around the Christological impasse is leading us toward what I would call an "egalitarian theology of the Trinity"—an understanding of the Trinity in which all three persons have equal rights and distinctive, though always interrelated, roles. Trinitarian theology affirms that the three persons are truly different from each other and one cannot be subordinated to the other, but they are also truly and essentially related to each other. This means that the work of the Spirit cannot be reduced to the work of the Word (even though both are essentially the same in their divine natures). As Saint Irenaeus reminds us, God as it were has "two hands"—the Word and the Spirit. They are both God's hands, equally so. One might say that God is ambidextrous, not favoring the right or the left.

Here Amos Yong voices a warning that we Christian theologians have not sufficiently been aware of: "So while discerning the Spirit is intimately connected with the Christ, this should not be understood in a way that subordinates the Spirit to Christ."[38] He admits that "those of us exploring a pneumatological approach to the religions are confronted decisively with the finality and normativity of Jesus Christ." But he adds, "Does it serve to finally resolve the relationship between pneumatology and Christology by subordinating the former to the latter?"[39] If the Spirit is truly different from the Word, then we can expect to find traces of that difference *ad extra*. What the Spirit is up to will not be able to be simply reduced to what the Word has revealed.

THE NEW TESTAMENT: EXCLUSIVE LANGUAGE IS CONFESSIONAL AND PERFORMATIVE LANGUAGE

But what about all the language in the Bible that *does* place Jesus in the center, to the apparent exclusion of any possibility of truth in other religions? "No other name . . . One mediator . . . Only begotten Son . . . No one comes to the Father except through me." We're biblical people. We have to take this language seriously. That means we have to ask not only what it meant but also what it means.

The New Testament scholar who has helped me most to figure out what it means is Krister Stendahl. He points out that all this talk about Jesus as "one and only" is essentially confessional language, not philosophical or ontological language. Or more personally, he calls it love language. The early Jesus-followers were speaking about the Jesus with whom they were in love, who had transformed their lives, whom they wanted others to know about. People in love are passionate about what they feel and exuberant in how they speak. They naturally use superlative language—"you are the most beautiful, the most adorable, the one and only." Such language is exclusive in order to be superlative. The primary intent is to be superlative, not exclusive.

The intent of such language is to say something positive about Jesus, not something negative about the Buddha. We misuse this language when we use it to degrade or exclude the Buddha or Muhammad. The intent of this "one and only" language, I would suggest, was essentially twofold: (1) to express the total, personal commitment of the Christian community to Jesus; and (2) to proclaim the universal meaning and urgency of what God had revealed in Jesus.

I am suggesting that we are faithful to this language primarily by affirming its *decisiveness* for Christian life and its *universal* significance and urgency for all peoples of all times. Exclusivity is not necessary to preserve what this language means for us today.

CONCLUSION

Allow me to conclude with a personal statement of faith: Recognizing that we are all fallible and that I may be fundamentally wrong, still, at this stage of my life—a fairly late stage coming after about forty-six years as a Christian theologian—I must confess my faith that Jesus is indeed the Way that is open to other Ways and that to be a faithful follower of Jesus I must recognize and engage the truth that the Spirit may be offering me in my Hindu and Buddhist and Muslim and Jewish and Native American brothers and sisters. Here I stand. I cannot do otherwise (unless Harold—with the Holy Spirit—can convince me otherwise!).

DIALOGUE AND Q&A

Harold Netland: You have to appreciate Paul's strong Lutheran conclusion. I know I will not persuade him to change his mind, but never underestimate the power of the Spirit. (*Audience laughter.*) Seriously, his comments at the beginning were very good and very appropriate. As Christians, we do need to be deeply committed to what we believe to be the truth. There is also a dimension of intellectual integrity which demands that to the best of our ability we approach issues with open minds, looking at the evidence and when necessary making adjustments. So I do appreciate those comments.

Paul did e-mail me and ask if he could use the term *fuzzy inclusivist* in referring to me, and I responded, "I've been called a lot worse." (*Audience laughter.*) Just a comment on that: I used to use those three categories: exclusivist, inclusivist, and pluralist. Of the three, the term *pluralist* is easiest to define, at least the way I define it. I have come to see, though, that those three categories really are not helpful, and in several recent articles, I have argued that we really need to drop them.[40] There are so many issues on the table. The categories are usually defined in terms of the question of salvation, but even if you're just looking at the question of salvation, it's very, very hard to fit the different, very carefully nuanced perspectives into just one of those three categories. And there are so many other issues on the table besides that question that I think forcing positions on theologies of religion into one of those three categories just is not helpful. In my response to Professor Knitter, I have five or six issues I wish to touch on. Some of these I will raise in the form of questions for clarification from Paul; in one of them, I will respond to a challenge he made; and then there will be one or two areas where we do frankly disagree.

Paul began by drawing the contrast between the first-century world and the present. Also, I believe that at the end of his opening statement, a similar kind of a contrast was operative. Here is my first question, and I mean it seriously: How exactly is the New Testament language and the world of the New Testament, i.e., the beliefs of the first followers of Jesus as we find this codified and expressed within the written Scriptures, how is that normative for us today? Because, as one reads or listens to Professor Knitter, it's very easy to draw the conclusion that the language used about Jesus in the New Testament is simply the product of that time, and that we need to think differently today because it's now such a different world. And so my question is simply: How in fact is what the New Testament says normative for us today?

My second question is as follows: How does Paul Knitter understand the concept of truth in religion? I define truth in religion in terms of beliefs and discussion of what I call defining beliefs, and so on. That's one way to do it. I don't get a clear definition or explanation from Paul, but his understanding of religious truth seems to be a function of two things—a religion is true if it can be a means to salvation and/or if we find people within the religion manifesting what Galatians 5 speaks of as the fruit of the Spirit: love, hope, joy, long-suffering, and so on. So my question here is simply: What do we mean when we say a religion is true or that Christianity cannot be the sole true religion? If we look at these qualities that we find in people—and I don't deny that you find peace and joy and so on in followers of other religions—but if that becomes the defining characteristic for the truth of a set of beliefs or a way of living, it seems to me that we must say that atheism is also true, because I certainly have known atheists who have peace, and joy, long-suffering, and patience in their lives, and so on. So that would be a second question.

Third question—and again, I'm not intending to be facetious here, Paul. I first encountered Paul's book *No Other Name*[41] when I was living in Tokyo. I read it and marked it up—as I do all good books—while riding the trains around Tokyo. Now, at that time, in the mid-1980s, Paul Knitter was clearly a pluralist, very much in the same kind of paradigm as John Hick, although articulating and nuancing things somewhat differently. In his later writings, he has begun using the wording of "mutualism," which seems to be a little bit different from Hick's model of pluralism, or is it? I'm not entirely sure on that. Now tonight—and I rejoice in this—he sounds very theistic, speaking in terms of God. So my question is simply this: Ontologically, what is the religious ultimate? Is it God the Holy Trinity? And in asking that, I fully admit that there is much to God the Holy Trinity that we don't understand, but for Christians, classically, God is the religious ultimate. It doesn't get any higher than that. Or is there something beyond the symbol of God that is really ultimate? This, of course, is the route that John Hick takes.[42]

We are moving quickly, but now to an area of admitted disagreement. First of all, though, let's start on agreement here. I do agree with Paul that religious violence is a huge, huge issue today. This has to be taken seriously by all of us, and we Evangelicals, as we do so often, have come late to the discussion and the issues on religious violence. So I'm in full agreement with him on that. Moreover, I would say we Evangelicals need to clean up our act in this area. I think our discourse, and especially the discourse of American Evangelicals—having lived outside the United States for many years, I'm sensitive to how others look at American Evangelicals—we have used Christian discourse to justify and to support social-political agendas that I certainly would want to question. So these would all be areas where I think Paul and I would agree. My question, however, is this: Is the commitment to the belief that there is a true religion, and that my religion or the beliefs that I embrace are true in a distinctive manner, is that in itself conducive to religious violence? I simply don't see the evidence for that claim. I simply don't see the evidence. Religious violence is an enormously complicated phenomenon. You're talking about issues of class, power, land, ethnicity—problems and disputes that go back for centuries. The belief that you are a special people blessed by God can be and often is used to justify abusing other people and violence; I don't question that, but is there anything in the belief that there is a true religion and that I happen to believe that this is the true religion, is there anything in that belief itself that *necessarily* leads to violence? I think, with all due respect, that is a very simplistic approach. Paul makes reference to the work of Charles Kimball.[43] But rather than Charles Kimball, I would recommend Mark Juergensmeyer on this issue.[44] I think Juergensmeyer offers a highly nuanced and perceptive discussion of that whole issue.

Let me finish here by addressing the issue of salvation in other religions. How do we know anything about salvation—about how we should understand the nature of salvation and the necessary conditions for realizing salvation? It's not something that you just read naturally off of the natural order. I would say it's God's revelation in the Scriptures and in the incarnation that tells us about salvation, and this includes of course the idea that God is love. But the same Scriptures that speak about God as love also speak about judgment. I wish they didn't. I wish they didn't; I'd love to excise those passages out of the Scriptures. But I don't see how we can appeal to the theme of God as love, which I firmly embrace, without also talking about this other theme that I find embedded throughout the Scriptures: judgment. And the fact, as I see it, is that not everyone ultimately will be saved. I don't want to dispute the theme that God is love. Paul Knitter has rightly emphasized that. I would simply say that's only part of the story. First Timothy 2:4 tells us that God wants all people to be saved and to come to a knowledge of the truth. Yes indeed, absolutely. But I am not a Calvinist; I do believe that people can and do resist God's grace, that they refuse God's offer of salvation. So I don't see the incompatibility between that affirmation and what I also see in Scripture as the reality that not everyone will be saved.

Well, I see I am out of time. I was going to comment also on love language and so on, but perhaps that will come up in the Q&A time. Thank you. (*Applause.*)

Paul Knitter: Thank you again, Harold. I think that many of the points that I had prepared to comment on your paper are probably going to touch on most of the questions you raised. If not, we'll talk further. I wanted to address three issues coming out of Harold's presentation. The first deals with religious language. The second deals with religious differences, which are a key point in your presentation. And then the third deals with the fact that all religions make claims of having the superior truth. I think the first two will touch on some of the questions you just posed for me, Harold.

First, concerning religious language, there's probably a pretty fundamental difference here—not an unbridgeable difference, but a difference—in our understanding of what it means to talk about God and things of God, such as salvation, Jesus, the incarnation, grace, and sin. First of all, let me state where we are in agreement. I do *not* want to avoid truth statements; in fact, I want to include propositional statements of truth. I don't want to boil everything down to Wilfred Cantwell Smith's "That's just how it moves me" (that's a paraphrase). Certainly, I don't want or to reduce religious truth solely to myth. However, I do believe (and I say this both because of the influence of my training and the teachers but also on the basis of my own experience) that all of our language about God is—and I know this is not going to go over well here—symbolic. As Paul Tillich, whose chair I occupy at Union Theological Seminary, reminded us, when we do experience the reality of God, the reality of Divine Mystery, the reality of God's truth in our lives, we also realize that what we are experiencing is beyond all of our clear, solid, definitive human comprehension. There's always a surplus; there's always more. So as true as it is that we have experienced God's reality right now—the reality of a God of love, or a God of support, or a God that empowers us to work for justice—as true as that is, and as much as we're ready to die for it, at the same time we know that there's more, that the reality of God also exceeds what we have experienced and what we know. And so our language becomes language that's more poetry than it is philosophy. It has to be. Religious language is inherently, incorrigibly, unavoidably symbolic.

Also, as symbolic, religious language is performative. It arises out of and leads to calling us to act in certain ways in the world. It calls us to *right living*. By that, I mean living our life in such a way that we find peace and purpose in our own lives and connect with others in love and compassion. The primary quality of religious language, therefore, is its power is to enable us to act in certain ways. So I do want to claim (you've heard me say this before) that right acting, orthopraxis, has a certain primacy over orthodoxy. The two, however, are essentially related. We cannot have one without the other (here I have some critical concerns about Buddhism), but the primacy is orthopraxis. So in all our religious language—that means when we speak about God as triune, when we speak about Jesus as divine, when we speak about our human predicament as sinful, when we speak about the world as having been created—we're using symbolic language. We have to take this language very seriously for it to empower us, but it's language that, while it is saying something very true, it's not saying everything that is true. It's saying something very important, important enough to die for, but it's not saying everything.

And because symbols are so powerful, because they always contain more than they say, we have to think about our symbols. As Paul Ricoeur reminds us, symbols give rise to thought. Here we face the daunting task of trying to unpack the truth of symbols in propositional statements. But the propositional statements are never going to be able to capture the fullness of what is communicated to us in that poetic, symbolic, metaphoric language of God as love, God as Trinity. So you see, religious truth, the truth of the symbol, is found in its ability to affect my life. Religious truth is truth for me when it opens me to meaning and purpose that gives me an inner peace and strength, and when it enables me to engage in a life in which I am furthering the well-being of myself and others.

For me personally, the truths and the symbols that so enable me to live my life I find primarily in Jesus Christ. And that means in and through the New Testament. So I can say not simply that the New Testament is true for me, but that it continues to be truth. It's true because it continues to work, because it continues to inspire, because it continues to animate the community. So the language of the New Testament is absolutely essential for me. It contains the first witness of the early community of Jesus-followers. And yet it is language that we can never say we have understood definitively, that we have understood finally. And as a good Catholic, let me add: we can never say that we have understood it infallibly. (On this point, the pope may disagree—but that's a Catholic issue). (*Scattered laughter.*)

The second issue I would like to explore further with you, Harold, has to do with the very real differences between religions. You speak about contrarieties. I prefer that word to "contradictions." If the differences between religions are contrary, they allow for complementarity. If they are contradictory, then we simply have to agree to disagree. This reminds me of the well-known Zen Buddhist image and reminder: We may need fingers to point to the moon. But the finger can never be the moon. So yes, our very different religious truth claims are different fingers pointing to the moon. And they are very important fingers, for there are truly different ways of approaching the moon. We need many fingers. But even when the differences between these fingers seem to contradict each other, because they can never be identified with the moon, it's possible that they may be pointing to the same moon!

I have found that most, certainly not all, of the contraries—the different fingers—that I have discovered in my exploration of other religions, and especially of Buddhism, have proven to be much more complementary than contradictory. This includes even the examples you have given of what you think are contradictions between Buddhism and Christianity: Christian claims that God created the world versus Buddhist convictions that there was not point of creation in time. Or even more fundamentally, the Christian assertion that there is a God and the Buddhist refusal to speak about a God. As you say, these certainly seem like out-and-out contradictions.

But I would urge you to be careful. Try to look more deeply, for we are dealing with symbolic language, or with fingers that point but can never be identified with what they are pointing to. I have found that what the Buddhists are suggesting to me, and to Christians in general, is that in a very real sense to think about God as a reality that exists as an object outside of ourselves, an object that we can identify, may be leading us to certain forms of idolatry; such language may end up capturing or reifying the mystery of God. What I'm saying here is that for me, my dialogue with Buddhism, and with the Buddhist assertion that there is no God as an entity that confronts me from the outside, has not only enabled me to appropriate the mystical content of our Christian tradition; it has also helped me, I think, to appropriate Saint Paul's talk about God as ultimate mystery (1 Cor. 2:7-8; Rom. 16:25; Col. 1:26-27). To unpack all this would take a book; in fact, it's the book I've been working on for quite some time.[45]

Finally, I think we need to talk more about superior-truth claims. There's no doubt about it, all religions, including Buddhism and the supposedly inclusive religions of Asia, have made claims that "my religion is better than yours." I don't want to deny that. And I don't want to deny that among particular religious truth claims or practices, some can be better than others—or some are true, and others are false. What I want to challenge are the sweeping, broad claims that my religion is on the top of God's list or at the end of the line. To put it somewhat cutely (I hope not crudely), I would like to challenge religious claims that seem to be saying, "My God is bigger than your God" or "My savior excludes your savior" or "My prophet is the final prophet over your prophet."

I want to explore the possibility that religions and religious believers, instead of making such final, absolute claims of superiority, would, rather, announce claims of universality. So in approaching the table of dialogue, religious believers will not announce that they have been given the superior or final truth over all others; rather, they will offer what they think are the universally meaningful or necessary truths that God has given them. So as a Christian, I would witness to what I have discovered in my religion, through Jesus Christ, and why I think it is true, important, powerful, and meaningful, not just for me, but also for you. And therefore I remain a missionary. All religious believers, if they take their beliefs seriously, have to be missionaries. They want to share the truth that they have been given.

But they make this witness and announce this message with what I would call "epistemic humility," which is quite different from the epistemic parity you criticize. Yes, I make my universal claims, but in the humble recognition that there may be universal claims coming from others (now I'm getting back to the Holy Spirit working in other religions) that could lay claim on me. Sometimes that will lead to contradictions where we have to choose one or the other. But we have to be careful about too quickly identifying contradictions. As I've said, for the most part, when I have encountered the universal claims of Buddhism, and often of Hinduism, I have found that they have enriched me in very unexpected ways; they have often enabled me, for instance, to reappropriate or to take another look at what the New Testament means.

I'll end with an example of a text of a New Testament passage that has come alive and claimed me through my dialogue with Buddhism in ways that

I don't think could ever have been possible without that dialogue. I'm talking about Gal. 2:20: "It is no longer I that live, it's Christ who's doing the living in me." Reading and praying over that text with my "Buddhist glasses" so to speak, I've found deeper meaning and power in it. That's just one example of such possibilities.

So I think that if we would recognize that our religious language is poetry, divine poetry, and if we take our poetry seriously but also humbly and then open ourselves to the poetry of others, maybe we'll end up being better Christians, and the world may be better off, too. (*Applause.*)

Netland: Let me briefly respond. I do want to leave time for questions, too. Two quick comments: Paul has rightly highlighted the importance of understanding religious discourse. It's a very complicated subject; some of you are familiar with that. Yes, symbols point to things. Poetry makes or can make affirmations, and in making affirmations, you rule out certain things. In speaking of propositions, I don't want to suggest that religious assertions are like physics equations. Propositions can be vague. Propositions can be precise. Of course we need to understand and admit that there is much in any statement about God that we don't fully understand. Take a simple reality like the microphone down there. In saying "There's a microphone on the stand," I'm making a true statement. There are all kinds of entailments that follow from that statement that I don't understand or couldn't be aware of. And so, yes, you do have to bear in mind the dimension that surpasses what we are aware of. Nevertheless, if religious discourse is going to have *any* purchase, if you're going to take the religious writings and the leaders from the different communities on their own terms seriously, there's something there that we do understand, and in making assertions some things are ruled out. And here I think, frankly, Paul and I do have somewhat different understandings of Buddhism, and it could be because Paul works more in the Mahayana tradition, while more recently I have been looking more at the Theravada tradition. Japan, where I grew up and then lived for ten years as an adult is Mahayana, so initially I was more familiar with the Mahayana tradition.

But more recently, I've been working in the Theravada tradition and exploring some of the earlier disputes in the Indian traditions between Buddhists, Hindus, and Jains and so on. The idea of religions themselves, as clearly identifiable, sharply different or distinct entities, is something of a modern notion, and we need to keep that in mind, so it's not like the followers of Gautama set out and said, "Let's start a new religion." There were significant similarities among various ancient Indian philosophical and religious groups. But don't miss the point that the followers of Gautama were seen by the traditional Brahmanical, or what today we call the Hindu, community as deviant and embracing views that were rejected as heretical. There were vigorous disputes among them over a number of questions, including "Does Brahman exist?" and between Hindus and Buddhists and Jains, like "Is there a substantial enduring soul, atman?" The literature is full of vigorous exchanges and what we today would call sharp analytic analysis of these claims.[46] And it was very, very important because all three communities believed that how you understand reality is *directly related* to whether you attain liberation. So these are not isolated or insignificant disputes. Either God exists or God doesn't exist. Hindus and Buddhists traditionally have acknowledged that this is an important ontological question and that both sides cannot be correct in what they affirm about the reality of Brahman. Much depends on how you define the concept of God, obviously. I have a list here of eight or ten Buddhist scholars who are familiar with the Christian understanding of God and simply flat out say, "Buddhism is atheistic; if that's what you mean by God, Buddhism is atheistic." Nagarjuna, the Indian philosopher so influential with the Mahayana, has an essay explicitly arguing against the possibility of there being a creator.[47]

So I want to take those kinds of disputes seriously and say they aren't just superficial disputes or language disconnects and that if you really understand what's happening, we're really on the same page here. I don't think we're on the same page. And I think that to admit that we are not ultimately in agreement about the reality of God is to take at least some of these traditional Buddhist communities seriously on their own terms. But I think from previous conversations with Paul that he and I have a little different understanding of the Buddhist tradition here on this point.

Knitter: Clearly, there have been the disputes that you point out, Harold, and I think you're better acquainted with them and have studied them more carefully than I. I want to take them seriously, but at the same time, maybe what were disputes then in that context, given that historical situation, don't necessarily have to be the same kind of disputes today.

Netland: Yes, that's fair.

Knitter: I think, as we engage in a world in which we're confronting the religious other not only more extensively but also more existentially than ever before, perhaps the context is such that we can look at some of these basic differences differently. Now, I say that not just to be nice. I want to be nice but also serious. In trying to do so, I realize, Harold, that our understanding of language, religious language, is not the same. The encounter with other religions, especially Buddhism, is requiring us Christians to ask ourselves just what we mean when we use our language about God. The word *God* itself is a symbol. The word *God* is a pointer. The word *God* doesn't capture what this reality of God is. The dialogue with Buddhism is urging Christians to look at the reality of God in a more nondualistic way than we have in the past. We have considered God and the world as two very distinct, divided, separate realities: God there, the world here. That is a bit exaggerated, I know. But there are very clear demarcations between the divine and the finite in Christian theology. My dialogue with Buddhism has pushed me to explore a more nondualistic, a more unitive and mystical understanding of God in which God is no longer an entity outside of me, but a power that has its very being within me.

Netland: Hmm.

Knitter: Now, if that sounds strange, I want to ask you what I ask myself: Is such a nondualistic understanding of God really that foreign to Christian tradition and experience? Such a nondualistic understanding of God is, I believe, contained, or can be reappropriated, in our symbol of God as spirit. I don't think we've really taken this central symbol of God as spirit seriously enough. I've been challenged to look more deeply into Jesus' admonition that we can truly worship God only if we remind ourselves that "God is spirit" and that we must worship God "in spirit" (John 4:24).

Netland: Hmm.

Knitter: Such a nondualistic God cannot be identified with the world, but at the same time cannot be found other than in the world. And so God and the world are not simply two. That's nondualism.

Netland: Hmm.

Knitter: But that doesn't mean that they're one! Rather, God is God, and we are humans, but we have our being in each other. This doesn't mean that we are God, but that we have our being in God, and that God has God's being in us. This is one of the ways in which Buddhism has nudged me toward a more unitive, personal understanding and experience of God. Maybe I'm way off

Christian base here. But I don't think so. My prayer life, thanks to Buddhism, has improved.

Netland: Yeah. Hmm. And, in fact, you are writing, or have finished writing, a book of how the study of Buddhism has affected you or helped you.

Knitter: Yeah, I've given it the audacious title of *Without Buddha I Could Not Be a Christian.*

Netland: There you go. OK. Hmm.

Robert Stewart: All right, let's open it up for questions. This aisle for questions for Paul Knitter, and this other aisle for questions for Harold Netland. We will alternate between the two.

Question 1: Dr. Knitter, you claimed at the beginning of your presentation that the context we're in today is different from what it was with the early church, and because of this, that Christians should change their perspective on inclusivism. However, when addressing issues of eternal existence, why would context determine the legitimacy of the specific truth claim about God?

Knitter: Wait, say that last part again.

Question 1: When addressing issues of eternal existence, why would context determine the legitimacy of specific truth claims about God?

Knitter: I'm not sure what you mean by eternal existence.

Question 1: God has always been who he was since all of eternity, and so if he always has been this one person, why would the context in which we are in right now change who he is?

Knitter: The very articulation that you used, "God is one person," is one way, a very important way, of understanding the mystery that is God. It's a way that grew up at a certain time in a certain place, and it is very key for us because it grew up in the New Testament period. But still, we may be able to understand the mystery of God in other ways, not fundamentally contradictory to what went before, but really different, and that's my point.

All of our language is always, as the postmodern philosophers tell us, socially constructed, always limited. I don't want to go too far with that, but there is something to what they're claiming. So as contexts change, we have perhaps the opportunity to understand, and to feel, the mystery of God in our lives in different ways.

Question 2: Hi, this is really for both of you, but from an Episcopal perspective to offer a different take on . . .

Knitter: That's Catholic, too. (*Laughter.*)

Question 2: The question I want to raise is one of generational perspective. I was in one of the last classes in the early seventies to have to worry about the draft, and my own personal quick observation of that float is that the combination of the civil rights movement and the antiwar movement caused a morality shift across all denominations, but I'm alert to it because I can see it because our prayer book in the Episcopal denomination changed in 1970. Back in that time, there was a lot of questioning of authority, including questions like "Who are we to judge anybody?" I'll also make the observation that a lot of people who didn't want to go to the Vietnam War headed for seminary. And a lot of those people are coming of age in all denominations and rising to positions of leadership. So my question for you is: Do you think there's some sort of generational bias such that we're imposing our own views on maybe some more traditional things in the Bible?

Netland: My short answer is that I'm sure that's the case, but could you be more specific?

Question 2: I'm just calling attention to words—the exact stuff that you're talking about—that we got very vague with language in trying to be inclusive within ourselves. What do we mean by justice, because that can mean a lot of different things to different people? I've learned to ask what you mean.

Netland: Can I just give a quick response?

Knitter: Oh, yeah!

Netland: I think, if I hear you, that what you're getting at is, "What is theology anyway? How do we, if we accept Scripture in any sense as normative or as divinely inspired, take a two-thousand-plus-year-old document and appropriate it for where we are today?" I have found David Wells's very short definition of theology very helpful. This is a very concise summary which won't do Wells's discussion justice, but essentially he suggests that theology involves us, from our perspective where we are located today, asking the question "What does it mean for us to be the recipient of God's revelation in this world at this time?"[48] And so implicit in this understanding of theology is that God has revealed himself to humankind, and there clearly are differences here on how we understand that, but I take God's revelation to be codified in Scripture and, to take the language out of Hebrews 1, the apex of God's self-revelation is in the incarnation. God's self-revelation then becomes normative, but then of course we have to ask the question "So what does it mean for me in 2009 where I am?"—I was going to say Chicago, but I guess this is New Orleans—"What does it mean for me to engage God's revelation in *this* context?" In that sense, every generation has to be reworking that question.

But the issue I was probing a bit with Paul was just in what sense then is that two-thousand-plus-year-old document, Scripture, normative for us today? I would say it's very, very normative, and that's why to me it's very important to try and understand the language of the apostle Paul, or the language of the Gospel writers and so on. One of my problems with pluralistic theologies of religions is simply that I think if the writers of the New Testament intended to put forward pluralistic views, they certainly had the resources to do so, and such pluralism would have been a very popular view in the first-century Mediterranean milieu. So the fact that I don't find that kind of language in the New Testament to me is significant.

Question 2: I'd agree.

Stewart: OK, thank you. Paul, did you want to respond?

Knitter: No, that's all right. (*Audience laughter.*)

Question 3: First, thanks for being here; it was a great debate. Dr. Knitter, I've read a number of your books, and I've enjoyed them thoroughly, and from them I get the distinct impression that you're first a liberationist—that's where your heart is, and that's how your praxis has played out. And from that your pluralism grows. Is that correct?

Knitter: Yes, yes.

Question 3: Now, I've read also some critiques of your writing, one in particular by Dr. Netland, that challenge the hermeneutic of starting with liberationism and working backward toward pluralism. How does that not put you on shaky hermeneutical ground? I would like you to address that, please.

Knitter: So, just to make sure I understand your question correctly, your first name is?

Question 3: Christopher.

Knitter: Christopher, you're referring to the shift in my thinking when I moved from "theocentrism," or God-centeredness, to "soterio-centrism," or salvation-centeredness.

Question 3: In order to substantiate your liberationism, if you think of liberation as the goal, the vehicle to get you there is pluralism. So you are working backward basically from the goal in trying to justify the goal by providing a means. Isn't that kind of hermeneutically backward?

Knitter: Well, I guess I wouldn't put them in such a neat "first this, then that" order. I understand the hermeneutical task more as a circle, not a straight line.

Question 3: Or a spiral . . .

Knitter: Or a spiral. That may be even better. I can respond to your question in the general context of my own personal faith journey and of my theological career. I began as a Catholic priest in a missionary order, the Society of Divine Word. Then I had to deal with the other religions, since I wanted primarily to convert them, so at that time, I tried to take the reality of religious pluralism seriously. Then, after I left the priesthood, got married, and became involved in social action in Cincinnati, especially through my wife, we took multiple trips during the eighties to El Salvador. We worked with the base Christian communities there and together with the Jesuits, six of whom were murdered because of their work for liberation. It was then that I realized that to be a Christian, I have to confront not just the many religions, but also the reality of the many poor. And I saw that both of those hermeneutical lenses can interpret each other. I realized that if we are really going to confront and do something about the structures of oppression that exist in our world, and which at that time I felt our government was supporting in what was going on in El Salvador, we need to draw on all the religious resources we can find, because religions have resources to confront oppression. But then I saw that that calling the religions to work together to promote human well-being and to confront oppression became a hermeneutical context in which you can carry on an even more effective interreligious dialogue. So I saw them as kind of a circle, with one feeding into the other. Does that help you?

Question 3: More or less, for right now.

Stewart: Great. Let's have another question.

Question 4: Dr. Netland, I agree with Dr. Knitter that there needs to be a great amount of dialogue among the faiths. How are we as Christians to claim Christ as the only way? How are we to reconcile that in light of what Scripture does declare in 1 Tim. 4:7 when it says to have nothing to do with irreverent or silly myths? How are we to reconcile that in light of our exclusive claims yet still having this pressing need to carry on discourse and dialogue with other faiths?

Netland: I guess I don't see the connection there, or let me put it a different way: I think that text and other similar texts like that in the New Testament are addressing in-house issues within Christian communities where you have division and discord and trouble of one kind or another. That's a qualitatively different situation than dealing with people who don't even profess any kind of allegiance explicitly to Christ.

I agree with Paul Knitter on the need for interreligious dialogue. We need to be engaged in dialogue. The word *dialogue* is a very tricky word, and especially among Evangelicals, it raises all kinds of red flags. At Trinity, when students object to interreligious dialogue, I say, "Fine, just substitute the word *conversation* for *dialogue*." We need to be talking with each other; we need to be listening to each other. We can learn from others; hopefully, they can learn from us. To put it in very, very crass terms that we Evangelicals understand and prioritize: How can you share the gospel with someone without engaging in conversation or dialogue? We need two-way listening. So dialogue has many forms. It can be informal; it can be formal, or ecclesiastical. We have many Muslim communities in the United States now. We have pastors who will invite Muslims for dinner in their church or in another more neutral site with parishioners simply for the sake of getting to know each other. This is wonderful, so I applaud all of that.

What I disagree with is the idea that you can't engage in *real* dialogue if you believe somehow that your religious claims are true and those that conflict with yours are false. That's where I say, "Wait a minute; why not?" My own sense, too, is that those from other faith traditions expect Christians to disagree with them. They don't think we all agree. And so I don't think they're surprised when we say, "You know I disagree with you on that, and here is what I think." Can you do this respectfully while also being convinced that God has revealed himself distinctively in the Scriptures and the incarnation? I don't see why not.

Are there people who are exclusivist in a negative sense, who are belligerent and socially intolerant of others and so on? Yes, of course there are. But you don't have to be that way. So my challenge to Evangelicals is "Let's join the conversation!" But you can do that while still being fully committed that God has distinctively revealed himself in the Scriptures and in Christ.

Knitter: I'm not against making truth claims in the dialogue. And I don't think that that's an impediment to dialogue at all. But I fear that it is an impediment to the dialogue if I make truth claims that I think I have fully and finally understood.

Netland: Hmmm.

Knitter: In other words, it is one thing to make a truth claim and to say, on the one hand, "This is it; anybody who disagrees with this is out," and, on the other hand, to say, "This is the truth claim I make; this is how I understand it; this is, I believe, what God has revealed to me, but"—this is what I meant by epistemic humility—"I recognize that my grasp of what I believe God has given me may be inadequate." In fact, it *is* inadequate. No one can understand God's revealed truth fully and finally. So I enter the dialogue with truth claims; I go in with commitment to my own truth claims. But I also go in with an openness through the dialogue to revisioning my truth claims. I think if I go in feeling that this is the truth in its propositional formulation, that God has given to me in my community, and it cannot be changed in any way, then I don't see how there's any dialogue possible. Rather, I engage other religious believers with this approach: "This is a truth claim that I do believe originates from God, but I can't claim that I know what this truth claim fully entails and how this truth claim may be clarified, deepened, corrected through a dialogue with you."

Netland: Maybe we can agree on this: Any really serious, sincere, intense discussion on these kinds of matters is, to some extent, going to leave both parties changed. I think we might disagree on the nature and the extent of the change, but just given the nature of a serious interreligious conversation, both parties are going to be affected and come away somewhat changed. I would certainly agree with that.

Knitter: I don't want to have the last word, but I have a statement that I think you would agree with. It comes from John Cobb. I don't have the exact formulation, but basically it is this: "The one fundamental prerequisite for dialogue, if you want to just boil everything down to what is necessary for dialogue, is that you enter the conversation recognizing that you have something to learn."

Netland: That is a good insight.

Stewart: The sad thing about this forum is that we never have enough time for the questions. But there are other avenues of asking questions. There is the reception and book signing. You can meet these men personally and shake their hands and so forth. I have found that a great way to get your question answered is to precede it with the question "Will you sign my copy of your book?" I've never met an author who wouldn't answer a question after you bought his book and asked him to sign it.

Notes

1. For argument supporting this claim, see Harold Netland, *Encountering Religious Pluralism* (Downers Grove, IL: InterVarsity, 2001), chs. 6–7; and Paul J. Griffiths, *Problems of Religious Diversity* (Oxford: Blackwell, 2001), chs. 1–3.

2. See, for example, Clark Pinnock, *A Wideness in God's Mercy: The Finality of Jesus Christ in a World of Religions* (Grand Rapids: Zondervan, 1992); John Sanders, *No Other Name: An Investigation into the Destiny of the Unevangelized* (Grand Rapids: Eerdmans, 1992); Millard Erickson, *How Shall They Be Saved? The Destiny of Those Who Do Not Hear of Jesus* (Grand Rapids: Baker, 1996); *What about Those Who Have Never Heard? Three Views on the Destiny of the Unevangelized*, ed. John Sanders (Downers Grove, IL: InterVarsity, 1995); and *Faith Comes by Hearing: A Response to Inclusivism*, ed. Christopher W. Morgan and Robert A. Peterson (Downers Grove, IL: InterVarsity, 2008).

3. I am using "religious pluralism" not as a descriptive term denoting religious diversity but rather as a term for a particular view about the relation among the various religions. In this sense, religious pluralism is the view that the major religions are all equally legitimate alternative ways of responding to the same divine reality, and that no single religious tradition can legitimately claim to be distinctively true or normative for all people. Religious pluralism in this sense is identified

primarily with John Hick, but Paul Knitter has also advocated versions of pluralism. See John Hick, *An Interpretation of Religion*, 2nd ed. (New Haven: Yale University Press, 2004 [1989]); idem, *A Christian Theology of Religions: The Rainbow of Faiths* (Louisville: Westminster John Knox, 1995); Paul F. Knitter, *No Other Name? A Critical Survey of Christian Attitudes toward the World Religions* (Maryknoll, NY: Orbis, 1985); *The Myth of Religious Superiority: A Multifaith Exploration*, ed. Paul F. Knitter (Maryknoll, NY: Orbis, 2005); *The Uniqueness of Jesus: A Dialogue with Paul F. Knitter*, ed. Leonard Swidler and Paul Mojzes (Maryknoll, NY: Orbis, 1997); and *The Myth of Christian Uniqueness: Toward a Pluralistic Theology of Religions*, ed. John Hick and Paul F. Knitter (Maryknoll, NY: Orbis, 1987). See also Peter Byrne, *Prolegomena to Religious Pluralism* (London: Macmillan, 1995); and idem, "It Is Not Reasonable to Believe that Only One Religion Is True," in *Contemporary Debates in Philosophy of Religion*, ed. Michael L. Peterson and Raymond J. VanArragon, 201–10 (Oxford: Blackwell, 2004).

4. Joanne O'Brien and Martin Palmer, *The Atlas of Religion* (Berkeley: University of California Press, 2007), 14.

5. Roger Schmidt et al. *Patterns of Religion* (Belmont, CA: Wadsworth, 1999), 10.

6. Ninian Smart, *The World's Religions*, 2nd ed. (New York: Cambridge University Press, 1998), 11–22; idem, *Worldviews: Crosscultural Explorations of Human Beliefs*, 2nd ed. (Englewood Cliffs, NJ: Prentice-Hall, 1995).

7. Ninian Smart, *The Religious Experience*, 5th ed. (Englewood Cliffs, NJ: Prentice-Hall, 1996), 5.

8. Griffiths, *Problems of Religious Diversity*, 21.

9. William P. Alston, *A Realist Conception of Truth* (Ithaca, NY: Cornell University Press, 1996), 5.

10. Wilfred Cantwell Smith, *Questions of Religious Truth* (London: Victor Gollancz, 1967), 67–68 (emphasis in original). See also Wilfred Cantwell Smith, *The Meaning and End of Religion: A Revolutionary Approach to the Great Religious Traditions* (San Fransisco: Harper & Row, 1962); and idem, "A Human View of Truth", in *Truth and Dialogue in World Religions: Conflicting Truth Claims*, ed. John Hick, 20–44 (Philadelphia: Westminster, 1974).

11. Hick, *An Interpretation of Religion*, 348.

12. For an elaboration of these points, see Harold Netland, *Encountering Religious Pluralism*, 197–211, 232–46.

13. This point is made nicely by William J. Wainwright, "Wilfred Cantwell Smith on Faith and Belief," *Religious Studies* 20 (September 1984): 353–66.

14. The Golden Rule is explicitly stated in the Analects of Confucius and is implicit in the writings of other religious traditions. See Confucius, *The Analects*, trans. D. C. Lau (London: Penguin, 1979), 12.2 and 15.24, 112, 135. See also John Hick, *An Interpretation of Religion*, 316–25.

15. See Sarvepalli Radhakrishnan, *Indian Philosophy*, vols. 1–2 (New York: Macmillan, 1923); Ninian Smart, *Doctrine and Argument in Indian Philosophy* (London: Allen and Unwin, 1964); and Richard King, *Indian Philosophy: An Introduction to Hindu and Buddhist Thought* (Washington, DC: Georgetown University Press, 1999).

16. On conflicting claims in the religions, see William A. Christian, *Oppositions of Religious Doctrines: A Study in the Logic of Dialogue among Religions* (London: Macmillan, 1972); idem, *Doctrines of Religious Communities: A Philosophical Study* (New Haven: Yale University Press, 1987); and Ninian Smart, *A Dialogue of Religions* (London: SCM, 1960).

17. See Griffiths, *Problems of Religious Diversity*, 31–37.

18. Keith Ward, "Truth and the Diversity of Religions," *Religious Studies* 26 (1990), 4–5.

19. Keith Yandell, "How to Sink in Cognitive Quicksand: Nuancing Religious Pluralism," in Peterson and VanArragon, *Contemporary Debates in Philosophy of Religion*, 191.

20. Christian, *Doctrines of Religious Communities*, 1–2, 5–11.

21. The literature on Christian theism is enormous. Helpful works that provide good reasons for believing that God exists include Richard Swinburne, *The Existence of God*, 2nd ed.

(New York: Oxford University Press, 2004); Stephen T. Davis, *God, Reason and Theistic Proofs* (Grand Rapids: Eerdmans, 1997); Keith Yandell, *Philosophy of Religion: A Contemporary Introduction* (London: Routledge, 1999). Helpful works on the incarnation in Jesus Christ include Stephen T. Davis, Daniel Kendall, and Gerald O'Collins, eds., *The Incarnation* (New York: Oxford University Press, 2002); Oliver D. Crisp, *Divinity and Humanity: The Incarnation Reconsidered* (Cambridge: Cambridge University Press, 2007); Murray J. Harris, *Jesus as God: The New Testament Use of Theos in Reference to Jesus* (Grand Rapids: Baker, 1992); Larry Hurtado, *Lord Jesus Christ: Devotion to Jesus in Earliest Christianity* (Grand Rapids: Eerdmans, 2003); Simon Gathercole, *The Preexistent Son: Recovering the Christologies of Matthew, Mark, and Luke* (Grand Rapids: Eerdmans, 2006).

22. See Eugene Thomas Long, ed., *Prospects for Natural Theology: Studies in Philosophy and the History of Philosophy*, vol. 25 (Washington, DC: Catholic University of America Press, 1992); and James F. Sennett and Douglas Groothuis, eds., *In Defense of Natural Theology: A Post-Humean Assessment* (Downers Grove, IL: InterVarsity, 2005).

23. This is a basic assumption underlying John Hick's model of religious pluralism. See John Hick, *An Interpretation of Religion*, ch. 13. See also Robert McKim, *Religious Ambiguity and Religious Diversity* (New York: Oxford University Press, 2001).

24. See Paul J. Griffiths, *An Apology for Apologetics: A Study in the Logic of Interreligious Dialogue* (Maryknoll, NY: Orbis, 1991); and Harold Netland, "Natural Theology and Religious Diversity," *Faith and Philosophy* 21, no. 4 (October 2004): 503–18. For a creative and thoughtful approach to natural theology, see C. Stephen Evans, *Natural Signs and Knowledge of God: A New Look at Theistic Arguments* (New York: Oxford University Press, 2010).

25. Helpful introductions to the subject include Paul F. Knitter, *Introducing Theologies of Religions* (Maryknoll, NY: Orbis, 2002); and Veli-Matti Kärkkäinen, *An Introduction to the Theology of Religions* (Downers Grove, IL: InterVarsity, 2003).

26. "The WEF Manila Manifesto," in *The Unique Christ in Our Pluralistic World*, ed. Bruce J. Nicholls, 15–16 (Grand Rapids: Baker, 1994).

27. Greer-Heard Point-Counterpoint Forum, http://www.greerheard.com/, accessed March 20, 2009.

28. *Global responsibility: In Search of a New World Ethic* (New York: Crossroad, 1991), xv.

29. Charles K. Kimball, *When Religion Becomes Evil: Five Warning Signs* (San Francisco: HarperSanFrancisco, 2002).

30. These last few paragraphs are drawn from my first lecture at Union Theological Seminary, published as "My God Is Bigger than Your God . . ."

31. Sharon D. Welch, *After Empire: The Art and Ethos of Enduring Peace* (Minneapolis: Fortress Press, 2004), 14.

32. David H. Jensen, *In the Company of Others: A Dialogical Christology* (Cleveland: Pilgrim, 2001), 190, 87, xii.

33. John B. Cobb Jr., "Beyond Pluralism," in *Christian Uniqueness Reconsidered: The Myth of a Pluralistic Theology of Religions*, ed. Gavin D'Costa (Maryknoll, NY: Orbis, 1990), 91.

34. Douglas John Hall, *Why Christian? For Those on the Edge of Faith* (Minneapolis: Fortress Press, 1998), 33.

35. Ibid., 34.

36. Amos Yong, *Beyond the Impasse: Toward a Pneumatological Theology of Religions* (Grand Rapids: Baker, 2003).

37. Ibid., 45–46.

38. Ibid., 169.

39. Ibid.

40. See Harold Netland, "Religious Exclusivism," in *Philosophy of Religion: Classic and Contemporary Issues*, ed. Paul Copan and Chad Meister, 67–80 (Oxford: Blackwell, 2008); and

idem, "Inclusivism and Exclusivism," in *The Routledge Companion to Philosophy of Religion*, ed. Chad Meister and Paul Copan, 226–36 (London: Routledge, 2007).

41. Knitter, *No Other Name?*.

42. See Hick, *An Interpretation of Religion*.

43. See Kimball, *When Religion Becomes Evil*.

44. See Mark Juergensmeyer, *Terror in the Mind of God: The Global Rise of Religious Violence*, 3rd ed. (Berkeley: University of California Press, 2003); and idem, *Global Rebellion: Religious Challenges to the Secular State, from Christian Militias to Al Qaeda* (Berkeley: University of California Press, 2008).

45. It has since been published: *Without Buddha I Could Not Be a Christian* (Oxford: Oneworld, 2011).

46. On the differences between Hindu, Buddhist, and Jain claims, see Smart, *Doctrine and Argument in Indian Philosophy*; King, *Indian Philosophy*; and John M. Koller and Patricia Joyce Koller, *Asian Philosophies*, 3rd ed. (Upper Saddle, NJ: Prentice-Hall, 1998). For an excellent study of the critique of the Hindu belief in Brahman by a Buddhist thinker, see Parimal G. Patil, *Against a Hindu God: Buddhist Philosophy of Religion in India* (New York: Columbia University Press, 2009).

47. See Nagarjuna, "Refutation of the View of God Being the Creator of the World and of the View of Visnu Being the Sole Creator of the Whole World," in *Papers of Th. Stcherbatsky*, trans. Harish C. Gupta, ed. Debiprasad Chattopadhyaya, Soviet Indology Series no. 2 (Calcutta: R.D. Press, 1969), 10–11. The Sri Lankan Buddhist scholar K. N. Jayatilleke claimed that "the Buddhist is an atheist and Buddhism in both its Theravada and Mahayana forms is atheism." K. N. Jayatilleke, *The Message of the Buddha*, ed. Ninian Smart (New York: Free Press, 1974), 105. Walpola Rahula asserts that, "According to Buddhism, our ideas of God and Soul are false and empty." Walpola Rahula, *What the Buddha Taught*, 2nd ed. (New York: Grove, 1974), 52. The Burmese Buddhist U Thittila states, "In Buddhism, there is no such thing as belief in a body of dogmas which have to be taken on faith, such as belief in a Supreme Being, a creator of the universe." U Thittila, "The Fundamental Principles of Theravada Buddhism," in *The Path of the Buddha: Buddhism Interpreted by Buddhists*, ed. Kenneth W. Morgan (New York: Ronald Press, 1956), 71. For a fascinating exchange over whether Buddhism is compatible with theism, see Perry Schmidt-Leukel, "'Light and Darkness' or 'Looking through a Dim Mirror'? A Reply to Paul Williams from a Christian Perspective," in *Converging Ways? Conversion and Belonging in Buddhism and Christianity*, ed. John D'Arcy May (Sankt Ottien, Germany: EOS Klosterverlag, 2007), 67–87; José Cabezon, "A Response to Paul Williams's *The Unexpected Way*," in May, *Converging Ways?*, 89–115; and Paul Williams, "Buddhism, God, Aquinas and Morality: An Only Partially Repentant Reply to Perry Schmidt-Leukel and José Cabezon," in May, *Converging Ways?*, 117–53.

48. See David Wells, *No Place for Truth, or Whatever Happened to Evangelical Theology?* (Grand Rapids: Eerdmans, 1993), 99–101.

2

Theologies of Religious Diversity: Toward a Catholic and catholic Assessment

Terrence W. Tilley

Judgments about the fittingness of various proposed theologies of religious diversity vary as much as the theologies do. All too often, however, people rush to judgment on the basis that a given theological proposal does or does not fit with the Bible or the tradition. But such a precipitous response all too often takes the Bible or the tradition as giving a single clear theology of religious diversity, a view belied by the great diversity of interpretations of Bible and tradition, by the variety of problems of understanding religious diversity, by the variety of proposed solutions by committed Christians, and by the lack of consensus within most denominations and between denominations about the judgments made or the criteria for making those judgments.

In what follows, I develop four rules from the Catholic Christian tradition that can be used to guide theologies of religious diversity.[1] I claim that these rules limn the "grammar" of the major statements proclaimed by the magisterium of the Roman Catholic Church during and since the Second Vatican Council (1962–1965).[2] I also suggest these as useful guides for the consideration of other Christians. At the end of this paper, I evaluate the approaches of Harold Netland and Paul Knitter, using these rules as criteria.[3] Each rule is articulated as a commandment. This is a tongue-in-cheek way to signal that there are other formulas possible, even if these formulations do validly articulate a particularly Catholic and generally Christian approach.

Four "Commandments" for a Theology of Diversity

I. THOU SHALT NOT DENY GOD'S UNIVERSAL SALVIFIC WILL.

The first rule, requiring us to acknowledge God's universal salvific will, distinguishes a Catholic approach from the narrow exclusivism characteristic of *some*Evangelical theologies. Such exclusivist views imply that either God did not desire to save all people (impugning God's creative goodness) or that God is not able to make that desire a real possibility for all people (impugning God's power).[4]

The key to this injunction is the document of the Second Vatican Council, *Nostra Aetate*, and the subsequent series of clarifications and expansions of that document. *Nostra Aetate* declared that "all peoples comprise a single community, and have a single origin, since God made the whole race of men dwell over the entire face of the earth" (§ 1). It went on to state, "One also is their final goal: God. His providence, His manifestations of goodness, and His saving designs extend to all men (cf. Wis 8:1; Acts 14:17; Rom 2:6-7; 1 Tim 2:4)" (§ 1). The document further asserted that the church rejects nothing "true or holy" in other religious traditions (§ 2) and that Christ died for the salvation of all (§ 4).[5]

This is not a new position but a development of an ancient one. In his summary of the teaching of the church fathers before Saint Augustine, Francis A. Sullivan, S.J., noted three points that they held in common. First, they had a "generally positive attitude on the possibility of salvation for both Jews and Gentiles who had lived before the coming of Christ."[6] While there was no clear consensus on just how God saved the holy ones of old, the ancient writers did not exclude them from salvation simply because they were not explicit members of the church. Second, they had a "uniformly negative attitude about the possibility of salvation for Christians who were separated from the great church by heresy or schism."[7] Those who refused to remain in the community enlivened by the love of God were effectively refusing God's love. So those who *put themselves* outside the church were putting themselves outside the community of salvation. Third, only when Christianity becomes established as the religion of the Roman Empire—and the actual, if perhaps all too often nominal, religion of most of its citizens—do writers exclude pagans and Jews from the circle of salvation. This is the point that the motto, *extra ecclesiam nulla salus* (outside the church there is no salvation), becomes rigidified. Sullivan concluded his analysis as follows:

If people were damned, it was not because God did not will their salvation; it was because they had refused the means of salvation he had provided for them. This does not mean that the judgment of guilt passed by Christian writers against heretics, schismatics, pagans and Jews was necessarily a correct judgment, or one that we can share. They may well have been wrong in their judgment about the guilt of the people who were outside the church. The important thing is that *if their judgment was mistaken, it was a mistake about the guilt of people, not about the justice or salvific will of God*.[8]

In sum, claiming that some were excluded from salvation was directed against those who left the church (before the establishment of Christianity as the official religion of the empire) or who would not join the church (after establishment)—and they were all "guilty" of refusing God's salvation by refusing to affiliate with the church. This is not directed to those who could not be guilty—those for whom association with the church was a practical impossibility.

The contrary view that God's salvific will is not universal is rooted in a reading of Saint Augustine, especially in his anti-Pelagian writings. However, if one attends to Augustine's rhetorical subtleties, one notes that he is not denying God's universal salvific will, but following a North African tradition of preaching to motivate "us" (and others) to avoid a dreadful fate. Threatening with fire and brimstone does not entail that one believes that God will actually throw some into eternal flames, just that God *can* do so if a person's life warranted it. Despite usual interpretations of Augustine, all people *may*be part of "us" who are spared by a gracious God. There is no reason not to hope so, especially if we live well.[9]

The universal salvific will of God may be universally effective, *pace* an all-too-common reading of Augustine's theology. In line with the earliest tradition and with Vatican II, then, any account that actually denies the universal salvific will of God is "outside the camp." The crucial point is this: whereas some ancient and medieval theologians presumed the moral guilt of those who were outside the church, Vatican II, along with some ancient theologians, presumes that those outside the church may well be morally innocent of rejecting salvation, and thus can be encompassed in the "us" whom God wills to be saved.[10]

But if those outside can be saved, then *how* can God save them? That leads to formulating a second rule.

II. THOU SHALT NOT DENY THE SUFFICIENCY OF GOD'S SALVATION IN AND THROUGH JESUS CHRIST.

The Second Vatican Council put it this way: "Christ . . . is the one Mediator and the unique Way of salvation" (*Lumen Gentium* § 14). In his encyclical *Redemptor hominis* (1979), Pope John Paul II noted that "every man . . . has been redeemed by Christ, and . . . with each man . . . Christ is in a way united, even when man is unaware of it" (§ 14). The International Theological Commission (1997) devoted a chapter of "Christianity and the World Religions" to the unique mediation of Jesus. It concluded that only "in Jesus can human beings be saved, and therefore Christianity has an evident claim to universality" (§ 49). It also stated that other "possibilities of salvific 'mediation' cannot be seen in isolation from the man Jesus, the only mediator" (§ 49).[11]

The early Christian texts on salvation through Christ alone were worked out in crucibles of conflict. They are weapons in a rhetorical battle. The anti-Jewish polemics in the Gospels of John and Matthew are the products of young and marginal communities of Jews devoted to Jesus as Messiah who were attempting to find their own identities as within the wide range of possibilities present in Judaism before and after the fall of the temple in 70 C.E. These texts, properly understood, do not license anti-Semitism or anti-Judaism. Similarly, the argument for the exclusive universality of salvation in and through Jesus characteristic of the patristic writers functions as polemics against apostates and opponents. Those who joined other sects, participated in mystery religions, or devoted themselves to the state religion were the targets of these blasts. It is an error to take them—or the anti-Jewish rhetoric in the New Testament—as if they were carefully articulated statements of theological principle rather than as shots fired in hot rhetorical battles. It is historically and theologically mistaken to take them literalistically as articles of faith.[12]

We need to note, however, some crucial points about this claim. First, it is not at all clear that Christian concepts of salvation are commensurable with notions of the final destiny of humanity found in other traditions, as Joseph A. DiNoia, O.P., and S. Mark Heim note.[13] Although some philosophers and theologians use "salvation" as if it were a generic concept for "human destiny" issues, this is not a precise use. It is, rather, the extension of a Christian term beyond the boundaries of the tradition in which it originated.[14]

Second, these rules do not guide God's acts, but our claims. Some of our Buddhist friends might believe that the Buddha-essence within us needs to be brought out and that over the course of many lifetimes, we might come to Nirvana or that Amidha Buddha will ultimately bring all into the Pure Land. Their rules guide them in their practices and relationships with those who share their tradition and those who do not; their rules do not guide the flow or power of the Buddha-essence or govern Amidha Buddha. These rules are not simple claims or "first-order assertions" about the way things are, but sophisticated theological guidelines for our practices, "second-order rules." This is not to deny that we can and sometimes should make first-order claims about salvation in and through Jesus Christ. Just how those first-order claims are to be formulated is a matter of significant theological debate.[15]

One cannot separate Christ from Christ's church. The quotation that began this section is part of a more complex whole: "This sacred Synod turns its attention first to the Catholic faithful. Basing itself upon sacred Scripture and tradition, it teaches that the Church, now sojourning on earth as an exile, is necessary for salvation. For Christ, made present in His Body, which is the Church, is the one Mediator and the unique way of salvation" (*Lumen Gentium* § 14). Nor is it possible to separate the church from the universal salvific will of God. Pope John Paul II wrote that "it is necessary to keep these two truths together, namely, the real possibility of salvation in Christ for all humanity and the necessity of the Church for this salvation" (*Redemptoris Missio* § 9). Hence, we need a third rule about the church.

III. THOU SHALT NOT DENY THE NECESSITY OF THE CHURCH FOR SALVATION.

This rule recapitulates what *extra ecclesiam nulla salus* explicitly articulates. Fr. Francis Sullivan's analysis suggests that the way in which the church is necessary is not a settled issue.[16] For example, the Congregation for the Doctrine of the Faith wrote in *Dominus Iesus*, quoting Pope John Paul II, "'the action of Christ and the Spirit outside the Church's visible boundaries' must not be excluded" (*Dominus Iesus* § 19).[17] Even the magisterium doesn't say *how* to articulate this point.

Yet because the church is the universal sacrament of salvation does not mean that other faith traditions are not *in some sense* willed by God to make available in some way the grace and truth of salvation.[18] Nor can we deny that the church has to be in mission. One of the criticisms of the practice of interreligious dialogue is that it evacuates the work of evangelization of its appropriate urgency. There seems to be an inconsistency between the practices of interreligious dialogue and evangelization. However, the Pontifical Council for Inter-Religious Dialogue construed this issue differently: "Proclamation and dialogue are thus both viewed, each in its own place, as component elements and authentic forms of the one evangelizing mission of the Church. They are both oriented towards the communication of salvific truth" (*Dialogue and Proclamation* § 3). These items need to be unpacked in the context of understanding the necessity of the church.

First, dialogue takes four diverse forms. *The dialogue of life* is the very practice of living together, supporting each other in a local context of religious diversity. *The dialogue of action* is the practice of collaboration across faith traditions to work for justice and development for all people. *The dialogue of theological exchange* is the practice of scholars seeking to understand more clearly their own heritage and to appreciate others' heritages as well—and, clearly, we can learn much about our own tradition by listening to and appreciating the testimony and criticism of others. *The dialogue of religious experience* emerges in the practice of sharing spiritual values and practices across traditions, as when Tibetan Buddhist and Western monastics share their traditions and practices (cf. *Dialogue and Proclamation* § 42). The significance of recognizing that dialogue takes multiple forms will appear at the end as we assess the various theological proposals regarding religious diversity.

Second, witness is the most effective proclamation.[19] Our practices, including the practice of believing, are our primary form of witness. The saying attributed to Saint Francis of Assisi, "Preach the Gospel always; if necessary, use words," is relevant here. The ways we use words and the purposes for which we use them vary. Christians want to evangelize the unchurched, spread the good news in lands that have never heard it, re-evangelize the lapsed Christians, and may even delight in the conversion of others to Christianity. Yet there are times and places in which explicit proselytizing provokes resistance and rejection by hearers, especially if there is a gap between our words and our other deeds. Recognizing and affirming the necessity of the church does not always demand verbal proselytizing, but it clearly demands witness. Members committed to the church witness in all they do to the beauty, truth, goodness, and justice that they find in the Christian tradition, and that they find the tradition advocating in and for the world. Alas, Christians' moral failures also function as witness to Christianity, but a profoundly negative witness. If our witness is not positive, our church loses credibility. This is not a claim about the way things should be, but about the way things are. That each form of dialogue calls for evangelization in the appropriate forms of witness seems obvious. Such witness makes the message credible in the context of dialogue.[20] In any event, coercion or tactics that undermine others' integrity are ruled out; tactics that provoke resistance should also be avoided.

The necessity of the church is connected with the sufficiency of Christ for salvation and the universal salvific will of God. The first three rules are clearly internal to the Christian tradition. The fourth rule is also internal to the tradition, but also seems one we ought to share with those who are not Christians.

IV. THOU SHALT AFFIRM THE DIGNITY OF EACH AND ALL HUMAN PERSONS.

One significant theme of the Second Vatican Council was the dignity of the human person. Descriptions of human dignity, its rootedness in God, and its implications for our life together are sprinkled through many of its documents.[21] Perhaps the strongest, and most astonishing (at the time) affirmation of human dignity as expressed in diverse religious traditions can be found in *Dignitatis Humanae*, the Declaration on Religious Freedom of the Second Vatican Council:

> This Vatican Synod declares that the human person has a right to religious freedom. This freedom means that all men are to be immune from coercion on the part of individuals or of social groups and of any human power, in such wise that in matters religious no one is to be forced to act in a manner contrary to his own beliefs. Nor is anyone to be restrained from acting in accordance with his own beliefs, whether privately or publicly, whether alone or in association with others, within due limits.
>
> This Synod further declares that the right to religious freedom has its foundation in the very dignity of the human person, as this dignity is known through the revealed Word of God and by reason itself. (§ 2)

The commitment to recognizing human dignity is not based merely in philosophical theory, but rather in the Catholic Church's understanding of divine revelation. This commitment is at the heart of Catholic teaching on social, political, and economic matters.

How to understand this rule and put it into practice remains underdeveloped. Robert Wuthnow has reported that participants in other faith traditions found Christians rather ignorant about other traditions.[22] The point is that Christians have not yet done a good job of recognizing the dignity of religious others. If they had, members of those faith traditions would not be calling for the increased respect and understanding that is needed to show that Christians accept their human dignity.[23] What Wuthnow values as the achievement of authentic pluralism is found not in the absence of faith, but in its full richness. As Rabbi Jonathan Sacks put it, "Difference does not diminish; it enlarges the sphere of human possibilities."[24]

Difference also must shape our understanding of the God who created each and all of us. The fact is that we belong to different faith traditions. However we may think God may work within and through those traditions, if we fail to recognize the intrinsic dignity of all as created in God's image and destined by God for communion with God, then we fail to observe this rule.

This difference prohibits religious imperialism. For to claim that our tradition is a diamond and the other traditions not precious stones is to deny the dignity of those whose lives have been shaped into what they are by their participation in those traditions. Heim and Sacks remind us that the unity of humanity is a unity of and in diversity. Those who would reduce our diversity to a minimalist vapid sameness in effect deny the dignity of each particular person. We are social by nature; part of who we are is materially shaped by the traditions and narratives that we live in and live out. The reductionism of diversity to "sameness in essence" neither respects the dignity of each and all nor avoids the most obnoxious form of intellectual imperialism—masked as "acceptance" of "what's 'really' the same as us." In doing so, we disrespect the other; we accept the others only as our mirror images, not as having the dignity of God's creatures, of being created in their real diversity in the image and likeness of God. They may even be our opponents, but they should not be our enemies; indeed, they are our friends because they are God's.

As Christians committed to human dignity, we must act in such a way that we respect the dignity of difference. This is not a flaccid relativism. Part of respecting others is confronting them in conversation when they have done what we find wrong or believe what we find inadequate. Evangelizing dialogue and witness is a requirement in such cases. Withdrawing into fideism, sectarianism, or solipsism is ultimately a terrible failure to recognize the dignity of others who are different from us. It is to cut them off from our part of the human community because their faith communities are not ours. That, in effect, is to deny them a place in God's community, the community of all of humanity. We may disagree profoundly with others in our community and work to change their minds and hearts on particular issues. We cannot abandon them. Abandonment of others affirms them as worthless to us; it is the ultimate denial of dignity.

Netland and Knitter: Do They Follow the Rules?

If these four rules do indeed express the "grammar" of the language that shapes the form of life that is Catholicism in particular—and are candidates for being recognized as the rules that do or should guide Christianity in general—how do the works of our primary speakers, Harold Netland and Paul Knitter, stand with regard to them?

Netland finds three issues that a theology of religious diversity needs to consider. What is the ultimate destiny of the unevangelized? How can Christians explain religious diversity? To what extent can Christians adapt and adopt practices and beliefs from other traditions in varied cultural contexts?[25] Although Netland does not claim to have developed a complete evangelical theology of religions, he has sketched its broad strokes.

With regard to the first question, Netland finds that despite a consensus on fundamental issues,[26] Evangelicals do not agree completely on the answer. Some find that only those who "hear the gospel and explicitly respond in faith to Jesus in this life can be saved."[27] These "hard exclusivists" or "narrow rejectionists" consign a vast majority of humanity—even those innocent of any actual sinful deeds—to eternal punishment. As noted in our discussion of the first rule, such exclusivists have to explain how it is that God does not desire to save all people and is yet all-good and all-just or that God wants that desire actualized but cannot do so despite being all-powerful. This challenge has led some Evangelicals to have a "wider hope" that some, perhaps even all, might be saved *not* through their own traditions (that would be an inclusivist approach not fully consistent with fundamental Evangelical claims) but through a combination of general revelation and divine graciousness.[28] Netland notes the perplexity and counsels that we cannot rule out such a possibility; while the Bible does not clearly license such a position as a proposition to be believed (it is far too speculative), it is certainly a hope that Christians can—and, I would claim, must—hold.[29] Hence, given our first rule, it is clear that an Evangelical "wider hope" position is in line with it, but it is not clear how a "hard exclusivist" or "narrow restrictivist" position can accord with this rule.

It is clear that Netland's position clearly exemplifies the second and third rules. All human beings are sinners and deserving of God's wrath. Yet the atonement effected by Jesus on the cross reconciles sinners to the Father.[30] For Netland, Christ's atoning work is sufficient to save all humankind, all sinners. Humans do not earn salvation (although perhaps they may refuse to accept it by remaining mired in sin or in rejection of God). The church as the community of the redeemed is to be in mission to all people.[31] While Netland's ecclesiology is not Roman Catholic with the latter's strong emphasis on the sacramentality of the church, clearly the church is God's arm working in the world. To affirm the "necessity" of the church might seem to undermine the doctrine of divine sovereignty. Yet the strong missiology of Netland's position suggests that it is of the essence of God's *church* to be in mission.[32] At minimum, this is an interesting alternative way of approaching the gist of the third rule.

In theory, Netland's approach supports the fourth rule. Indeed, is it not a sign of respect for each and all to see them as worthy of hearing the truth about God? However, there is some substantial tension here in Netland's practice. His conclusion from his earlier analysis of the ten criteria for judgment of the truth of faith that "one is justified in accepting the Christian faith as true *because it is the only world-view that satisfies the requirements of all the . . . criteria*"[33] has been challenged not only for the adequacy of the criteria, but also for the fairness of his application of them to other traditions.[34] His more recent work seems fairer, but when it comes to the central particular analysis of moral realism in truth in comparing Christianity and Zen (specifically the view of Masao Abe), Netland seems not to exercise interpretive charity and to afford the religious other the respect he deserves.[35] Netland quotes an important conclusion in a sentence from Abe and then comments on it: "'While in a human, moral dimension the Holocaust should be condemned as an unpardonable, absolute evil, *from the ultimate religious point of view even it should not be taken as an absolute but a relative evil.*' From the perspective of ultimate reality—that is, emptiness—we cannot condemn the Holocaust as evil, since moral categories do not apply on that level."[36] The criticism of Abe presumes that we can get to the perspective of ultimate reality, a point that Abe would deny. The inference that we cannot on Abe's view condemn the Holocaust is simply invalid. Abe must maintain silence about the ultimate viewpoint, and Netland does not show how he knows that ultimate viewpoint (some Christians and Jews have construed the Holocaust as horrible yet tolerated by God) and how one can call God good if God tolerates such evil in God's creation. For if God tolerates it, is it not good, at least comparatively? Or is nothing intolerable for God? And if the Holocaust is not intolerable for an all-good God, what is?

My point is not to decide this issue. My point is simply to show that Netland's position may tend to neglect the true diversity of religious practices and belief and disrespect the dignity of each and all who are different, even though Netland's theory requires respect for diversity and dignity. Those of us who have stopped seeking to hear the truth from others because we already have the truth (and one cannot seek for what one has—it is a conational impossibility) may tend to a certain intellectual imperialism. This seems to me a point that a supporter of a "wider hope" must take care about, for not to attend to such listening can all too easily violate the fourth rule.

If Netland's work is in some tension with our rules, what of Paul Knitter's? Knitter's work has moved from a theocentric, pluralist theory, very similar to that of John Hick's work, to a mutualist approach focused on Christians and others working together for social justice.[37] In so doing, Knitter's move shows that the criticisms of those like Netland who accuse a pluralistic position of an untenable relativism—a position with which I am in sympathy—do not obviously apply to Knitter's mutualist position.

Concern for human welfare is common to many faith traditions.[38] This concern and action to realize human welfare provides ground—properly "shaky ground"—for interreligious cooperation. This ground is "shaky" because it is no foundation but is the ad hoc practice of mutual cooperation. Such interreligious cooperation becomes more solid with "dialogue." That is, the point is not to engage in a dialogue to find common ground to get started. The "starting point can be clarified or corrected after one starts" working for common goals.[39] The point is not to build intellectual edifices, but to feed the hungry and understand how to overcome the social evil of hunger. In such cooperative action to ameliorate particular evils, shared understandings can emerge. Authentic interreligious dialogue is not a necessary *foundation* for cooperation, but the *result* of sharing the work and talking about it.

Knitter, in contrast to pluralists, has reversed the relationship of theory and practice.[40] The mutualist starting point, the turn to praxis, marks Knitter's moving away from philosophical foundationalism to using shared praxis as the fundamental point for connections and for common effort between faith traditions. This move also offers his position the opportunity to avoid denying Christ's uniqueness or traditional views of God or the church.[41]

The heart of mutualism is God's universal salvific will. Mutualism easily accords with our first rule. Knitter holds that Jesus is a unique and necessary mediation of God's salvific will, but God's universal salvific will also holds open the possibility that other mediations are or can be on par with Jesus Christ.[42] Hence, the mutualist christological posture does seem to deny "the sufficiency of salvation in and through Jesus Christ."

However, the issue is not settled. In an era when understanding salvation as wrought by the atoning blood sacrifice of Jesus suffering as our substitute has become less than credible as a theory of reconciliation, the issue of what salvation means must be reconsidered.[43] Liberation theology revamped soteriology to include social and this-worldly components as well as individual and next-worldly components. Knitter's understanding is worth considering:

> Followers of Jesus would be better off if they understood (and felt) Jesus more as a *sacrament* of God's love than a *satisfaction* for God's justice. In the technical language we've already encountered, the way

Jesus "saves"—that is, the way he enters people's lives and connects them with God—can be understood better as a *representative cause* rather than as a *constitutive cause*. More simply: Jesus "saves" people not by fixing something but by showing something. He doesn't have to fix or rebuild the bridge between God and humanity by responding to God's demand for satisfaction for humanity's sinfulness. Rather, his task is to reveal or show humanity that God's love is already there, ready to embrace and empower, no matter how often humans have lost their way in selfishness and narrow-mindedness. In other words, Jesus shows that the "bridge," or the relationship between God and humans, already exists; they just don't know where to find it or are not able to trust that it can be found.[44]

In this passage are the seeds of an orthodox flower.[45] If Jesus is truly a *sacrament* of God, then Jesus does not merely represent, but himself empowers those who walk in his way. The "showing" of a bridge is not a mere pointing out but is an exercise in enabling people to find it and to learn how to walk on it. When Jesus shows us the way, he also gives us the way.[46] It is possible that the mutualist tradition—though with some tensions and some questions still needing exploration—fits the second principle.

Our third rule is "Thou shalt not deny the necessity of the church for salvation." Once again, some of Knitter's claims seem to conflict with this rule. However, Knitter does not deny the *necessity* of the church for salvation. That mutualists deny the *sufficiency* of the church for salvation is not startling, but merely puts them in company with most contemporary inclusivists.

However, if Jesus is understood as the sacrament of God and the church as the sacrament of salvation, then it is the duty of the church to show as an effective sacrament, as Jesus did, the salvation wrought by God. Again, this showing is not simply proclamation of truths, but transforming witness. If the church's communication is to be effective, that is, to be the means that God uses to change others, then the church is necessary to continue on that divine communication. The image of the church as the body of Christ is important here. In this world, we can do nothing without our bodies. If God in Christ shows how God saves, then the church is necessary to keep hope alive and to remember in powerful practices, not just empty words, the way to life eternal.[47] Knitter has not formally violated the third principle, but his position is in tension with it. Then again, Netland is in tension with this principle, but for a different reason.

That mutualism fits the rule regarding human dignity seems obvious. Pluralism affirms a rough parity among religions and also the ability of non-Christian believers to encounter the transcendent. These seem to avoid any form of religious prejudice. However, mutualism is superior to pluralism on this specific issue because it does not tend to render differences among faith traditions superfluous as pluralism too easily can.[48] Properly understood, mutualism also should not succumb to intellectual imperialism or flat relativism, although such tendencies seem an all-too-common social and personal expression of sin.[49]

In sum, I find that Netland and Knitter diverge in different ways from the central thrust of the principles of a particularly Catholic and generally Christian approach to the problem of religious diversity. Yet even if the principles are correct and our colleagues here are in tension with them, the exploration of how to live in and live out our citizenship in God's commonwealth, the *basileia tou theou* (the reign of God) proclaimed by Jesus, is not finished. We all benefit from the ongoing debates of how to live faithfully in a pluralistic culture set in a global world, a context far from first-century Palestine, where our faith tradition was given its initial distinctive shape in the discipleship of Jesus' first followers. I believe we need to learn from each of them in order to shape adequate Christian theologies of religious diversity.

My own view is different. I do not believe these problems are soluble on a theoretical level. All we can do is to live as faithful disciples who commit ourselves to living together in peace with our diverse neighbors, who collaborate across faith traditions to work for justice and development for all people, who work to understand more clearly our own heritage and to appreciate and learn from others' heritages as well, and who share spiritual values and practices when appropriate across our diverse traditions (cf. *Dialogue and Proclamation* § 42). In the end, it is beyond our ability to comprehend how God will ultimately resolve the diversity, so our challenge is to work for more authentic practice in this world and have faith that God will care for all in the next.

Notes

1. This section of the paper is based on Terrence W. Tilley et al., *Religious Diversity and the American Experience: A Catholic Approach* (New York: Continuum, 2007), 47–63.

2. I put most of these rules as proscriptions rather than prescriptions. Prescriptions tell us what to do or believe. Proscriptions tell us what *not* to do or believe. Proscriptions allow for creativity in theology in that they remind us not to make certain moves as we build a theology in and for our faith tradition. Proscriptions admittedly sound negative, but prescriptions are actually

more constraining. Proscriptions leave room within a tradition for constructing new theological understandings in a way that prescriptions seem at times to exclude. Perhaps this is why the classic councils precisely proscribed what Christians were not to say ("Si quis dixerit . . . anathema sit") rather than prescribed what Christians were obligated to believe.

3. Tilley et al., *Religious Diversity and the American Experience* explores Knitter's journey (93–109); this paper marks my first exploration of Netland's approach. This evaluation is intended to be irenic rather than disputatious. Although there are significant elements in both positions that I cannot assent to (and some I would actively oppose as a theologian), the present focus is on the specific central issues involved in a theology of religions by considering the central strengths of the two approaches.

4. In 1 Tim. 2:1-6, there is a "proof text" for this view. Of course, there are many other proof texts that proponents of almost any view on the range of God's offer of salvation can quote from the Bible. And some Catholics will wonder how this squares up with the tradition of *extra ecclesiam nulla salus*, but that issue is discussed under rule III. I neither accept nor reject the proposition that people are able to refuse to accept God's will that they be saved, so we have to acknowledge that it may be possible that people have the freedom and ability to thwart God's will and do so. Hence, it may be possible that God's salvation is not universally effective. Even if it is possible for some to refuse God's grace, whether any actually do so is not a question relevant to my project.

5. This universalism is not unique to *Nostra Aetate*. In the Constitution on the Church, *Lumen Gentium*, the council declared that "all are called by God's grace to salvation" (§ 13). Members of other faith traditions are related to the people of God "in various ways" (§ 16). The Pastoral Constitution on the Church in the Modern World, *Gaudium et Spes*, noted that God's grace acts in the people's hearts in unseen ways and that we "ought to believe that the Holy Spirit in a manner known only to God offers to every man [*sic*] the possibility of being associated with this paschal mystery" (§ 22), a theme taken up in the decree on mission, *Ad Gentes* that declared that Christians are to "share in cultural and social life by the various exchanges and enterprises of human living. Let them be familiar with their [others'] national and religious traditions, gladly and reverently laying bare the seeds of the Word which is hidden in them" (§ 11). A series of papal encyclicals and other documents from Vatican offices reinforced this point: God calls all people to union with God—God is the origin and the final end, the destiny, of humanity.

6. Francis A. Sullivan, *Salvation outside the Church? Tracing the History of the Catholic Response* (New York: Paulist, 1992), 27.

7. Ibid.

8. Ibid., emphasis added.

9. As Sullivan put it, Augustine was understood to be claiming the following: "that the universally contracted guilt of original sin was sufficient to justify God in condemning not only infants who died without baptism, but also adults who died in ignorance of Christian faith. There is good reason to believe that it was his effort to reconcile the exclusion of these two categories of people from salvation with the justice of God that led St. Augustine to his theory about the consequences of original sin for the whole human race." See ibid., 37. Medieval theologians generally rejected this view regarding the unbaptized babies (ibid., 46) and only accepted that God would damn people for sin they actually committed. Yet even Augustine, ever the rhetorician, is not certainly to be understood as making this point as one that Christians must believe. As a polemicist, Augustine is notoriously inconsistent across his broad range of writings. His understanding of the freedom of the will varied remarkably over the course of his long polemical career. In one of the few documents Augustine wrote as an instruction from him as a pastor and bishop rather than as a polemicist, the *Enchiridion*, a very odd rhetorical picture appeared. Compare Terrence Tilley, *The Evils of Theodicy* (Washington, DC: Georgetown University Press, 1991). Augustine's description of the way things have gone in the world in *Enchiridion* included the observation that not all people are redeemed. This leads to an obvious question: Why are some not redeemed? To deny that God could redeem them would deny God's omnipotence. To deny God's

will to save all would deny God's benevolence. How did Augustine the bishop deal with this perplexity? Augustine taught the resurrection of the flesh: all people are resurrected. He then responds to various questions about the resurrection of those who were miscarried, deformed, had their bodies dissolved, or deviated significantly from the norm in height or girth, etc. Having solved these problems, he affirms that *we* will rise in our bodies without internal or external defect to ease and happiness. Augustine then turns to the resurrection of the bodies of the damned. Those who are not liberated by Christ will be raised to endless damnation. In his *Enchiridion*, there is a profound rhetorical difference here between the "we" who are to be saved and the "those" who are to be damned. If one is sensitive to the rhetoric of and audience for *Enchiridion*, the contrast is essential. Augustine is addressing a believer. His audience included only those who will be raised to felicity. Whosoever is not liberated by Christ is "them," outside his audience. Whatever Augustine may have written for other audiences, in this instruction the audience's redemption is presumed. Hence, in *Enchiridion*, Augustine dismissed out of hand the importance of many of the speculative issues, especially those which have nothing to do with "us." They need not worry "us." Augustine never materially identified "them." Implicitly, all who read *Enchiridion* with the rhetorical force that he wrote it must read it as an instruction to "us." The key point is that even Augustine did not—when he was writing as a teacher of the Christian faith—identify materially who is damned, but only implied that they are not "us." The extent of the "us" was left unclear—indeed, "us" may be so extensive as to include all just people at least since Abel. At one point, he even described the church as beginning from Abel and consisting in all the just. Sullivan, *Salvation outside the Church?*, 30. And while Augustine is typically taken to be saying that God both wills the salvation of all, but that "they" do not deserve it and God is justified in damning them, it may be better to understand him as saying that God wills the salvation of "all of us" and finally leave the extent of that "all of us" undetermined.

    10. See Sullivan, *Salvation outside the Church?*, 151.

    11. Numerous other texts might be cited, but they would only simply reiterate the claim that Jesus Christ is the unique and sufficient mediator of divine salvation. This affirmation is not always articulated clearly. "Christianity and the World Religions," for example, snips quotations about Christ as the mediator of salvation from earlier biblical and patristic authors but fails to follow its own rules for interpreting those texts. "The context— literary, sociological, etc.—is an important means of understanding, at times the only one, texts and situations; contexts are a possible place for truth, but they are not identified with truth itself" (§ 101). As they note, we cannot understand the meaning of an utterance, text, monument, artifact, life, or movement apart from the context(s) in which each lives and moves and has its being. However, in its section on "fundamental theological presuppositions" (§ 32–49), the commission uses proof texts from the Bible and the fathers of the church as if these propositions extracted from their context simply showed Christ's universal normativity for salvation. They give little consideration to intratextual contexts, much less the situations in which and the purposes for which the texts were composed. For example, the document simply cites patristic authors Justin Martyr and Clement of Alexandria, who claimed that the Greeks stole ideas from Moses and the prophets (§ 44), without ever noting that those claims are defensive polemical rhetoric. These latter claims are not merely historically unverifiable but also likely to be simply false. By neglecting the opportunity to contextualize and analyze such claims, the ITC document is inconsistent with its own theory of interpretation.

    12. This rule leaves open the questions of how to understand the relationships between the salvation God wrought in and through Jesus Christ and the salvation that God wills for all of humanity. Beyond notions that salvation in Jesus Christ is in some way a fulfillment and completion of other patterns of salvation, theologians have proffered Spirit Christologies and Trinitarian accounts of God's salvific action. See Jeannine Hill Fletcher, *Monopoly on Salvation? A Feminist Approach to Religious Pluralism* (New York: Continuum, 2005), 62 and below. What is precluded is suggesting that some other mediator is also a "Son and Word of the Father." *Dominus Iesus*, § 10. Vatican documents have criticized formulations of Trinitarian accounts and Spirit-Christologies. Their critiques generally can be seen as applying another classic maxim, *opera*

trinitatis ad extra indivisa sunt. In a proscriptive form, we might formulate this as "Do not treat the works of the members of the Trinity in, on, and for the world as separable from each other's." What is attributed to the work of the Father is also that of the Son and Spirit. What is said to be the work of the Son is also that of the Father and the Spirit. The work of the Spirit cannot be separated from the work of the Son or Father. One cannot ascribe salvation outside explicit association with the Christian community to the Spirit *rather than* the Son. Nor can one separate the work of the Word of God from the actuality of the Incarnate One. This proscription simply blocks the path of a theological view that would separate God's works for the world as if the persons of the Trinity could be said to be operating in some way independently of each other. This proscription does not block appropriate theological distinctions but reminds us that there are theological shoals in this area.

13. See J. A. DiNoia, "Varieties of Religious Aims: Beyond Exclusivism, Inclusivism, and Pluralism," in *Theology and Dialogue: Essays in Conversation with George Lindbeck*, ed. Bruce D. Marshall, 249–74 (Notre Dame, IN: University of Notre Dame Press, 1990); idem, *The Diversity of Religions: A Christian Perspective* (Washington, DC: Catholic University of America Press, 1992); S. Mark Heim, *Is Christ the Only Way? Christian Faith in a Pluralistic World* (Valley Forge, PA: Judson, 1985); idem, *Salvations: Truth and Difference in Religion* (Maryknoll, NY: Orbis, 1995); idem, *The Depth of the Riches: A Trinitarian Theology of Religious Ends* (Grand Rapids: Eerdmans, 2001).

14. Properly speaking, coming to Nirvana or the Pure Land, being absorbed in the ocean of being, or fading from life in Hades are not concepts of "salvation." Each of these concepts clearly obtains its significance from within the respective faith traditions that generate them. The generic use of the term *salvation* may be misleading or even intellectually imperialist. Such generic talk of salvation hides the fact that our talk of salvation in Christ may not have clear parallels in other traditions. The works of Catholic theologian J. Augustine DiNoia, O.P., and Baptist theologian Mark Heim highlight the differences. The conceptual structures of the faith traditions that give these terms their sense may be incommensurable. It is not at all clear that they could properly understand or evaluate such assertions.

15. I have chosen to avoid the linguistic quagmire where proponents battle over jots and tittles in Christology. These battles have led to convoluted theories of religious diversity that are of purely academic, not practical, interest. Is Jesus Christ as "constitutive" or "normative" for salvation? What is the difference? In what sense must we understand the "unicity" of salvation in Christ? Is he unique as savior? In what sense? How is his "finality" compatible with the unabrogated covenant God made with Israel? The rule that seems to us to underlie these claims is better understood by using the philosophical understanding of necessary and sufficient conditions. For our purposes, we can say a condition is necessary if for a state of affairs to obtain, the condition must be actual. We can say a condition is sufficient for a state of affairs just in case that if the condition obtains, then the state of affairs obtains. To say that Jesus Christ is sufficient for salvation is to say that the actuality of his person and work brings salvation; we do not say that Jesus Christ is necessary for salvation, because that would be an inappropriate constraint on God's power. See Tilley, "'Christianity and the World Religions': A Recent Vatican Document," *Theological Studies* 60 (June 1999): 323. For that reason, we say Jesus Christ is unique. Nothing else is needed other than Jesus Christ (sufficiency), and no other sufficient condition obtains (uniqueness).

16. Sullivan, *Salvation outside the Church?*, 156.

17. How this action and how the church's involvement in it are to be understood remains open. The key may be found in the Second Vatican Council's Pastoral Constitution on the Church in the Modern World: "While helping the world and receiving many benefits from it, the Church has a single intention: that God's kingdom may come, and that the salvation of the whole human race may come to pass. For every benefit that the People of God during its earthly pilgrimage can offer to the human family stems from the fact that the Church is *the universal sacrament of salvation,* simultaneously manifesting and exercising the mystery of God's love for humanity." *Gaudium et Spes* § 45, referring to *Lumen Gentium* § 15 (emphasis added). By introducing the idea of the church as a sacrament, the council effectively opens up the issue of how

the church as sacrament of God is necessary. Regarding the ways in which God's saving grace comes to people, the "Council limited itself to the statement that God bestows it 'in ways known to Himself.'" *Dominus Iesus* § *21*, citing Vatican II, *Ad Gentes* 7.

18. A key argument of Jacques Dupuis is that the various faith traditions can be construed as willed and used by God for the salvation of humanity. I have argued that this interpretation of the efficacy of other traditions is compatible with official Catholic teaching as presented in *Dominus Iesus*. Tilley, "Christian Orthodoxy and Religious Pluralism," *Modern Theology* 22 (January 2006): 51–63. One need not—and must not—assert that other religious traditions are sacramental as is the church. However, one can also affirm that in some way these traditions can be willed by God as vehicles of some sort to bring those who have no access to the church (or perhaps those who are so appalled by some of the actions of members of the church) and thus cannot participate in the sacramental life of the church directly. Also see the debate continued in Gavin D'Costa, "'Christian Orthodoxy and Religious Pluralism': A Response to Terrence W. Tilley," *Modern Theology* 23, no. 3 (2007): 435–46; Tilley, "'Christian Orthodoxy and Religious Pluralism': A Rejoinder to Gavin D'Costa"; Gavin D'Costa, and Terrence W. Tilley, "Concluding Our *Quaestio Disputata* on Theologies of Religious Diversity," *Modern Theology* 23, no. 3 (2007): 463–68; Perry Schmidt-Leukl, "On Claimed 'Orthodoxy,' Quibbling with Words, and Some Serious Implications: A Comment on the Tilley-D'Costa Debate about Religious Pluralism," *Modern Theology* 24, no. 2 (2008): 271–84; and Terrence Tilley, "Orthodoxy and Religious Pluralism: A Comment," *Modern Theology* 24, no. 2 (2008): 291–92.

19. As Paul Knitter put it, "Witnessing is based on the desire and need to share what one has found to be true and precious" with others. Paul F. Knitter, *The Myth of Religious Superiority: Multi-faith Explorations of Religious Pluralism* (Maryknoll, NY: Orbis, 2005), xi.

20. Walter Ong, S.J., has suggested that the use of the Greek term *katholicos* as one of the marks of the church is significant. "Realizing Catholicism: Faith, Learning and the Future," in *Faith and the Intellectual Life: Marianist Award Lectures*, ed. James Heft, S.M. (Notre Dame, IN: University of Notre Dame Press, 1996), 31–33. Using Greek when formulating the marks in Latin, when the Latin form *universalis* was available to complement the other three marks ("one, holy, apostolic"), suggests that "catholic" and "universal" are not quite the same thing. Ong suggests that the universality of the church consists not in the extent of the church, but in its distribution as "the leaven in the lump." The church does not cover the world or own the world, nor is it simply worldwide. Rather, it is to be found everywhere that the breath of the Spirit raises the lump of the world into the bread of life. In this sense, the church may be a sacrament not by its universality understood as a characteristic of its extensiveness, but by its catholicity, by its obligation not to be the world, but to raise the world into new life in the Spirit. This is another way of suggesting that the center of evangelization may not be proselytizing, but witness. The necessity of the church is a sacramental necessity. God acts in and through the church as God acts in and through the bread and wine of the Eucharist. This necessity can be understood in a number of ways. Just as the sacrament of baptism classically was construed as having three modes depending on the circumstances (baptism of water as the ordinary way, of blood for those catechumens who were martyred before being baptized, and of desire for those who were not Christians but oriented to the Good that is God in their lives), so perhaps we can think of the sacramental presence of the church as multimodal depending on the circumstances Realizing that sacramentality in practice may well require different practices to represent and effect the grace of God in the world, to be the leaven in the lump. To reduce this sacramentality to one mode, e.g., proselytizing, would certainly not be required by the present rule and, arguably, would be an inept way of living by it—especially in light of our fourth and final rule.

21. The Second Vatican Council in its Pastoral Constitution *Gaudium et Spes* proclaimed: "There is a growing awareness of the exalted dignity proper to the human person, since he stands above all things, and his rights and duties are universal and inviolable. Therefore, there must be made available to all men everything necessary for leading a life truly human, such as food, clothing, and shelter; the right to choose a state of life freely and to found a family, the right to

education, to employment, to a good reputation, to respect, to appropriate information, to activity in accord with the upright norm of one's own conscience, to protection of privacy and to rightful freedom in matters religious, too. (§ 26)" This affirmation of this dignity is rooted in the Christian conviction that all people are created in the image of God and called to communion with God. *Gaudium et Spes* § 12, 19. *Nostra Aetate* found that there is no basis "in theory or in practice for any discrimination between individual and individual or between people and people arising either from human dignity or from the rights which flow from it. Therefore, the Church reproves, as foreign to the mind of Christ, any discrimination against people or any harassment of them on the basis of their race, color, condition of life or religion" (§ 5).

22. Robert Wuthnow, *America and the Challenges of Religious Diversity* (Princeton: Princeton University Press, 2005), 72.

23. Rabbi Jonathan Sacks finds that the greatness of the God of Abraham, Isaac, Jacob, and Jesus is that the divine unity is great enough to encompass and even love diversity. "*God is the God of all humanity, but between Babel and the end of days no single faith is the faith of all humanity.*" Jonathan Sacks, *The Dignity of Difference: How to Avoid the Clash of Civilizations*(New York: Continuum, 2003), 55 (emphasis original). Like Vatican II, Sacks called for respect for and positive appreciation of the human search for God in all its forms. "The challenge to the religious imagination is to see God's image in one who is not in our image. That is the converse of tribalism. But it is also something other than universalism. It takes difference seriously" Ibid., 60. The challenge for those of us who believe in the intrinsic dignity of humankind created by God is to recognize "the dignity of difference." Like Vatican II, Rabbi Sacks recognized that our faith traditions are not private. They are involved in the social, economic, and political dimensions of our existence. Hence, as the council did, he noted that our faith "involves justice, not merely in the narrow sense of the rule of law and the transparency of procedures, but also in the substantive sense of conferring on all members of society an honoured place." Ibid., 121. The rule that we are to affirm human dignity involves that as we cherish our own lives, "then we will understand the value of others. We may regard ours as a diamond and another faith as a ruby, but we know that both are precious stones." Ibid., 209.

24. Ibid.

25. Netland formulates these issues in terms of statements rather than questions, but for the purpose of oral exposition, describing his answers to these questions is preferable. See Harold A. Netland, *Encountering Religious Pluralism: The Challenge to Christian Faith and Mission* (Downers Grove, IL: InterVarsity, 2001), 319.

26. Netland presents the pillars of a "biblical theology" in a series of six propositions. An Evangelical theology of religions must necessarily work out of this framework. Netland acknowledges that there are differing statements to articulate a biblical theology but finds that the thrust of these propositions limn the evangelical approach. First, "the one eternal God is holy and righteous in all his ways." Netland, *Encountering Religious Pluralism*, 315. Worry about members of other faith traditions' ultimate destinies is tied up with a sense of God's righteousness, which implies fairness to all God has created. A traditional strong exclusivism seems to count against God's fairness, as some see God as holding people responsible for not responding to the call from God—a call of which they knew little or nothing. Second, "God has sovereignly created all things, including human beings, who are made in the image of God." Ibid. Eschewing any hint of dualism, the Christian doctrine of creation is inevitably linked to the doctrine of the fall as explaining why humans have at least functionally "lost" the image of God evinced in human sinfulness—that is the fourth proposition. "The biblical teaching on creation is rich with implications for understanding religious others." Ibid., 316. Third, "God has graciously taken the initiative in revealing himself to humankind, and although God's revelation comes in various forms, the definitive revelation for us is the written Scriptures." Ibid. Evangelical and Catholic theologians differ thematically at this point in an interesting way. Netland centers the discussion of this point on the distinction of general and special revelation, the former being revealed to all humans in some way, the latter being God's gift to humanity of the Scriptures. Netland also notes

that others outside those who have received the Scriptures—Jews and Christians—may have received special revelations from God as well. Catholic theologians might not disagree with any of those points but tend not to find "revelation" the crucial category, but rather "grace" working in, on, and through "nature" to be the central focus. Catholics find the grace of God to be found sacramentally in Jesus Christ and the church he founded and to focus the issues on the ways in which God's grace—God's gracious presence—is available in, to, and through (if at all) traditions other than the Christian. Fourth, "God's creation, including humankind, has been corrupted by sin." Ibid., 318. Like most Catholic theologians, Netland finds that sin "is both personal and social in its manifestations, it is found both in the individual and collectively in human cultures and societies." Ibid. All people justly face divine wrath unto eternal punishment because of sin—a very difficult doctrine to understand. Fifth, "In his mercy God has provided a way, through the atoning work of Jesus Christ on the cross, for sinful persons to be reconciled to God." Ibid., 319. Netland seems to support a substitutionary doctrine of the atonement. Sixth, "The community of the redeemed are to share in the gospel of Jesus Christ and to make disciples of all peoples, including sincere adherents of other religious traditions, so that God is honored throughout the earth." Ibid., 323. While one might dispute whether the biblical text is aware of other developed faith traditions in the contemporary sense, the importance of the evangelizing impulse is clearly part and parcel of the Christian tradition. However, whether Jews are to be evangelized (would this not impugn God's fidelity, since God did make a covenant with the Jewish people and clearly not all Jews have explicitly rejected Jesus Christ?) and whether evangelization should be *ad gentes* (to the nations or peoples) or *inter gentes* (among the nations or peoples) are open questions. For a discussion of the latter (*inter gentes*) approach, see Terrence Tilley, *The Disciples' Jesus: Christology as Reconciling Practice* (Maryknoll, NY: Orbis, 2008), 252–60 and the literature cited there.

    27. Netland, *Encountering Religious Pluralism*, 320.

    28. Ibid., 321.

    29. In effect, Netland is wisely saying that we Christian theologians do not need to decide whether any humans have exercised their freedom to reject God's revelation and grace so thoroughly as to damn themselves. Netland's view aligns nicely with that of Karl Rahner's (although Rahner's theory is "inclusivist," finding that some can be saved even if they know not the name of the One who saves; Rahner's term was "anonymous Christians"). Writing for the *New York Times*, Eugene Kennedy offers this summary and quotation of Rahner's position. Kennedy writes, "Rahner has consistently described a vision of the universe in which all men and women ultimately will be saved by a loving God who is beyond our comprehension. 'An orthodox theologian,' Rahner says dryly, 'is forbidden to teach that everybody will be saved. But we are allowed to *hope* that all will be saved. If I hope to be saved, it is necessary to hope that for all men [*sic*] as well. If you have reason to love one another, you can hope that all will be saved.'" Eugene Kennedy, "Quiet Mover of the Catholic Church," *New York Times Magazine* 23, September 1979, 66–67. The refusal to deny God's universal salvific will is rooted in our faith in God's love for all creation and our hope—not our explicit belief—that God will bring each and every part of it to its ultimate fulfillment.

    30. Netland, *Encountering Religious Pluralism*, 319.

    31. Ibid., 323.

    32. Ibid., 323–25.

    33. Harold A. Netland, *Dissonant Voices: Religious Pluralism and the Question of Truth* (Grand Rapids: Eerdmans, 1991), 193.

    34. Netland has acknowledged and responded to such criticisms. Netland, *Encountering Religious Pluralism*, 294–307. He rightly points out that if there are no criteria that can be used across the "boundaries" of faith traditions, then we have no way out of relativism. Granted that there may be differences in application of the criteria, if we can talk across traditions, then we can talk about what is true, beautiful, good, and just across traditions even if we might dispute just what better or best satisfies those criteria. Netland also recognizes the logic of comparison. See ibid., 182–92, for example. One cannot simply compare tradition *T* with tradition *U* in some

general manner. Rather, one can compare tradition T with regard to topic or thesis q with tradition U with regard to q or to a q' that is analogous in U to q in T. So one might compare Christianity on creation *ex nihilo* with Theravada Buddhism on *prattitya-samutpada* (dependent co-origination) and ask which, if either, accords better with the results of modern science. Or one might compare Islam and Christianity on the crucifixion of Jesus and evaluate which better accounts for what are or seem to be facts establishable by historians' investigations. I also applaud Netland's recognition that the *conditions* that make a statement true or false are distinct from the *criteria* by which we judge those statements true or false. Ibid., 198; but compare 145–46, where he seems to fall into the trap of conflating the truth of a belief with the warrant for believing; unfortunately, the polemics involving skepticism and "truth" as discussed in modernity has misled him, I believe, at this particular point. Nonetheless, I do not agree with his view regarding the relationship of propositional to personal truth; my own views can be found in *Inventing Catholic Tradition* (Maryknoll, NY: Orbis, 2000), 156–77; and *Faith: What It Is and What It Isn't* (Maryknoll, NY: Orbis, 2011), 102–28.

35. Rabbi Jonathan Sacks has called for genuine respect among those of differing faith traditions through the practice of listening and speaking that forms authentic conversation. The root of this call is a profound understanding of creation. Sacks wrote, "God, the creator of humanity, having made a covenant with all humanity, then turns to one people [the Jews] and commands it to be different, *teaching humanity to make space for difference. God may at times be found in human other, the one not like us*. Biblical monotheism is not the idea that there is one God and therefore one gateway to His presence. To the contrary, it is the idea that *the unity of God is to be found in the diversity of creation*." Sacks, *The Dignity of Difference*, 53; emphasis original. While one might disagree with particular points Sacks made, a crucial aspect of this fourth rule is to listen to what others are saying in *their* terms and not to interpret them presupposing *your* terms.

36. Netland, *Encountering Religious Pluralism*, 307. Netland cites Masao Abe, "Kenotic God and Dynamic Sunyata," in *Zen and Western Thought*, ed. William R. LaFleur (Honolulu: University of Hawaii Press, 1985), 52–53.

37. The discussion of Knitter's work is based on Tilley et al., *Religious Diversity*, 93–109. Knitter's move toward a religious mutualism based on working for justice began as a result of his own collaborative pursuit of greater justice in the 1980s. Knitter recounted meeting two refugees from El Salvador in 1983 who had been persecuted for fighting for human rights in their home country. This encounter changed Knitter's entire posture for dealing with the question of religious diversity. Within a year, he and his wife were participating in an ecumenical group attempting to assist political refugees in a war-torn Central America. Knitter followed this ecumenical experience by participating in a Hindu-Christian dialogue in India that viewed the promotion of justice as an indispensable component of meaningful dialogue. Knitter, *One Earth, Many Religions* (Maryknoll, NY: Orbis, 1995), 1–22. These real-life collaborative pursuits of justice affected Knitter's own scholarly writing. His essay "Toward a Liberation Theology of Religions" documented his evolution from a theologian who grounded his theory in philosophical principle to a theologian who reflected on the practices of Christian groups working for justice. (John Hick and Paul Knitter, eds., *The Myth of Christian Uniqueness: Toward a Pluralistic Theology of Religions* [Maryknoll, NY: Orbis, 1987], 186–88.) Knitter's use of liberation as a starting point for interreligious dialogue and cooperation is significant for several reasons. First, Knitter is influenced by the recent tradition of liberation theology that refuses to separate liberation in this world from salvation in the next. Second, Knitter's shift from a theocentric pluralism toward a justice-based mutualism should force his critics to rethink their standard critique of pluralism. It may no longer apply to his work. Pluralists tend to violate our second and third principles; Hick certainly has no use for them. Yet this does not necessarily apply to Knitter's mutualism. Although classic pluralist theory cannot fit the principles we have articulated, Knitter's moves bring him more in line with classic Catholic principles while retaining many of the gains that pluralism sought. Finally, Knitter has taken the lead in attempting to show that the mystical and prophetic strands in non-Christian religions provide practical starting points for interreligious cooperation and dialogue. This last

point is particularly important if Knitter is to preserve respect for the dignity of others. Paul F. Knitter, "Is the Pluralist Model a Western Imposition?" in Knitter, *The Myth of Religious Superiority*, 39.

38. Knitter has argued that concerns with salvation or soteriology are a point of convergence between religions. In Knitter's usage, "salvation" is a very broad concept, entailing liberation from suffering and oppression in personal, social, political, and religious spheres of our lives. Knitter names this orientation toward human well-being as "Soteria" or "the ineffable mystery of salvation." He defined Soteria as being fundamentally concerned with the liberation of the poor and nonpersons.

39. Paul Knitter, "Toward a Liberation Theology of Religions," in *The Myth of Christian Uniqueness: Toward a Pluralistic Theology of Religions*, ed. John Hick and Paul Knitter (Maryknoll, NY: Orbis, 1987), 187–88.

40. Like some postmodern theologians, Knitter has moved away from the concern to find foundations for what we do and believe, and moved to a position that recognizes the primacy of practice over theory. Knitter's use of the word *ineffable* in describing salvation recognizes that no particular faith can express the entire mystery of salvation. (Who knows how to describe with any reliability the furniture of heaven, the temperature of hell, the bliss of Nirvana, or the identity of atman with Brahman or, finally, even whether these concepts refer to one or many forms of salvation?) By focusing on the promotion of justice, Knitter's approach avoids the traps of taking one's own ideological or religious commitments as a foundation for cooperation. Rather, the very work helps participants to understand what Soteria is both for themselves and for others. Knitter's focus on Soteria does not impose any specific views of God on potential participants in cooperative efforts between different religious groups. Knitter also recognizes that not all faith traditions understand salvation the same way, but that this is to be expected if salvation is an ineffable mystery. He simply proposes that "shared praxis" offers a starting point for discussion that contains a smaller threat of ideological hegemony. Knitter, "Toward a Liberation Theology of Religions," 187. Knitter discussed the divine in Jesus in terms of a "Spirit Christology" rather than a "logos Christology." Knitter, *Introducing Theologies of Religions*, 142–45. He noted that attempting to preserve the uniqueness of Jesus without diminishing the importance of religious figures found in other traditions forces one to walk a tightrope. He argued that conceiving of Jesus as "spirit-filled" is helpful because Jesus is an essential but not exhaustive representation of the divine mystery available to all religious traditions. Jesus was focused on instituting the reign of God in his preaching and life. He did not focus on his own status or establishing a religious tradition separate from Judaism. Jesus' emphasis on establishing the kingdom of God mirrors the role of the Hebrew prophets who were moved by the Spirit. Knitter's position has continued to evolve. Knitter has added an explicit concern for ecological well-being to his understanding of Soteria. Knitter, like any good pluralist, has tended to focus more on what unifies than what divides the world's religious traditions. In this quest for commonalities, Knitter came to the (rather obvious but often ignored) conclusion that the earth itself provides the common context for all human religious experiences. The divine is experienced in different ways at different times and places. Expressions so different as to be incommensurable speak of those experiences. But the earth, in all its limited diversity, is the common site for all religious reflection. Hence, ecological concerns are an area for forming a common purpose among differing religious communities. Knitter, *One Earth, Many Religions*, 112–13. One only need survey the locations in which religious communities function, and one can easily find common problems that face multiple religious communities. Knitter identifies poverty, victimization, violence, and patriarchy as common sources of suffering confronting most religious communities. Knitter, *Introducing Theologies of Religions*, 136–37. Increasingly, degradation of the environment—natural, political, and social—is a concern of all. Religious cooperation in particular places to understand and alleviate these problems can lead to dialogue. Common understanding of what is wrong about poverty or patriarchy cannot be guaranteed, but even small ameliorations of patterns of oppression can be celebrated as signs of hope. Knitter's focus on common problems reflects the "can-do pragmatism" of his nation. The

U.S. context certainly features both religious diversity and serious obstacles to justice. Pursuit of justice is a practical staring point, not a theoretical foundation for, interreligious cooperation. Knitter, "Toward a Liberation Theology of Religions," 188. However, as the cooperation of many from different faith traditions in the civil rights movement showed, focus on a goal on which diverse folk can agree can promote deeper understanding through witness and action. In this sense, Knitter's evolution toward praxis has produced a serious "sited" theology of religions. Knitter's position is so nuanced in comparison to many other pluralists that James L. Fredericks also evaluated it separately from other pluralist theologians. Fredericks contends that Knitter's commitment to social justice helps Knitter avoid religious relativism. Fredericks also claims that Knitter is moving further away from a position of pluralism because not all religious traditions are concerned with the sort of justice that Knitter seeks. James L. Fredericks, *Faith among Faiths: Christian Theology and Non-Christian Religions* (New York: Paulist, 1999), 132. Knitter's notion that concerns for ecology and justice can serve as opportunities for interreligious cooperation and dialogue still rings true after Fredericks's critique. However, the notion that Knitter may be using semi-exclusive ethical claims to critique cultural and religious conduct is perhaps valid. The notion that most religious traditions contain an interior concern for suffering caused by patriarchy is a claim that Knitter will need to be able to defend as a non-Western imposition. Knitter has worked diligently to avoid this criticism, and for now, his work as editor of *The Myth of Religious Superiority: A Multifaith Exploration* serves as evidence that he is more than sensitive to concerns that the pluralist position is only attainable within a Christian context. This work, as already noted, contains essays from authors of various religious traditions who support the pluralist position. Knitter, "Is the Pluralism Model a Western Imposition?"

41. Paul F. Knitter, *Introducing Theologies of Religions* (Maryknoll, NY: Orbis, 2002), 146–48.

42. Ibid., 154.

43. For a survey that addresses this point, see Lisa M. Cahill, "The Atonement Paradigm: Does It Still Have Explanatory Value," *Theological Studies* 68, no. 2 (2007) 418-32. She recognizes the value of religious images and thought about the atonement but seems to find little explanatory value in atonement theology.

44. Knitter, *Introducing Theologies of Religions*, 152–53.

45. One can understand Knitter's concept of a "representative cause" as merely showing the way. Indeed, if one assumes that representation signifies as a text does, then what Jesus does is simply to reveal what is already there, as Knitter puts it. In that case, the mutualist position is in serious tension with, or even in serious violation of, our second principle. Knitter does not deny that Jesus is unique. That Jesus is God's symbol or sacrament is affirmed. In the context of contemporary understandings of language such as speech act theory (see Tilley, *The Evils of Theodicy*), symbols and sacraments are never *mere* representations, but, when effective, literally *effective*communications that change the receiver. Given this understanding of how language works, the salvation wrought in and through Jesus is clearly sufficient. Whether a Spirit Christology like Knitter's falls within the limits of Catholic orthodoxy is another question. Roger Haight has noted that many do not accept Spirit Christology as orthodox. Roger Haight, S.J., *Jesus: Symbol of God* (Maryknoll, NY: Orbis, 1999), 445. However, the move toward Spirit Christology seems to be made out of motivations to uphold God's universal salvific will and respect the dignity of the non-Christian other rather than an attempt to "demote" Jesus. If a Spirit Christology is seen as an alternative model to a Logos Christology, rather than a substitution for it, then it is possible that this sidestream of the tradition is a viable course.

46. As any extremely powerful exemplar does, Jesus showed people how to live in and live out the reign of God and in that showing enabled them to do just that if they would but respond to his action. If this is a form of "exemplarism" in Christology, it is not the sort of exemplarism that is merely exemplary, but is powerfully, empoweringly exemplary. As such, it may not fall under the strictures raised against exemplarism, that the redemption in Christ is merely an ethical model of what love means.

47. Knitter's projects promote the four types of dialogue noted above. The church is also to proclaim and serve the kingdom of God. *Dialogue and Proclamation*, § 59. This proclamation of the kingdom of God is far more christocentric than Knitter's Soteria. However, Knitter has pointed out that Christians working for Soteria need not jettison their specific beliefs and practices. Knitter, "Toward a Liberation Theology of Religions," 187.

48. Fredericks, *Faith among Faiths*, 116.

49. Knitter's pursuit of human welfare and liberation is motivated from a deep commitment to the universality of human dignity. It also allows for him to focus interreligious activity on a common problem rather than on an "absolute reality" that erases difference. Knitter's christological and ecclesiological claims seem to be in some tension in that they do not represent as well as some think they ought the principles of a Roman Catholic theology of religions. This raises the question of whether a mutualist approach can fit the rules. James L. Fredericks has argued that Paul Knitter's liberative pluralism is so nuanced that it is beginning to occupy a different space than other versions of the pluralist response (Fredericks, *Faith among Faiths*, 119, 132, 135), a position with which I agree. John Paul II and Benedict XVI have stated that the impulse toward peace and human welfare is present within all faith traditions and open to all peoples. This means that one could engage in Knitter's collaboration on common problems even if one possessed a more traditional Christology and ecclesiology. Thus, Knitter's move toward common problems as a source of common ground among divergent faith traditions has provided the church with a great gift. Moreover, even if the words are untraditional, it remains possible that a mutualist model communicates the heart of the tradition well. Certainly Knitter would claim so. As Robert Wuthnow noted, interreligious cooperation must be focused on a specific problem and local if it is to be both productive and sustained. Wuthnow, *America and the Challenges of Religious Diversity*, 303. Knitter's practical approach to religious cooperation meets Wuthnow's criterion. The mutualist model for understanding religious diversity also challenges Catholics to be judged by the fruit the church bears. Knitter, *Introducing Theologies or Religions*, 135–36. In this way, the model can serve as a corrective to any prideful tribalism or intellectual imperialism. It also can serve as a promising bridge to the world. Working for liberation and justice might be one way in which the church can bear effective witness to the reconciling activity of God revealed in the activity of Jesus Christ—healing, forgiving, reconciling, and working to realize God's reign.

3

No Other Name: The Gospel and True Religions

S. Mark Heim

I would like to focus on three aspects of the word *true* in the question "Is Christianity the only true religion?" In one sense, we use the word *true* to mean "the real thing." This is true coffee, not an imitation. That person is exhibiting true integrity, not a semblance of it. What is true is authentic. For a religion to be true in this respect means that at its origins and in its ongoing life, it is not hypocritical (carried out for reasons other than the ostensible ones), and it is no mere epiphenomenon of some other causal factor (as, for instance, if all religion were explained purely as a psychological pathology). In another sense, we use the word to mean verified or verifiable by experience. Analytical philosophers in the twentieth century regarded a proposition as meaningful only if one could specify a set of circumstances that would count as verifying (or, in other formulations, falsifying) it. For a religion to be true in this sense means that, so far as we can judge, those who pursue it actually achieve the states or conditions it promises. The true is the realizable. In yet another sense, we take true to mean descriptively accurate, at the furthest reach of our epistemological horizon. In this sense, it is not true to say that electrons are in orbits around the nucleus of an atom, analogous to those of planets around the sun, since their behavior is described much more precisely in terms of quantum mechanics. For a religion to be true in this sense would mean that its account of the world within which truth of the first two types are at play is the most accurate and comprehensive one.

Keeping these three meanings in mind, I would say (1) that Christianity is not the only true (authentic) religion, nor is its authenticity necessarily of a different sort than others. (2) I do not believe that Christianity is the only true (realizable) religion. But I believe Christianity is the uniquely saving religion.

My faith does not rest in generic qualities of Christianity as a religion, but in the decisive saving significance of Jesus Christ for all humanity. There is full communion with God only in communion with Christ. (3) I do believe that Christianity is the most fully true (descriptive) religion. I further believe that one mark of the truest religion (or religions) is the capacity to recognize and affirm distinctive elements of truth in others. The adequacy of one's own tradition is correlative with the ability to make room for what is valid in others. My religion could not be true if it had no means to recognize that others are as well, in various facets of these three dimensions.

We generally use a typology—exclusivism, inclusivism, pluralism—in the area of religious pluralism. Exclusivism is the view that only one religion is true and all others are false, inclusivism the view that the benefits of the one truest religion can be accessed from within others which are at least partially true. Pluralism is the view that all major religions are independently valid. But these categories are nearly useless, given the uncertainty of what we mean by "true."

In a concrete and straightforward sense, every religion is the only true one. There is no way to live a Jewish life except the Jewish way. Every other way is false in that it is not truly Jewish. Exclusivism is just common sense. In one sense, inclusivism seems obvious, too. No religion is without its commonalities with others. If honoring your parents has value in Christianity, then it must have value when practiced in another tradition as well. There is truth in both. At one level, pluralism is plainly right. If the question is about religion's ability to perform certain descriptive social functions, then the answer is clear: many religions have demonstrated their independent ability to animate advanced civilizations, maintain moral systems, and provide meaning for human life. They are all true.

The typology originates in an agreement between the most liberal and most conservative theologies of religion that there is and can be only one religious end, one actual religious fulfillment. The typology then chooses up sides on the means to that end: one way or many. The typology was originally formulated with an implicit focus on Christian salvation as its reference point, though not all religions share the concept or seek its realization. This specifically Christian term, referring to a concrete hope, has been thoroughly blurred into an all-inclusive positive possibility. And the blurring comes from both sides, from exclusivist Christians who assume all possible forms of good subsist in a salvation whose only alternative is utter evil or torment and from pluralist Christians who assume the aims of all religions are essentially identical. The pluralist knows that the particularities of all religions are finally insignificant.

The exclusivist knows that the particularities of all religions but one are insignificant. Both are mistaken.

We can illustrate the blurring tendency I am describing by taking a very simple example. In a colloquial way, some picture a resolution to issues of religious pluralism by envisioning an afterlife somewhat on the model of a parliament of world religions. This final, peaceful realm is one where Jesus and the Buddha, Shankara and Muhammad, Confucius and Mahavira and Moses, along with shamans, bodhisattvas, and spirit guides of all descriptions converse and commune together. They share their varied appreciations for awesome, divine mystery, each seeing and celebrating the value of the other's truth. We rarely note the heavy religious bias in such a picture. This may sound strange, since it sounds to many like an eminently egalitarian approach. What I mean is that this vision is an outright rejection of many religious traditions' ultimate aims. The heaven pictured is a place of personal and interpersonal relations. By virtue of its very categories, this picture of a final human end would be unacceptable or inconceivable for the Buddha or Shankara, the great sage of Vedanta. In fact for many religious traditions, this scenario could be at most a kind of kindergarten metaphor, a preliminary and quite unsatisfactory way station. Of course, it is not a full description of salvation in Christian terms either, but it encompasses many of salvation's categorical essentials: relation, the integrity of personal selves, communion-in-difference, even a personal relation with Jesus for everyone.

It is hard to see how we can take the religions seriously and at the same time regard all the distinctive qualities that are precious to each one as essentially unimportant in terms of religious fulfillment. Religious traditions agree that the ends they seek are closely linked with the distinctive ways of life that they prescribe. We are often told that it is important to study traditions in their unique texture, to understand them on their own terms. But it is hard to see why that would be so if we know in advance that specific differences do not correspond to any variation in religious outcomes.

Is there a perspective that honors the *distinctive* testimony of the various faith traditions as religiously significant? Are there conditions under which various believers' accounts of their faiths might be extensively and simultaneously valid? A positive answer to these questions would affirm the various religious traditions in a much more concrete sense than either liberal or conservative theologians allow.

The key to such a perspective is recognition that religious paths may in fact lead persons to the distinctively varied states that they advertise. If different religious practices and beliefs aim at and constitute distinct conditions of human fulfillment, then a very high proportion of what each tradition affirms may be true and valid, in very much the terms that the tradition claims. This is so even if deep conflict remains between the religions regarding priorities, background beliefs, and ultimate metaphysical reality. Two religious ends may represent two human states that it is utterly impossible for one person to inhabit at the same time. But there is no contradiction in two different persons simultaneously attaining the two ends. Adherents of different religious traditions may be able to recognize the reality of both ends, though they are not able to agree on the explanation of how and why the two ends exist or on the priority they should be given. On these terms, salvation (the Christian end) may differ not only from conditions humans generally regard as evil or destructive but also from those that specific religious traditions regard as most desirable and ultimate. We can avoid the deadlock of the instrumental question over what will get you there ("one way or many ways?") by asking with real openness "way to *what?*"

Gandhi wrote, "Religions are different roads converging to the same point," and asked, "What does it matter if we take different roads so long as we reach the same goal? Wherein is the cause for quarreling?"[1] But I ask, "What if religions are paths to different ends that they each value supremely? Why should we object?" A famous verse of the Bhagavad Gita is often quoted on the presumption that it indicates the identical goal of all religions: "Howsoever people approach Me, even so do I welcome them, for the paths people take from every side are Mine."[2] But Krishna's declaration in the voice of supreme Brahman appears an equally good charter for a diversity of religious ends, affirming that people will realize different receptions corresponding to their different approaches to ultimate reality. If human beings form their ultimate desires freely from among many options, and then through devotion and practice are able to see those desires actually realized, there is no reason to complain about the process but ample room to differ over which end we should seek. Pluralism looks real. The best explanation for this appearance is that it is real.

Salvation is communion with God and God's creatures through Jesus Christ. It is the Christian religious end, if you like. This does not mean that there are not other religious ends, quite real ones. It only means that Christians do not hope to achieve them, and they believe that God has offered greater, more inclusive gifts. Christians believe that salvation, the God who offers it, the relations it presupposes, and its priority in divine purpose are objectively real. But salvation has to be accepted. It has to be evaluatively true, or it is not realized. Other religious traditions can legitimately take the same reciprocal view of their own religious aim: it is real and supreme, but it can be realized only by those who accept it as so.

A religious end or aim is defined by a set of practices, images, stories, and concepts that has three characteristics. First, the set provides material for a thorough pattern of life. It provides a framework that encompasses all the features of life, practical and sublime, current and future. Second, at least some of the elements in the set are understood to be constitutive of a final human fulfillment and/or to be the sole means of achieving that fulfillment. For instance, for Christians, there is a texture of such elements making reference to Jesus Christ. Relation with Christ is believed to be integral to the deepest human fulfillment itself. Some Buddhists may maintain that all the teachings and instruments used to follow the dharma way are ultimately dispensable, even the eightfold path itself. But they can be discarded only *after* use, and nothing else is fit to serve the same purpose. One may pass beyond them, but everyone must pass through them. The way and the end indwell each other. Third, for any individual or community, the religious pattern is in practice exclusive of at least some alternative options. Living in accord with the set of stories and practices necessarily involves choices. "The ascetic life leads to peace" and "The sensual life leads to joy" may both be accurate reports. But we can practice the observance of one more comprehensively only at the expense of the other. The conflict between the two is profound not because one is false, but precisely because both are true. For our purposes, it makes no difference that there may be a tantric claim that some particular combined practice of asceticism/sensuality will lead to peace *and* joy. This is itself a practice that, if followed, rules out either of the other two paths in their particularity.

Some fulfillments may be similar enough that the paths associated with them reinforce each other to some degree, as typing and piano playing may both train the fingers. Some ends may simply pose no direct obstacle, one to the other, save the intrinsic division of finite effort needed to pursue both, as with marathon running and single parenthood. Yet other ends are so sharply divergent that a decisive step in the direction of one is a move away from the other: strict nonviolence and participation in armed revolution. It is obvious that many goods or secondary goals may overlap on the paths to different religious realizations. Discipline is a quality essential to learning the piano or a new language. It is connected with both these different ends, but it is not identical with either of them. If discipline itself were the primary aim, then music or a language would themselves become instrumental means and not ends at all. What for some is an instrument is for others an end. In the two particular cases we have mentioned, discipline is an intermediate or instrumental shared aim. If we focus on that end alone, we can view music or language learning as a varied set of resources for achieving the same human quality. We can do a similar thing with religions, so long as we change the subject, looking toward some such intermediate aim and away from what the religions themselves characteristically seek.

There is an interesting dynamic balance in the relation of religious ends. The more similar the aims, the more sharply contention arises over whether one path should supersede another. If the aims are nearly identical, this tendency is very powerful. To take a trivial example, if the end in view is word processing, few would not take sides between computers or typewriters as the more adequate tools. On the other hand, the more incommensurable religious ends appear, the less they contend for the same space. Losing weight and learning Spanish are separate aims with their distinct requirements. Though they have less concretely in common, there is a proportionally smaller impetus to substitute one for the other. These dynamics are key elements in understanding religious conflict and the possibilities for mutual understanding.

It is certainly possible to fail to actualize any religious end. Instead of achieving one among alternative fulfillments, a person may attain none at all. There are human conditions, whether contemporary or eschatological or both, that no valid religious view seeks as its final end or regards as consistent with its end. Such would be states of perennial suffering, of thorough ignorance, of malicious destructiveness toward self or others. On this point there is ample room for common cause among the faiths, for spiritual and practical cooperation to overcome these conditions, even from differing perspectives. There is an enormous difference between a lack of religious fulfillment of any description and the achievement of *some* religious fulfillment.

As I have described it here, the hypothesis of multiple religious ends is not committed to any particular metaphysical view. I have developed it for reasons that are mainly Christian, but in principle it could just as easily be adopted by others. It involves recognizing other religions as true in the sense that they actually lead to the experienced ends they advertise. But even where such mutual recognition exists, it reflects conflicting metaphysical assumptions—the Buddhist assuming that the Christian end exists within a universe correctly characterized by the analysis of the dependent co-arising of phenomena, and the Christian assuming that the Buddhist end exists within a universe shaped by a Trinitarian creator God. The universe does have some ultimate character or order, and to accept multiple religious ends does not mean to propose ontological chaos. There is no logical reason why a universe with a single religious ultimate might not also encompass a variety of religious ends.

According to its own account of that ultimate, each tradition will have to provide a specific account of how/why that pluralism would be consistent with its nature.

One (or more) of the religions may in fact describe that ultimate order more accurately than others. In addition to being authentic and achieving what it aims at, a "true religion" in this sense means one that best describes the world in which religious ends exist. On this point, we all think our religion the one true one.[3] This situation is epistemologically unavoidable. The apologetic challenge for each faith is to explore how the reality of the others makes sense in its own particularistic terms.

Recognition of diverse religious ends is the condition for recognition of the decisive significance of our religious choices and development, a significance that the particularistic witness of the individual religions collectively affirms. We can expect a fulfillment in line with the "one and only" path that leads us to it. There is no cogent reason to assume that all of us—the vast majority against their prior conditioning and desires—will experience only one among these religious ends or some undefined condition beyond any of them, whether in an eschatological future or here and now. Our conditions of religious fulfillment are significantly constituted by the expectations, relations, images and practices that we bring to them. The lives that lead to the rewards of a Buddhist monastic, a Muslim imam, a Hindu Brahman priest, or a Baptist deacon have unique textures. In these cases, it is not hard to note generic similarities: textual devotion, communal structures, ritual practices. But for any person who wishes to attain a religious fulfillment, generic elements alone are entirely insufficient. The person will need particular texts, a specific community, discrete rituals.

In the characteristic religious dialectic, as we progress toward the realization of our aim, we at the same time develop an ever deeper and clearer desire for that end itself above all others. Religious consummation is the entrance into a state of fulfillment by one whose aspiration has been so tuned and shaped by particular anticipations of that state and by anticipatory participation in aspects of that state that this end represents the perfect marriage of desire and actuality. It is a dream come true for one whose dream has been tuned to the specific desire for that particular gift and no other. Religious ends are not extrinsic awards granted for unrelated performances, like trips to Hawaii won in lotteries. To take a Buddhist example, no one is unhappy "in" nirvana or arrives at it unready. This is because the state of cessation is an achievement that life on the right path makes possible. The end is not "enjoyed" until a person becomes what the path to the end makes her or him. The way and the end are one.

We can certainly point to great figures in varied religious traditions who exhibit some common moral and spiritual qualities. But we can hardly deny the different textures of these achievements. If our selected devotees all strike us as having a claim to be good people, it still appears that one would have to choose between one way of being good and another. It is also clear that people in various traditions pursue and claim to participate in religious attainments other than or in addition to moral transformation. There are, of course, interesting cases of the combination of religious traditions, cases where people may follow both Buddhist and Confucian paths, for instance. This only reinforces the point we have been making. Were they not exclusive paths to distinct ends, there would be no need to follow two ways, since the same range of ends could be achieved in either one alone. Both are practiced because each constitutes a unique pattern, yielding distinct benefits, benefits in this case regarded as compatible and complementary.

To me as a Christian, it appears to make perfectly good sense to say two kinds of things. First, we may say that another religion is a true and valid path to the religious fulfillment it seeks. We may agree with the Dalai Lama, for instance, when he says, "Liberation in which 'a mind that understands the sphere of reality annihilates all defilements in the sphere of reality' is a state that only Buddhists can accomplish. This kind of *moksha* or *nirvana* is only explained in the Buddhist scriptures, and is achieved only through Buddhist practice."[4] There is no way to the Buddhist end but the Buddhist way.

Second, we may say what the book of Acts says of Jesus Christ, that "there is salvation in no one else, for there is no other name under heaven given among mortals by which we must be saved" (Acts 4:12 NRSV). There is a relation with God and other creatures made possible in Christ that can only be realized in communion with Christ.

On these terms, each tradition can acknowledge the *reality* of the religious end sought by the other, in terms largely consistent with those used by that tradition itself. After describing the Buddhist end, the Dalai Lama says, "According to certain religions, however, salvation is a place, a beautiful paradise, like a peaceful valley. To attain such a state as this, to achieve such a state of *moksha*, does not require the practice of emptiness, the understanding of reality. In Buddhism itself, we believe that through the accumulation of merit one can obtain rebirth in heavenly paradises."[5] The Christian end, then, is something like one of the pleasant interludes that Buddhists may enjoy between births as a reward for merit on their path toward true release. As a kind of mirror image, a Christian might say that Buddhists do not attain Christian salvation, as their aim does not lead to that personal relationship with God which is salvation. Instead, they attain peace, cessation of all desire, and emptiness of self. The Buddhist end is then something like a transitory mystical state Christians might experience in the course of their path toward personal communion with God.

These are classically inclusivist views, which interpret other faiths ultimately in the categories of the home religion. But each recognizes the distinctive reality of the other's religious end, and so recognizes a diversity of religious ends. Each regards the other's ultimate as penultimate, leaving open the further possibility of transformation. There is no necessary contradiction in these two accounts of possible human ends, though there is a decisive divergence in their evaluative frameworks for these ends, and there are contradictions in the metaphysical assumptions associated with each framework. Both accounts could be flatly wrong. But there is no logical reason that both cannot be descriptively correct. In fact, if one of the writer's characterizations is correct, it implies a very substantial measure of truth in the other. Accepting different religious ends allows for mutual recognition of extensive *concrete* substantive truth in another tradition. Ironically, this degree of mutual agreement about particulars is ruled out by those who insist the Buddhist end and the Christian one must be the same.

As I have noted, the hypothesis of multiple religious ends is not committed to any particular view of the religious ultimate. My interest in the hypothesis is grounded in part in the way that it validates particularistic Christian confession, but as such, the hypothesis also supports those in other religious traditions who are committed to the distinctive truth of their confession. I believe that the true order for religious diversity is rooted in the God of Christian confession. Christians can understand the distinctive religious truth of other religions as rooted in connections with real dimensions of the triune God.[6] I am convinced, for instance, that the Theravadan Buddhist end is, in fact, as that tradition claims, a cessation of suffering. In that concrete respect, it is similar to salvation. But realization of this end relinquishes (as unreal) a whole range of possible relations with God and others whose presence is essential to the end Christians seek. In that respect, it is similar to what Christians mean by loss. The fact that it may be "the same ultimate reality" behind distinct religious experiences does not by any means require that they result in the same religious end.

If we give "religious end" an abstract meaning—the achievement of *some* religious fulfillment among several possible alternatives and/or the use of religion to serve some generic social role—then we can say that many if not all paths truly achieve religious ends. There is an "any-way" sign at most forks on the religious journey. Each road will get you to a real destination, but not the same destination. If, in contrast, "religious end" is a religious fulfillment of some determinate nature, as described by one of the traditions, then it is clear that it is constituted by certain features to the exclusion of others. There is a one-way sign at many turnings on the religious journey. In either case, we must acknowledge that all these paths link with each other, that crossover travel is a real possibility. At most points, a two-way traffic sign is appropriate. Roads can bear travelers over the same ground toward different destinations, whether those travelers pass in opposite directions or go side by side for this overlapping leg of their trip.

The hypothesis of multiple religious ends offers the most coherent foundation to ground three elements I believe are essential for an effective understanding of religious pluralism, even if they are ordinarily thought incompatible. The first element is the religious significance of careful study of faith traditions in their particularity. The second is the recognition of distinctive and effective religious truth in other religions, truth that contrasts with that of my own faith. The third is the validity of witness on the part of any one faith tradition to its "one and only" quality, and indeed to the superiority of its end in relation to others. An authentic religious pluralism acknowledges a diversity of religious ends. This implies that religious witness is also in order. Where witness can have no meaning, it is dubious whether dialogue may either.

This approach shifts the focus away from flat claims of truth and falsehood and toward concrete religious alternatives. We ask not, "Which religion alone is true?" but, "What end is most ultimate, even if many are real?" and, "Which life will I hope to realize?" Let us presume for the moment that the following ends are actual possibilities: the cessation of self, the realization of an absolute single self that is "nondual," communion with the triune God. These are real human possibilities, whose attainment depends significantly on the practice and aspiration of the person who attains them. The ends are not identical, and in reaching one, we will not automatically attain others. That is, in approaching religious differences, emphasis falls on the contrast of their *positive* ends. The Christian gospel is not just preached against false religions, but it is witnessed as an alternative among other true religions.

Notes

1. Mahatma Gandhi, *Hind Swaraj, or, Indian Home Rule*, rev. ed. (Ahmedabad: Navajwan, 1939), 36.

2. Bhagavad Gita 4.11. The translation is given in Anantanand Rambachan, "My God, Your God, Our God, No God?," *Current Dialogue* 33 (July 1999).

3. If, like some pluralist thinkers, we distinguish between our religious tradition and our particular view of the way the universe actually is, then this point still holds completely, with the small difference that the actual religion in question is now the pluralist theory.

4. H. H. the XIVth Dalai Lama, "'Religious Harmony' and Extracts from *The Bodhgaya Interviews*," in *Christianity through Non-Christian Eyes*, ed. Paul Griffiths, Faith Meets Faith (Maryknoll, NY: Orbis, 1990), 169.

5. Ibid.

6. This is worked out in some detail in S. Mark Heim, *The Depth of the Riches: A Trinitarian Theology of Religious Ends*, Sacra Doctrina (Grand Rapids: Eerdmans, 2001).

4

General Revelation, Inclusivism, Pluralism, and Postmodernism

Millard J. Erickson

Central to the discussion of the validity and efficacy of world religions is the doctrine of general revelation. While Christian exclusivists insist that a proper relationship with God requires knowledge of him through his special revelatory work, inclusivists contend that the knowledge of God available to all persons makes such a relationship possible, even for those who have never heard the gospel explicitly. To pluralists, the term *general revelation* appears somewhat ethnocentric. They prefer the nomenclature of *natural theology*, holding that the adherents of all religions are related to the same God, although they construe him according to the understanding of him found in their own sacred writings.

While the doctrine of general revelation has had a long and varied history, certain periods have proven to be epochal. In those times, because of particular issues impinging on the discussion, the topic has been explored in much greater detail and depth than at other times. One of these was in the time of Augustine, when the sacking of Rome brought forth charges that the adoption of Christianity had been responsible for such an adverse occurrence. To reply, Augustine found it necessary to appeal to evidence that would have been familiar to those who did not accept the authority of the Christian Scriptures. Then when Christianity found itself in contact with non-Christian religions, again some common arena of discussion was needed, so Thomas Aquinas developed his fourfold proof of the existence of God. In the sixteenth century, as the conflict between Rome and the Reformers was vigorous, the issue was the status of grace, so the exclusiveness of the church's revelation was at stake. Then in the twentieth century, twice the church found itself endorsing what turned out to be evil. The first was during World War I, when some leading churchmen were among the ninety-three intellectuals who endorsed the Kaiser's war policy as a working of God.[1] Then in the 1930s, the church proclaimed Adolf Hitler to be God's good gift to the world. In each case, Karl Barth saw what he believed to be a mistake based on the blurring of the distinction between general revelation and special revelation or, more accurately, the confusion of thinking that there was some knowledge of God available apart from Jesus Christ. His criticism of these liberal conceptions spilled over into a dispute with his fellow neo-orthodox theologian, Emil Brunner, not only over the status of a general revelation, but also over the integrity of the image of God in humans, enabling them to discern the true God within nature, and even the issue of the ability to receive the special revelation without some divine particular enablement.[2]

All of these debates, however, took place within a context that assumed a certain objectivity to knowledge and its objects. Thus, a rational discussion and debate could be conducted over the extent of knowledge available through the natural world and the validity of various religions, based on this. Although such a conception of truth and knowledge is often depicted as restricted to the modern period and especially the Enlightenment, it was also shared by the era commonly referred to as premodernism.

Postmodernism, however, casts the discussion in an entirely different light. While there are many varieties of postmodernism, for purposes of our discussion herein, we may think of postmodernism as a philosophy that affirms the following statements:

1. All human knowledge is conditioned, that is, affected by the historical and cultural situation in which it is found. There is therefore no purely objective knowledge.
2. There is no common human nature that can be assumed in all persons. This means that there is no common rationality among all persons, no laws of logic inherent in everyone.
3. There is no purely sterile standpoint from which truth can be known neutrally.
4. Reality is never known directly or in terms of uninterpreted facts. All knowledge is interpreted knowledge.
5. There is no metanarrative, no all-inclusive explanation of reality, valid for all persons. Attempts to construct such holoscopic theories either fail or become the means of suppressing contrary views, and thus of oppressing those who hold them.

The thesis of this chapter is that the movement known as postmodernism, if accepted as true, has far-reaching effects on the doctrine of general revelation, especially as it bears on the question of the relationship of human beings to God.

Definition of General Revelation

The definition we will be working with in this paper is that general revelation is the knowledge of God through means available to persons at all times and places. It thus does not require a knowledge of sacred Scriptures or of the events described therein. In the Christian formulation of the doctrine, it is God's work, his revelation, rather than human discovery, that is being considered.

It should be noted that this is a theological definition and one made from the perspective of Christianity. It assumes that such knowledge of God as may exist is the result of God's initiative in making himself known. From a philosophical perspective, or even from a broad approach of comparative religions, it should rather be termed natural theology, or the knowledge of God obtainable apart from any particular religious document or institution.

Traditional Loci of General Revelation

As usually conceived, general revelation consists of three types:

1. *Nature.* God's handiwork is seen in the physical and animate creation he has made. A number of biblical texts are believed to support this contention, most notably the nature Psalms and Romans 1. This is something external to the human, although presumably the complexity of the human body would also be part of it.

2. *The moral constitution of the human.* In Romans 2, Paul speaks of the law written within, which leads the person to do the works of the law, even though he or she does not possess that written law. This has sometimes been seen as involving actual content of what is right and wrong, and in the thought of some others, is simply the moral impulse that there is such a thing as right and that one ought to do it.

3. *God's providential working in history.* In addressing the Lycaonians in Acts 14, Paul spoke of how God had given a witness of himself. Some also believe this can be seen in the fortunes of nations, which God causes to rise and fall.

Of these three, the first two, if genuine, are clearly available to anyone, although presumably a blind person would have difficulty in seeing the starry heavens above, and a psychopath or sociopath would have difficulty recognizing the moral imperative within. Such, however, are unusual situations, so that we might say that these sources of knowledge are accessible by any normal person. The third classification is somewhat more problematic, since some of the data of God's providence require being in a special location or having access to certain historical data. The more common elements, however, such as the sending of weather and the resulting bearing of crops, are as available to inspection as are the phenomena of creation.

I would suggest a fourth locus, which is seldom mentioned but is rather widely utilized: *shared human experience*. A considerable amount of contemporary preaching draws on experiences that are familiar to the listeners—experiences such as loneliness, rejection, insecurity, and the like. These are experiences that to varying degrees everyone can relate to, and they become the basis for much persuasion, whether that is acknowledged overtly or not. In a day in which there is a relatively lesser popular interest in the natural sciences than there is in human relationships, this can be considered a manifestation of God, not necessarily by particular occurrences, but by virtue of the common humanity with which he endowed us.

Attempts to Do Theology in a Postmodern Age

With the rise of postmodernism, theology has entered a whole new era. The rules by which the theology game is played are, if theology accepts postmodernism, completely changed. We may examine several attempts to do theology on this new basis.

Liberation Theology

If we consider postmodern theologies in terms of the classifications utilized by David Ray Griffin, then what he terms liberationist postmodern theology is a significant option.[3] We may see here as well a marked move from a greater reliance on a scriptural basis to more attention being given to experiential and thus more universal factors. It is not that liberation theology does not utilize Scripture, but rather that the scriptural base is rather narrow, focusing on passages dealing with oppression and political/economic liberation. This suggests that such passages are especially selected for emphasis because they fit criteria derived from some other source.

We do not have to search far to discover that other source, for Gustavo Gutierrez makes that clear in his very definition of theology, that it is reflection on praxis in light of God's word.[4] Here, theology is not so much a cool, detached, objective examination of an ancient text as it is involvement in practical behavior, intended to minister to the needs of the poor.

As such, the basis of the theology is something of universal accessibility. It is the experience of poverty from which theology begins, and it is actual involvement in that experience. While not all theologians are personally poor, by identification with the poor, they may empathetically share in their experience.

Thinking of liberation theologies more generally, it is not just poverty but oppression the experience of which forms the basis of this reflection on praxis. Whether that oppression is economic, political, gender, or even ecclesiastical, the experience that leads to the theology is that of the weak being oppressed by those with the ability to exercise power over them.

PROCESS THEOLOGY

Many process theologians are quite clear that they consider themselves postmodern, in the sense that they are not intending to follow the older metaphysical approach. Their postmodern theology, however, is what Griffin terms "constructive postmodernism."[5] They are definite in declaring that their endeavor is one of natural theology, of drawing from experiences that should be accessible to everyone.[6] Thus, the idea that reality is of the nature of event or process rather than of substance is attested to by common experiences of perception. Here we note that reality as we experience it is not merely a smooth, continuous flow of events, blending into one another, but rather a sequence of discrete occurrences.[7] This is supplemented by a more technical source of data, drawn from physics, according to which, in quantum mechanics, it is possible to predict either the location or the velocity of a particle, but not both. While the former is commonly experienced by everyone, the latter is more restricted to scientists but in theory would be available to anyone able and willing to make the effort to acquire knowledge of that field.

We should note, however, that process theology also draws on much the same sort of experience as does liberation theology. This is seen in the list of qualities of God or types of gods that process theology rejects.[8] Many of these characteristics of the rejected god are attributed by Scripture to him. So in this case, the natural theology is not simply seen as supporting or harmoniously supplementing the content of special revelation, but as contradicting it.

JAMES MCCLENDON

The late James McClendon was a pioneer in postmodern theology and was especially known for his unique development of narrative theology. In his book *Biography as Theology*, McClendon's doctrinal insights are not based upon exegesis of particular biblical passages, but rather on the examination of the biographies of several Christian leaders such as Martin Luther King Jr. and Dag Hammarskjöld.[9] He contends that such biographical studies can provide content for theology. This is indicated quite clearly by the subtitle of the book:

How Life Stories Can Remake Today's Theology. In order to draw upon these life stories, however, it is not necessary to examine the Bible per se. Rather, one may simply consult the biographical data available or, if necessary, write one's own biography of the individuals concerned. Note, however, that this, on the strictest terms, is not special revelation, at least not in the usual sense of that term in Christian theology. Rather, since it does not assume direct familiarity with the canonical Scriptures, it by default must be considered a case of general revelation.

J. RICHARD MIDDLETON AND BRIAN J. WALSH

J. Richard Middleton and Brian J. Walsh in their interestingly titled book *Truth Is Stranger than It Used to Be*, describe the Christian faith in narrative and even dramatic terms. The biblical narrative is a great drama that, however, is unfinished. It ends with the work of the church in the first decades following the life of Christ. By way of analogy, suppose that we were to find an unfinished play of Shakespeare's, which all Shakespearean scholars judged to be authentic. The problem, however, is that the conclusion is lost and presumably unrecoverable. What then is to be done? Rather than having a Shakespearean scholar or a collection thereof attempt to reconstruct the final act, Middleton and Walsh advance a different solution. Their recommendation would be to assemble a group of experienced Shakespearean actors, who would proceed, in the spirit of Shakespeare, to finish out the play by impromptu reproduction.[10]

The analogy they are suggesting is applied to the church. In a sense, the Bible is an unfinished play, in which the long final chapter has not yet been written. What we as Christians today are to do is to complete the drama by living the Christian life, as a continuation of the trajectory found in the Bible. Implicit in this is the idea that the Holy Spirit who was at work in the characters who lived in biblical times is also at work in believers today.[11]

Note, however, that the church today is much more accessible to examination than was the church in biblical times. In a sense, one could contend that what Middleton and Walsh are advancing is a claim for the extension of special revelation, first temporally, so that the canon really should not be considered closed in the early centuries. However, it is also possible to regard this as an extension of accessibility of these events such that the knowledge of the life of the church would be available to anyone willing and able to examine the public accounts, and thus this would be general revelation.

STANLEY GRENZ

In the thought of the late Stanley J. Grenz, we find an attempt to formulate a new approach to Evangelical theology. Grenz was concerned to do theology in a way that would appeal to a generation of postmodernists. In his judgment, the Evangelicals of the previous generation had structured their theology on the basis of modernism. This meant that they placed a great deal of emphasis on doctrine as a first-level phenomenon, which gave actual information about God. He cites as a typical definition of theology that of Klaus Bockmuehl, that it is a compilation of Christian doctrine, based on Scripture. While this was a useful definition of theology in time past, says Grenz, it is no longer serviceable as a basis for Evangelical theology.[12] Instead, he proposes and states repeatedly this alternative: "Christian theology is the believing community's reflection on its faith."[13]

Part of the reason for this changed conception is Grenz's revised definition of Evangelicalism. In the modern period, he says, Evangelicals understood their religion as basically a matter of beliefs, or commitment to a set of doctrines. Instead, says Grenz, Evangelicalism should be thought of primarily as an experience, the experience of new birth.[14] Doctrine arises as the believing community reflects on this faith, drawing out the doctrines that the experience both presupposes and those it implies.[15]

This shift is significant for the topic of our consideration. Whereas the earlier definition of doctrine required access to the Bible, this latter definition does not. It only requires access to, or observation of, a faith community. One could formulate an understanding of theology simply by using the methodology of sociology of religion, without needing the tools of exegesis. Like history, the life of the church is exposed to anyone's examination. It may be the Scriptures at second hand, but it is nonetheless possible without direct knowledge of Scripture. To the extent that the church is a social institution, it is the object of study by sociology of religion.

This presents a real dilemma for Grenz. On the one hand, as I have sought to argue, with theology being based on the church's experience, that is accessible to all persons and thus is universal. On the other hand, however, postmodernism in general is quite averse to metanarratives, or universal theories, which claim to account for everything and to everyone at all times and places. Yet Grenz, as an Evangelical, wants to maintain the supremacy and uniqueness of Jesus Christ but at the same time to do so from the perspective of postmodernism. He struggles mightily to offer a rationale for this contention, and part of the problem is that postmodernism contends that there is no such thing as a neutral point from which judgments of truth and falsity can be made.

He finally offers this rationale: that Christianity is the supreme religion because it does a better job than does any other religion of community building, as it defines community.[16] That, however, begs the question of the nature of community.

IMPLICATIONS FOR A POSTMODERN THEOLOGY

We have seen that postmodernism, with its tendency toward rejection of authority, has a natural inclination away from reliance on any special revelation and a much greater sympathy for general revelation. In actual practice, the various types of postmodernism draw their content from sources available to anyone willing to examine them.

This means that, in practice, the theology flowing from this general revelation is something of a universal theology, since its sources are not restricted to any one segment of the human race. In the modern period, this led to a theology that was something of the lowest common denominator. The most common representative of such a theology was deism, a generalized kind of god. Ideally, the god that everyone should believe in was the same. This was believed to be the truth about deity and what should be believed by everyone. As more specific content was given to such a view, it led to various sorts of inclusivism. For example, Karl Rahner held that there were "anonymous Christians," who held to the essentials of Christian belief on the basis of a common experience, even if they called themselves by the names of other religions or even considered themselves to be atheists.[17]

In a postmodern setting, however, general revelation leads to a quite different conclusion. Rather than experiencing the same object in the same way, different persons, conditioned by historical and cultural factors, have differing perceptions of the same reality. The attempt to make any one narrative a metanarrative, normative for everyone everywhere, results in such a narrative being used oppressively against those who dissent. Further, no one can possibly know all of reality in order to be able to formulate a true metanarrative. Thus, metanarratives are both impossible and undesirable.

Here we find, then, an internal contradiction within postmodernism between a universalizing tendency and an anti-universalizing tendency. This tension is inherent in a philosophy that rejects metanarratives, by what is actually a metanarrative of sorts in itself, and that opposes foundationalism but is itself a foundationalism, albeit of a somewhat unusual type.[18] It seems likely that the resolution will be through a different response than that which modernism worked out, where a universal and general view was adopted.

The most likely response of postmodernism is not an inclusivism but rather a pluralism of one of two types. The first would follow the neo-Kantian model advanced by John Hick, in which there is a reality that he refers to as the One, but which is perceived rather differently.[19] These religions are really the same thing, but differently expressed, much the way one language might be spoken in different dialects or with differing accents. The pluralism of religions is really a variety of expressions of the one religion, resulting from filtering the same basic reality through differing cultural categories.

The other kind of pluralism is more radical and would correspond to more radical varieties of postmodernism. Here the variety results not from differing perceptions of the same reality, but from different realities. The adherents of different religions are actually responding to different objects. This would be more like a polytheism or even a henotheism.

On the surface of it, the type of pluralism just described would seem to be immune to postmodernism's objection to metanarratives. On closer examination, however, this can be seen not to be the case. Pluralism is not the narrow type of religious narrative represented by any of the particular religions. It is, however, still a religious worldview, although of a general or generic variety, as contrasted with materialistic or humanistic visions of reality. It rests on the assumptions of a universal rationality and objective knowledge that postmodernism opposes.

IS POSTMODERNISM THE FINAL WORD?

These seem to me to be the options resulting from the idea of general revelation in a postmodern context. Another option, however, is to challenge the validity and appropriateness of postmodernism, which I prefer and have advanced in print.[20] This suggests that the alternative to postmodernism is not merely a return to modernism, but to what I term, rather satirically, *postpostmodernism*, which recognizes postmodernism's valid points of insight but insists that rational thought and indeed living cannot long persist on the basis of a wholesale adoption of its tenets.

The major difficulty for postmodernism, it seems to me, is that if it succeeds in arguing that all knowledge is conditioned, then that insight applies to postmodernism as well. I personally think their contention is correct and held it long before postmodernism was on the scene. What is impressive is how those who contend that there is no neutral place from which to contemplate options use this to neutralize competing theories but then proceed as if this did not apply to their own view. That, however, appears illegitimate and even disingenuous. What I have argued in its place is that we acknowledge the fact of our own conditionedness but then make every possible endeavor to minimize the conditioning effect. This would include such steps in the self-discovery process as writing one's own intellectual autobiography and interacting with those of differing cultures and perspectives. It also would mean taking steps consciously to compensate for the effect of these conditioning factors on our beliefs and perspectives. Beyond that, it means being willing to be contrarian. By that is meant simply being willing to challenge the commonly held conceptions of the times. It does not mean being disagreeable or cranky. It does mean asking hard questions, being skeptical, insisting on justification for contentions being advanced.

Having said all of this, what is the status of postmodernism? If the postmodernists are correct that all beliefs are conditioned, then if we take this at simple face value, we must say, "And so is that statement," and proceed to ignore it. We might give the postmodernist the courtesy of simply saying, "Well, that's your opinion," and hold our own nonetheless. Suppose, however, we are to follow Derrida, who insisted that while everything was to be deconstructed in the name of justice, that justice was not deconstructible any more than deconstruction itself.[21] For if that were not the case, then, as Caputo put it, there would be no point to deconstruction, a very good observation indeed.[22] If, however, we are among those pesky contrarians, we will ask, "Why should not deconstruction be deconstructed, too?" and will presumably receive one of two answers. Either deconstruction or, more generally, postmodernism is not to be deconstructed, or it is not to be considered conditioned because it is an exception to the rule or there are exempting conditions why the rule should not be applied. In the former case, then, the rule must actually be restated as "All theories are conditioned except the theory that all theories are conditioned." That, however, would be a mere flat assertion, not an argument, and circular in nature as well. The other approach would be to say, "All *An* is *X*. This is *Ap*. Therefore, this is not necessarily *X*." Since one of the bases of deconstruction is the presence of contradictory elements within a view,[23] this requirement of not deconstructing deconstruction not only permits, but requires, its own deconstruction.

The difficulty with both of these moves is that they prove too much. If they succeed, they fail. For if there is one exception to the rule, then why may there not be other exceptions as well? Similarly, if there are exempting conditions, so that this view is not really an instance of the rule, then may there not be other theories that are not instances of the rule as well? The problem is that if this view is not an instance of the type of thing to which the rule applies, then we must ask of what it is an instance. Thus far, that has not been done, at least not satisfactorily.

The problem is that if postmodernism is true or correct, then on its own terms it is false or at least relative. It will not do to say as sociologists of knowledge Berger and Luckmann said, "To include epistemological questions concerning the validity of sociological knowledge in the sociology of knowledge is somewhat like trying to push a bus in which one is riding."[24] The early Wittgenstein said, "My propositions are elucidatory in this way: he who understands me finally recognizes them as senseless, when has climbed out through them, on them, over them. (He must so to speak throw away the ladder, after he has climbed up on it.) He must surmount these propositions; then he sees the world rightly."[25]

The alternative would seem to be Wittgenstein's next statement: "Whereof one cannot speak; thereof he must be silent."[26] This, however, is exactly what the postmodernists do not do. It would be fine if the postmodernist were to say, "I am a postmodernist, and postmodernism is the truth for me, and you are a modernist, and modernism is the truth for you." Better yet, it would be desirable if the postmodernist were willing simply to hold his postmodern view in silence or at most to say, "This is what I believe," but never suggest that anyone else should accept it. As soon, however, as the postmodernist advances his view as something that others should adopt and believe as well, then an implicit assumption has been made of some area of neutrality, where discussion between those from different paradigms can be conducted. Postmodernists, contra their theory, really seem to be saying that postmodernism is true and modernism is false, or at least that postmodernism is preferable to modernism. This situation is seldom if ever faced, however. In a panel on postmodernism, I once raised a question about the status of the discussion we were having about different paradigms: was the discussion itself modern, postmodern, or what? The disappointing response of a postmodern Evangelical theologian on the panel brought that line of query to a halt: "I don't understand the question."

That, however, is *the* question, and evading it will not advance the discussion. Derrida himself saw this clearly when he said, "We have no language—no syntax and no lexicon—which is foreign to this history; we can pronounce not a single destructive proposition which has not already had to slip into the form, the logic, and the implicit postulates of precisely what it seeks to contest. . . . One must reject even the concept and the word 'sign' itself—which is precisely what cannot be done."[27] Until, however, the postmodernist is willing to face this dilemma head on and deal with it, we may feel justified in proceeding with the discussion of general revelation and its relevance to the issues of exclusivism and inclusivism.

If we are willing to acknowledge and accept this shortcoming of what we might term "hard postmodernism," there may still be a way of incorporating some postmodern insights into what we might term "soft postmodernism." Since, however, these insights are not unique to postmodernists, they may be included in what we might term instead soft modernism, postpostmodernism, or what Griffin labels "reconstructive or restorative postmodernism."[28] It is a view that acknowledges the limited and conditioned nature of every belief yet is unwilling to accept the idea of a plurality of truths. It takes steps to counter the limitations of one's situation in time and space and to seek a unifying truth.

One leading postmodern philosopher even gives a hint that such a metanarrative is possible. Richard Rorty tells of how he went to the University of Chicago seeking a unifying view that would tie together the manifold considerations in his life, from the Trotskyism he had been taught from childhood to the wild orchids that grew near his family's vacation home in New Jersey. He tried Platonism and various other philosophies but finally despaired of finding such a comprehensive scheme. He acknowledges that "I decided that only religion—only a nonargumentative faith in a surrogate parent who, unlike any real parent, embodied love, power, and justice in equal measure—could do the trick Plato wanted done." For him, however, this was not an option: "Since I couldn't imagine becoming religious, and had gotten more and more raucously secularist, I decided that the hope of achieving a single vision by becoming a philosopher had been a self-deceptive atheist's way out."[29] His later writings confirm this commitment to a secularist, and even an antireligious, stance.[30]

It is the possibility that Rorty admitted that I believe could be pursued at some length. While the God described is likelier to be found in special than in general revelation, general revelation would once again become a meaningful concept and a useful element in an objective theology. The issue of inclusiveness and even pluralism is therefore still a viable topic of discussion.

Notes

1. Karl Barth, *God, Grace and Gospel* (Edinburgh: Oliver and Boyd, 1959), 57–58.

2. *Natural Theology: Comprising "Nature and Grace" by Emil Brunner and the Reply "No!" by Karl Barth*, ed. John Baillie, trans. Peter Fraenkel (London: G. Bles, 1946).

3. David R. Griffin, "Introduction: Varieties of Postmodern Theology," in *Varieties of Postmodern Theology*, ed. David R. Griffin, 1–7 (Albany: State University of New York Press, 1989).

4. Gustavo Gutierrez, *A Theology of Liberation: History, Politics, and Salvation*, 15th anniversary ed. (Maryknoll, NY: Orbis, 1988), xxix.

5. David Ray Griffin, "Introduction: Varieties of Postmodern Theology," in David Ray Griffin, William A. Beardslee, and Joe Holland, *Varieties of Postmodern Theology* (Albany: State University of New York Press, 1989), 3.

6. John B. Cobb Jr., *A Christian Natural Theology: Based on the Thought of Alfred North Whitehead,* 2nd ed. (Louisville: Westminster John Knox, 2007).

7. John B. Cobb Jr. and David Ray Griffin, *Process Theology: An Introductory Exposition* (Philadelphia: Westminster, 1976), 14–16.

8. Ibid., 8–10.

9. James McClendon, *Biography as Theology: How Life Stories Can Remake Today's Theology* (Nashville: Abingdon, 1974).

10. J. Richard Middleton and Brian J. Walsh, *Truth Is Stranger than It Used to Be: Biblical Faith in a Postmodern Age* (Downers Grove, IL: InterVarsity, 1995), 182–83.

11. Ibid., 184.

12. Stanley J. Grenz, *Revisioning Evangelical Theology: A Fresh Agenda for the 21st Century* (Downers Grove, IL: InterVarsity, 1993), 62.

13. Ibid., 81, 84, 87, 88, 91, 92.

14. Ibid., 32–34.

15. Ibid., 92.

16. Stanley J. Grenz, *Renewing the Center: Evangelical Theology in a Post-Theological Era*, 2nd ed. (Grand Rapids: Baker, 2006), 285–94.

17. Karl Rahner, "Anonymous Christians," *Theological Investigations* (London: Darton, Longman & Todd, 1969), 6:390–98.

18. Timm Triplett terms this type of foundationalism "contextual foundationalism." Triplett, "Recent Work on Foundationalism," *American Philosophical Quarterly* 27, no. 2 (1990): 101.

19. John Hick, *Problems of Religious Pluralism* (New York: St. Martin's, 1985), 96.

20. Millard J. Erickson, *Truth or Consequences: The Promise and Perils of Postmodernism* (Downers Grove, IL: InterVarsity, 2001).

21. Jacques Derrida, "Force of Law: The Mystical Foundation of Authority," in *Deconstruction and the Possibility of Justice*, ed. Drucilla Cornell, Michael Rosenfeld, and David Gray Carlson (New York: Routledge, 1992), 14–15.

22. John Caputo, in *Deconstruction in a Nutshell: A Conversation with Jacques Derrida*, ed. John Caputo (New York: Fordham University Press, 1997), 131–32.

23. Derrida, "Force of Law," 9.

24. Peter L. Berger and Thomas Luckmann, *The Social Construction of Reality: A Treatise in the Sociology of Knowledge* (New York: Anchor, 1966), 13.

25. Ludwig Wittgenstein, *Tractatus Logico-Philosophicus* (London: Routledge and Kegan Paul, 1955), 189.

26. Ibid.

27. Jacques Derrida, *Writing and Difference* (Chicago: University of Chicago Press, 1978), 280–81.

28. Griffin, "Introduction," 5–6.

29. Richard Rorty, "Trotsky and Wild Orchids," in *Wild Orchids and Trotsky: Messages from American Universities*, ed. Mark Edmundson (New York: Penguin, 1993), 41–42.

30. Richard Rorty, "Universalism and Truth," in *Rorty and His Critics*, ed. Robert I. Brandom (Malden, MA: Blackwell, 2000), 21–22.

5

Is Christianity the Only True Religion, or One among Others?

John Hick

The likelihood is that you are a Christian. So the question I am raising is inevitably an uncomfortable one. For you may have taken it for granted, for as long as you can remember, that of course Christianity is the only true religion, or at least much the most true. I myself became a Christian by Evangelical conversion when a law student, and it was part of the package of belief that I accepted wholeheartedly that Christianity is uniquely superior to all others, and the world in process of being converted to Christian faith.

But that was some sixty years ago. In those days, like most of my generation, I had never met anyone of another faith and knew virtually nothing about the other world religions—and the little that I thought I knew has turned out to be largely caricature. But the present generation is generally much better informed. And today we all know, when we stop to think about it, that people of the other world religions have exactly the same view of their own faith as we do of ours.

In other words, the religion that seems so obviously superior to anyone depends in the vast majority of cases on where he or she happens to have been born. Someone born into a devout Muslim family in Egypt or Pakistan or Albania (or for that matter in England) is very likely to grow up as a Muslim; someone born into a devout Hindu family in India (or again in England) is very likely to be a Hindu; someone born into a devout Buddhist family in Thailand or Sri Lanka or Burma (or once again England) is very likely to be a Buddhist, just as someone born into a devout Christian family in this country is very likely to be a Christian; and so on.

There are, of course, and always will be individual conversions for individual reasons in every direction both to and from each of the great world faiths, and generally we must presume that this is a right move, but such conversions are statistically marginal in comparison with the massive transmission of faith from generation to generation within the same religion. So normally, the religion that you accept—or, of course, the religion that you reject—is the one into which you happen to have been born. I think that this is obvious and undeniable, although theologians all too seldom reflect on its implications.

So why do many—in fact, probably most—Christians believe that Christianity is uniquely superior to all other faiths, the one and only true religion?

Well, above all, the New Testament says so. We read in John's Gospel that Jesus said, "I am the way, and the truth, and the life; no one comes to the Father, but by me" (14:6), "I and the Father are one" (10:30), "He who has seen me has seen the Father" (14:9), and "[B]efore Abraham was, I am" (8:58 RSV). In these texts, all from John's Gospel, does Jesus not clearly claim to be God, or God the Son, incarnate, and is he not claiming that his is the only path of salvation and thus the only true religion? So in the Acts of the Apostles, we read that "there is salvation in no one else, for there is no other name [than that of Christ] under heaven given among men by which we must be saved" (Acts 4:12).

I must say a little about this New Testament basis of the belief, although it would require a whole week, or more likely a whole year, to discuss it properly. But most New Testament scholars today do *not* believe that Jesus, the historical individual, claimed to be God incarnate. That doesn't mean that they don't believe that Jesus was in fact God incarnate, but they don't think that he himself taught that he was. In case this comes as a surprise to some, I will give some brief quotations. I'm going to quote only from distinguished New Testament scholars who personally believe strongly that the church has been right in believing that Jesus was God incarnate. They believe this with their whole heart. But nevertheless they hold, on the basis of the evidence, that Jesus did not himself claim this. Referring first to those New Testament sayings which I quoted a minute ago—"I am the way, the truth, and the life," etc.—Professor Charlie Moule of Cambridge, the doyen of conservative British New Testament scholars, writes, "Any case for a 'high' Christology that depended on the authenticity of the alleged claims of Jesus about himself, especially in the fourth Gospel [i.e., John's], would indeed be precarious."[1] Also in Cambridge, Canon Brian Hebblethwaite of Queen's College, a notable defender of the orthodox doctrine, says, "It is no longer possible to defend the divinity of Jesus by reference to the claims of Jesus."[2] Then the late Archbishop Michael Ramsey (previously a New Testament professor) said, "Jesus did not claim deity for himself."[3] Again, perhaps the leading New Testament scholar in this country today, Professor James D. G. Dunn, after examining minutely every relevant text in all four Gospels and indeed throughout the New Testament, writes that "there was no real evidence in the earliest Jesus-tradition of what could fairly be called a consciousness of divinity."[4] These are all people who accept the traditional incarnation doctrine but who are also part of the scholarly consensus that the historical Jesus did not himself teach this. It is generally held today that the great "I am" sayings of the fourth Gospel, which I quoted a minute ago, cannot be attributed to the historical Jesus but are words put into his mouth by a Christian writer some sixty to seventy years later, and also that Jesus' sayings in the Synoptic Gospels cannot be taken to constitute a claim to be God incarnate; as Dunn says, "There was no real evidence in the earliest Jesus-tradition of what could fairly be called a consciousness of divinity."

If this comes to anyone as a bit of a shock, that is because although theologically educated ministers of the church know this, they do not mention it in their sermons. And I must confess that I myself have never said it in a sermon, but only in settings such as this. This silence has been going on for a very long time, and of course the longer you put off saying something difficult—difficult to the hearers—the harder it becomes to say it. When some years ago, 1977, a group of us, who included the Regius Professor of Divinity at Oxford, and a former Regius at Cambridge, then Warden of Keble College, Oxford, and the Principal of Cuddesdon Theological College, Oxford, and others, published a book called *The Myth of God Incarnate* in which we discussed this question openly and frankly, we were attacked and reviled, not for saying what the scholarly world had long known, but for saying it so publicly and with such an alarming title. But today, more than twenty years later, the whole subject is much more openly discussed, and I don't have any hesitation in discussing it here.

It's also well known today—another theme of that book—that the term *son of God* was widely used in the ancient world. Jesus was by no means the only person to whom the term was applied. In particular, within Jesus' own religion, Judaism, Adam was called the son of God, and is so called in Luke's Gospel, where Jesus' ancestry is traced back to "the son of Seth, the son of Adam, the son of God" (*tou Seth tou Adam tou Theou*; 3:38), angels were called sons of God, Israel as a whole was called God's son, and indeed any outstandingly pious Jew could be called a son of God. And the ancient Hebrew kings were enthroned as son of God; hence the words of Psalm 2:7, "Thou art my son, this day I have begotten thee." But no one within Judaism thought that God literally begot sons. The phrase *son of God* was clearly metaphorical. The phrase *son of* meant "true servant of," or sometimes "given a special divine mission by," or more generally "in the spirit of." The term was a very familiar metaphor within Judaism and never implied deity. But as Christianity expanded beyond its Jewish roots into the Greco-Roman world, the metaphorical son of God was gradually transformed in Christian thinking into the metaphysical God the Son, second person of a divine Trinity. And it is this epoch-making development that is under question today.

Now, in the discussions of the last twenty or so years, the idea that Christianity is the only true religion and only source of salvation, and that only Christians are saved, is today generally called exclusivism, in distinction from the two other main positions, called inclusivism and pluralism.

However, today the majority of Christian theologians and church leaders have moved away from this strict exclusivism to what is called inclusivism. This concentrates primarily on the question of salvation and is the view that salvation is indeed through Christ alone in virtue of his atoning death on the cross, but that this salvation is not confined to Christians but is available, in principle, to all human beings. So non-Christians also can be included within the sphere of Christian salvation—hence the term *inclusivism*. People of good will outside the church can be said to have an implicit Christian faith, or to be anonymous Christians, or to be in such a state that they *will* respond to Christ as their lord and savior when they confront him after death. On this view, Christianity remains the only true religion, but those who do not know Christ can also benefit from his atoning death. This position was adopted by the Catholic Church at the second Vatican Council in the 1960s and is the position of the present pope and also of a majority of theologians within the other mainline Christian churches, including the Church of England, the Methodists, the United Reformed Church, Baptists, etc.—except in each case for their fundamentalist wings. Its attraction is that, on the one hand, it preserves the traditional conviction of the unique centrality/normativeness/superiority of Christianity, but on the other hand, it does not involve the horrifying implication that only Christians can be saved. This is why it is today so attractive and remains such a popular position.

But it does have its negative side. If we think for a moment of the analogy of the solar system, with God as the sun at the center and the religions as planets revolving around that center, the inclusivist position says in effect that the life-giving light and warmth of the sun falls directly only on our earth but is then reflected off it to the other religions, which thus receive it at second hand. Or in terms of economics, this is a kind of trickle-down theory of salvation. We Christians are the spiritually rich at the top, but our riches trickle down in varying measure to the people of the other world religions below. And just how realistic this is will depend on what we mean by salvation.

If you define salvation as being forgiven and accepted by God because of the atoning death of Jesus on the cross, then salvation is by definition Christian salvation, and Christianity is by definition the only true religion. That is to settle the matter by definition. Suppose, however, that instead of doing this, we start with the realities of human life around the world as we find it and mean by salvation something concrete, something that can take place progressively in people's lives, something that is meant to begin here and now in this life and to make a manifest difference. We can describe it as the gradual transformation of men and women from natural self-centeredness to a new orientation centered in the divine reality that we call God, liberating us into love and compassion for our fellow beings. On this view, it is those who love their neighbors, who have compassion—that is, feeling with and for others—and who give something of their time, energy, intelligence, resources to those in much greater need both far and near, who are on the path of salvation. Or again, putting it in biblical terms, it is those whose lives embody what Saint Paul called the fruit of the spirit, which he described as "love, joy, peace, patience, kindness, goodness, faithfulness, gentleness, self-control" (Gal. 5:22)—to which we must, I think, add a commitment to social justice as an expression of love—who are on the way of salvation. It's not a question of "Are you saved or not saved?" but of the direction in which you are going, the path you are on.

Now the call to self-transcending love and compassion comes to humanity through a number of channels. Jesus taught that we are to love and value our neighbors as we love and value ourselves, even to love those who regard themselves as our enemies, so that "you may be sons of your Father who is in heaven; for he makes his sun rise on the evil and on the good, and sends rain on the just and on the unjust" (Matt. 5:44-45). Others hear the call to an equal concern for all in the Hebrew Scriptures in such divine commands as "You shall love your neighbor as yourself" (Lev. 19:18), or in the teaching of the Talmud, "What is hateful to you, do not do to your neighbour. This is the entire Torah; the rest is commentary" (*Babylonian Talmud*, Shabbat 31a). Others again hear it in such Hindu teachings as one on which Mahatma Gandhi based his life: "If a man give you a drink of water and you give him a drink in return, that is nothing. Real beauty consists in doing good against evil. . . . The truly noble know all men as one, and return with gladness good for evil done."[5] And yet others hear it in such Buddhist teachings as "As a mother cares for her son, her only son, all her days, so towards all living things a man's mind should be all-embracing."[6] And yet others hear it in the Qur'an, where we read, "Repel evil with what is good. Then you will find your erstwhile enemy like a close, affectionate friend" (41:34), or in the teachings of the Sufis of Islam, such as this parable of Rumi's:

> God rebuked Moses, saying, "I fell sick, thou camest not." Moses said, "O transcendent One, what mystery is this. Explain, O Lord!" God said again to him, "Wherefore didst thou not kindly ask after me when I was sick?" Moses answered, "Lord, thou never ailest. My understanding is lost." God said, "Yea, a favourite and chosen servant of mine fell sick. Consider well: his infirmity is My infirmity, his sickness is My sickness."[7]

You see, such ideas are genuinely Christian, but they are also genuinely Jewish, Islamic, Hindu, and Buddhist.

There is, in fact, a basic moral outlook which is universal, and the concrete reality of salvation consists in a spiritual transformation whose natural expression is unrestricted love and compassion. I stress the word *basic*, because what is common to the different faiths is this truly basic principle, not the specific moral codes which have developed within different societies at different times and places and in different circumstances. These latter reflect the particular historical circumstances in which they were formulated and are not immutable but ought to develop as societies change, and when they don't, they can produce evil instead of good. We see this, for example, in some of the harsh rules of desert life in parts of the Old Testament and in parts of the sharia of Islam, and also, in a lesser way nearer to home in current debates within the churches about the ordination of women, about the remarriage of divorced persons, and about homosexuality. New moral sensitivities and new scientific knowledge rightly enter into the development of our specific social norms.

But the *basic* moral teaching of the religions remains the same. It constitutes the universal ideal. But how does it actually work out in people's lives? Do Christians in fact respond to it better than the rest of humankind? Are Christians in general better human beings, morally and spiritually, than non-Christians in general? This is the question that I would invite you to focus upon. In order to answer it, of course, one has to get to know people of other faiths, and this is much easier for some than for others. Birmingham, for example, where I live, is a multifaith city. There are eighty thousand or more Muslims, large Sikh and Hindu communities, a smaller but long-established Jewish community, and growing numbers of Buddhists and Baha'is.

When you go into the mosques, synagogues, gurdwaras, and temples, as well as churches, something strikes you, or at least has struck me, very forcibly. On the one hand, all the externals are different. When you go into a Hindu temple, for example, the sights, colors, sounds, smells are those of India, and you can easily imagine yourself back there. And not only what the senses perceive, but also the language, the concepts, the whole way of thinking are distinctively Hindu. And the same is true in their different ways of each of the other places of worship. But at a much deeper level, it seems evident that essentially the same thing is going on in all these other places as in our Christian churches: namely, men and women are coming together under the auspices of some ancient, highly developed tradition which helps them to open their minds and hearts "upward" to a higher divine reality which makes a claim upon the living of their lives. And the basic claim is, in each case, as I illustrated a few minutes ago, the same. So it seems right to say with the thirteenth-century Muslim writer Jalaludin Rumi, writing about the religions of his time, "The lamps are different, but the Light is the same: it comes from Beyond."[8]

But further, it is a very common experience of Christians in such a city as Birmingham that when you get to know some of your neighbors of other faiths—and you meet them today in every walk of life, but particularly when you know individuals and families—you do not find that they are in general any less loving and caring, any less honest, any less likely to help a neighbor when someone next door is ill or in some trouble and needing friendly support, any less law-abiding, any less concerned for the good of society, any less ready to make sacrifices for the education of their children, any less faithful in the practice of their religion than are our Christian fellow citizens in general. I do not say any more, but I do say not any less. There are good and bad people, and all degrees of goodness and badness, within each faith community, including Christianity, but it does not seem that Christians in general stand out as morally and spiritually superior to everyone else.

And there's another kind of encounter that has been to me equally important. Partly in the course of interfaith dialogue over a number of years with Jews, Muslims, Buddhists, Hindus, and Sikhs, and from time spent in the heartlands of these other faiths, I have had the very good fortune to come to know a small number of individuals whom I regard as, in Christian terms, saints—saints in the sense that they have largely transcended the ego point of view and become channels of the higher divine reality. Such all-too-rare individuals are extremely important to us, because they make it much easier for us to believe in the higher reality to which the religions point. And they are to be found not only within Christianity but within each of the great faith traditions.

And although this is a huge topic which I cannot open up here, I do not think that history shows Christian civilization through the centuries to have been morally superior to all other civilizations. It is an unpleasant business to compare historical evils, but since many people take it for granted that Christianity has a manifestly cleaner record than the rest of the world, I would just remind you of the centuries-long persecution of the Jews, the Crusades, the burning of witches and heretics, the conquest and exploitation of what today we call the Third World, the carrying off of so many of its people as slaves, the history of Christian Europe through the twentieth century, which saw two terrible wars between Christian nations in which tens of millions were killed, and the Jewish Holocaust, and churches supporting fascist dictators in Italy, Spain, Brazil, El Salvador, Chile (the most recent being General Pinochet), and for a whole generation supporting apartheid in South Africa. And so it just does not seem to me that Christians, either individually or collectively, are manifestly better human beings than the rest of the human race.

But—and this is the question that we now have to ask ourselves—is this what you would expect if our traditional doctrines are straightforwardly true? According to these doctrines, we have a uniquely direct knowledge of God in Christ, a uniquely direct access to and relationship with God in prayer and worship in the name of Christ, and the direct presence of God with us in the sacraments of the church. Would you not then expect all this to make a visible difference in the lives of Christians? Would you not expect the fruits of the spirit to be more evident in Christians than in non-Christians? I suggest to you that we should expect that, because otherwise the unique superiority of Christianity would be mere rhetoric. But then, on the other hand, can we honestly claim that Christians are, in fact, morally and spiritually better human beings, in general, than non-Christians?

You see where all this is pointing—to the conclusion that perhaps Christianity is not after all the one and only true, or one and only salvific, religion. So this brings us to the third option that I mentioned for understanding the global religious situation. I've said a little about exclusivism and more about inclusivism. The third option, generally called pluralism, holds that there is not just one and only one point of salvific contact between the divine reality and humanity—namely, in the person of Jesus Christ—but that there is a plurality of independently valid contacts and independently authentic spheres of salvation, which include both Christianity and the other great world faiths.

In developing this pluralist point of view, I am assuming that religion is our human response to a transcendent reality, the reality that we call God. And as it is a *human* response, there is always an inescapably *human* element within it. To remind ourselves of this, look at the histories of both Judaism and Christianity. The image of Yahweh reflected in the Old Testament develops over the centuries from a violent tribal god who commands the Israelites to engage in genocide against the original inhabitants of Palestine ("Go and smite Amalek, and utterly destroy all that they have; do not spare them, but kill both man and woman, infant and suckling, ox and sheep, camel and ass"; 1 Sam. 15:3) to the universal Lord, blessed be He, of later and modern Judaism. Within Christianity, for quite a long period of time in the medieval world, most Christians thought of God as a terrible figure who would send most human beings to eternal hell, and before whom they trembled in terror, expecting to be judged by the equally terrible figure of Christ, and their Christian faith was largely one of dread. Life's calamities—disease, death, droughts, plagues, floods, and so on—were seen as God's punishments for human sin. And because life was so precarious, they thought that God must be very angry with his human creatures. For mercy, they looked to their local saints and to the figure of the Virgin Mary, who might intercede on their behalf. It was only in the thirteenth and fourteenth centuries that Jesus came again to be thought of by many as manifesting divine love, which is how most of us think today. Now, is it God's nature that has changed through the centuries, or is it our human images of God that have changed? Clearly, it is our human images of God.

So, in other words, between ourselves and God as God is in God's ultimate transcendent being, there is a screen of varied and changing human images of God—not graven images but mental images, or pictures, or concepts of God. And our awareness of God is always through and in terms of these human images. We worship God through our own images of God, to which our human ideas and cultural assumptions have inevitably contributed. These mental images differ considerably not only between religions, but also within a given religion. In fact, if we could see into one another's minds now, I believe we would find a great range of images or concepts of God.

But how can this be? The basic principle involved was stated long ago by Thomas Aquinas when he said, "Things known are in the knower according to the mode of the knower."[9] This is a principle that was taught in a much more massively systematic way by the philosopher Immanuel Kant and has been strongly confirmed since by cognitive psychology and the sociology of knowledge. "Things known are in the knower according to the mode of the knower," and the mode of the knower differs as between the different religions and the different cultures and histories within which they have arisen. This, I suggest, is the basic clue to a religious understanding of the fact of many religions each producing, so far as we can tell, equally valuable fruits in human life.

I've been concentrating so far mainly on the question of salvation. But what, more briefly, about the different and often incompatible teachings of the different religions? What about their conflicting truth claims? For example, for Christians, God is a Trinity of Father, Son, and Holy Spirit, whereas for Jews and Muslims, God is strictly unitary; for Christians, Jesus was the second person of a divine Trinity, whereas for people of all the other religions, he was a great prophet or teacher or guru but was not literally God walking on earth. Again, for the monotheisms, the ultimate reality, the absolutely real, is an infinite person, but for Buddhism, for example, the ultimate reality is not a person but a reality beyond the scope even of the personal/impersonal distinction. And, of course, on a less basic level, there are innumerable other differences between the teachings of the different faiths. But how can this be if they are all responses to the same ultimate reality that in Christian language we call God?

Well, if we accept the distinction between the divine reality as it is in itself and as variously imaged by us, then our Christian doctrines are about the ultimate divine reality as conceived by us, in distinction from that reality as it is in itself. And the different truth claims of the different religions are claims about *different* manifestations of the Ultimate to different human mentalities formed within different human cultures and different streams of religious history. As such, they do not contradict one another. That Muslims, for example, think of the divine and experience the divine as the Qur'anic Allah is not incompatible with the fact that Christians think of the divine and experience the divine as the heavenly Father of Jesus' teaching or, more theologically, as the Holy Trinity. In other words, what are called the conflicting truth claims of the religions do not in fact conflict, because they are claims about different human awarenesses of the divine, made possible by the fact that, to quote Aquinas again, things known are in the knower according to the mode of the knower.

But there is something else important to be said before I finish. There is a valid sense in which, for those of us who are Christians, Christianity *is* the only true religion, the only one for us. For we have been formed by it. It has created us in its own image, so that it fits us and we fit it as no other religion can. And so for most of us who are Christians, it is the right religion, and we should stick with it and live it out to the full. But we should also be aware that exactly the same is true for people formed by the other world religions. They also should stick with the religion that has formed them and live it out, though in each case gradually filtering out its ingrained claim to unique superiority.

So the bottom line, I am suggesting, is this: we should live wholeheartedly within our own faith, so long as we find it to be sustaining and a sphere of spiritual growth, but we should freely recognize the equal validity of the other great world faiths for *their* adherents, and we can also be enriched by some of their insights and spiritual practices. We should not see the other religions as rivals or enemies, or look down upon them as inferior, but should see them simply as different human responses to the divine reality, formed in the past within different strands of human history and culture. And we should seek a friendship with people of other faiths, which will do something to defuse the very dangerous religious absolutism that is being exploited in almost all the conflicts going on in the world today. To support religious absolutism is to be part of the problem which afflicts humanity. But we can be part of the solution by setting an example of transcending that absolutism.

Notes

1. C. F. D. Moule, *The Origin of Christology* (Cambridge: Cambridge University Press, 1977), 136.

2. Brian Hebblethwaite, *The Incarnation: Collected Essays in Christology* (Cambridge: Cambridge University Press, 1987), 74.

3. Michael Ramsey, *Jesus and the Living Past* (Oxford: Oxford University Press, 1960), 39.

4. James D. G. Dunn, *Christology in the Making: A New Testament Inquiry into the Origins of the Doctrine of the Incarnation* (Philadelphia: Westminster, 1980), 60.

5. Mahatma Gandhi, *Autobiography: The Story of My Experiments with Truth,* trans. Mahadev Desai (Washington, DC: Public Affairs Press, 1948), Volume 1, ch. 10.

6. *Sutta Nipata*, 143.

7. Jalālu'l-Dīn Rūmī, *Rumi, Poet and Mystic*, trans. R.A. Nicholson (Oxford: Oneworld, 1978), 65.

8. Ibid., 166.

9. Thomas Aquinas, *Summa Theologica* II/II, Q.1, art. 2.

6

John Hick's Monotheistic Shadow

Paul Rhodes Eddy

The British scholar John Hick has spent a lifetime investigating a wide range of issues related to the philosophy of religion. Today, Hick is most widely known for his articulation and defense of religious pluralism. In barest terms, Hick's mature pluralist philosophy of world religions holds, "The great world faiths embody different perceptions of, and correspondingly different responses to, the Real from within the major variant ways of being human; and that within each of them the transformation of human existence from self-centeredness to Reality-centeredness is taking place."[1]

The most critical conceptual problem facing Hick's pluralist project involves the de facto existence of radically conflicting human conceptions and experiences of the divine. The most obvious—and problematic—of these differences is the fundamental conceptual dichotomy between those religions that view the divine as a personal being and those that view it in terms of a nonpersonal principle, force, or "absolute." Thus, from the very beginning of his move to pluralism in the early 1970s, Hick's central apologetic project has been the construction of a viable solution to this problem of the apparently conflicting conceptions of the divine.[2]

Despite his best attempts, however, one of the most persistent charges leveled against Hick's pluralism over the years is that it continues to privilege a personal over a nonpersonal conception of the divine. More specifically, the charge has been made that Hick's ostensively tradition-neutral pluralist philosophy of religions hides, in fact, a cryptomonotheism at its very core. Here, "mono-theism" is to be understood as over against any sort of pluralistic conception of ultimate reality, on one hand, and any form of impersonal monism on the other.

This paper is composed of two major sections. First, I will trace the history of the charge of cryptomonotheism in its several forms and Hick's respective counterresponses. Finally, I will argue that, while Hick's mature pluralist apologetic does surmount some of the earlier forms of this critique, it nonetheless remains vulnerable to the charge of cryptomonotheism at several critical junctures.

JOHN HICK AND THE CRYPTOMONOTHEISM DEBATE

STAGE ONE: THE "COPERNICAN REVOLUTION"

In the early 1970s, Hick announced his move to a pluralist theology of religions, which in his eyes amounted to a "Copernican revolution" in terms of its theological magnitude.[3] With this move, Hick immediately felt the force of the conflicting conceptions of the divine problematic. His initial response to this problem was two-pronged, involving both theological-conceptual and experiential facets.[4] Hick begins by suggesting, "The Hindu distinction between Nirguna Brahman and Saguna Brahman is important and should be adopted into Western religious thought."[5] In briefest terms, Nirguna Brahman literally means "God without attributes," God as the self-existent, utterly transcendent reality that is beyond all human categories, including the "personal." Saguna Brahman, on the other hand, refers to "God with attributes," God as in relation to creation and thus experienced in personalistic categories. By dislocating the Nirguna-Saguna dichotomy from its specifically Hindu context, and by emphasizing God's infinite nature, Hick argues that "the one ultimate reality is both Nirguna and non-personal, and Saguna and personal, in a duality which is in principle acceptable to human understanding."[6]

Second, Hick goes on to support this distinction by suggesting that, when it comes to actual religious experience, all the major religious traditions exhibit some type of parallel dichotomization in regard to the divine. As examples, he offers the personal God Iswara and the nonpersonal absolute Brahman found within Hinduism. And within Christianity, he notes that the typically personal conception of God has been complemented by the idea of God as beyond personal by various Christian mystics.[7]

In spite of his attempts to rinse the nonpersonalistic Brahmanic privilege from the Nirguna-Saguna cloth, it was not long before Hick's religious pluralism was charged with covert Vedanta Hinduism.[8] Interestingly, at the same time, Hick's pluralist model also became the target for charges of cryptotheism.[9] One can identify two primary foci with regard to this latter accusation. First, in spite of his attempts to equalize the conceptions of a personal God and a nonpersonal absolute, Hick nonetheless continued to grant the moniker *God* most-favored terminological status when describing the ultimate divine reality. Hick was to wrestle with this terminological problem for the next decade.

Second, one of Hick's explicit motivations for his "Copernican revolution" involved the Christian idea of the God of universal love.[10] However, once the nature of ultimate reality is delimited in a manner such that whatever is said of it must be as appropriate to nonpersonal as to personal categories, the universally concerned "God of love" upon which Hick's original pluralist move depended is revealed as parochially Christian—or, at best, parochially theistic. Thus the paradox: to be consistent, Hick was forced to remove from the center of the universe the very conception of a loving God that led him to remap the universe of faiths in the first place. In essence then, the earliest charge of cryptotheism was tied to the observation that Hick assumes as a primary impetus for his pluralist revolution the very thing—i.e., the centrality and universality of the personal God of love—that it must explicitly reject if it is to be successful.[11]

STAGE TWO: THE NEO-KANTIAN MOVE

In 1976, Hick unveiled what was to become the conceptual hallmark of his mature pluralist model.[12] By adopting the Kantian noumenon-phenomenon distinction and relocating it from the realm of sensory to religious experience, Hick produced what arguably has proven to be the most sophisticated philosophical defense of a religiously realist pluralistic philosophy of religions.[13] In brief, Hick argues that both personalistic and nonpersonalistic conceptions of ultimate reality are "divine phenomena constituting forms in which the unknown divine noumenon impinges upon human consciousness. The status of these divine phenomena . . . is thus comparable with that of the phenomenal world in Kant's critical philosophy."[14]

By the early 1980s, Hick was developing this neo-Kantian proposal in full force.[15] Although the Nirguna-Saguna dichotomy continued to appear in his writings, it now functioned merely as an explicitly Hindu *analogy* to the noumenal-phenomenal mechanism.[16] Hick made it a point to emphasize that his new model was "a significantly different hypothesis" from this Hindu analogy, in regard to which it has only a "partial resemblance" at best.[17] In fact, he saw it as the critical path that avoided both a crypto- (nonpersonal) Vedantism and a crypto- (personal) theism.[18]

Hick also adjusted the two elements of his model that had drawn the most fire. These modifications served both to fine-tune his neo-Kantian proposal and to thwart charges of crypto-anything. First, Hick addressed the terminological problematic in regard to the divine noumenon, exploring various possibilities so as to privilege neither a personal nor a nonpersonal conception of ultimate reality. He experimented with a number of terms, including *God* (in a qualified sense), *the transcendent, the Eternal One, the Ultimate,* and *divine Reality.* By 1983, however, Hick had settled on what would prove to be his term of preference: *the Real.*[19]

Second, one notices that from the early 1980s onward, Hick no longer explicitly appeals to the "God of love" defense for his pluralistic move. This change signals another conscious effort on Hick's part to further distance his noumenal Real from the Christian God, which is now viewed as merely one of its many possible phenomenal manifestations. A related change in his presentation also is worthy of note. At roughly the same time, Hick for the most part ceased describing his pluralistic shift in terms of the Copernican analogy. Hick has clarified the reason for this departure: it marks the conscious shift on his part from addressing the problem of religious diversity as a Christian theologian to facing it as a *theologically neutral* philosopher of religion.[20]

In spite of these adjustments, Hick's pluralistic model continued to attract charges of cryptotheism. Here, one of Hick's most enduring critics comes to the fore of the discussion: the Roman Catholic inclusivist Gavin D'Costa. According to D'Costa's initial critique, despite the adoption of the neo-Kantian mechanism, Hick's Copernican revolution remains covertly theistic for at least three reasons.[21]

First, although Hick has adopted the neo-Kantian mechanism and tradition-neutral terminology, and has discontinued his explicit "God of love" defense, such moves only serve to intensify the question of just what grounding his pluralist move now carries. Once one ontologically disengages the Christian God of love from the noumenal Real, Hick's primary impetus for the pluralist shift should be disengaged as well. The fact that his project continues to steam ahead undaunted reveals that some form of covert theism must still be powering this pluralist craft. And it would seem to be a fundamentally "christological" theism at that, in that God's universal love is definitively revealed *only* in Jesus Christ.[22]

Second, and I believe more importantly, D'Costa pointed out that Hick's post-Copernican conception of the eschaton remained fundamentally theistic. This type of charge was such that it challenged not only Hick's pluralistic model, but also his long-standing method of apologetic for meaningful God-talk and a robust religious realism. For even subsequent to his pluralist move, one finds Hick arguing for an eschatological vision that "implicitly rejects the *advaitist* view that Atman *is* Brahman, the collective human self being ultimately identical with God, in favor of the more complex *vishishtadvaitist* interpretation of the Upanishads, which is in turn substantially in agreement with the christian conception of God as personal Lord, distinct from his creation."[23] Thus, in D'Costa's summary words, "On Hick's premises, religious truth claims are verified in the eschaton and his Copernican eschaton is distinctly theistic, thereby smuggling 'God' from the *centre* to the *end* of the universe of faiths—thereby creating the same problems prior to the epicycle."[24]

Finally, D'Costa noted a vestigial strand of implicit theism running through Hick's post-Copernican theodicy.[25] Although it was developed prior to his pluralist move,[26] Hick continued to apply his "Irenaean theodicy" on this side of the Copernican divide whenever the problem of evil cropped up.[27] The problem here, again, is that his Irenaean theodicy is fundamentally grounded upon the notion of a personal God of universal love.[28] Thus, Hick is again found writing in his pluralist stage as if the ultimate Real is—in the end—best described in theistic terms.

STAGE THREE: TYING UP LOOSE ENDS—MYTHOLOGY, ESCHATOLOGY, AND COSMIC OPTIMISM

By 1985, Hick began offering substantive responses to these criticisms, each of which served to modify not only his pluralistic model, but his life-long theological project as well. Four important moves can be identified.

First, in a 1985 Postscript to a reprint of his earlier article "Eschatological Verification Reconsidered," Hick significantly reworks his previous theistic eschatological scenario:

> It seems likely that the different expectations cherished within the different traditions will ultimately turn out to be partly correct and partly incorrect. It could be that in a mind-dependent *bardo* phase immediately after death these expectations will be fulfilled in the experience of believers—Christians, Hindus, Muslims, and so on each encountering what their different traditions have taught them to anticipate. But as they advance beyond that phase . . . [they] will themselves develop, becoming gradually more adequate to the reality. . . . It may well be that the final state will prove to be beyond the horizon of our present powers of imagination.[29]

Hick went on to address this issue in his monumental work, *The Interpretation of Religion*. He begins by easily explicating how the notion of eschatological verification is compatible with the theistic religions. The problem, as always, arises in regard to the question of how to preserve a place of equality for the various nontheistic traditions' postmortem scenarios, while nonetheless providing the requisite elements necessary for the (eschatological) verification of prior (terrestrial) religious claims. Thus, for example, in regard to the Advaita Vedanta Hindu scenario, he writes, "If, then, in the eschaton all consciousnesses have united into a single consciousness, and if this was predicted in a theory propounded by some of the individual consciousnesses before they united, it would seem that the unitary consciousness may be said to have verified that theory in its own experience. The eternal Self will know (and indeed knows now) that It is the one ultimate Reality underlying the illusorily finite egos."[30] Thus, with such moves, Hick purports to put to rest any charges of covert eschatological theism.[31]

A second critical shift, one parallel to the first shift, is made explicit in *Interpretation of Religion*. In a section devoted to an analysis of the "naturalistic option," Hick once again calls forth his Irenaean theodicy—with its inherent personalist-theistic presumption—as a response to the problem of evil.[32] However, twelve chapters later, in the course of a discussion on the fundamentally mythological character of religious language, he attaches an appendix entitled "Theodicy as Mythology." Here, Hick effectively neutralizes the charge of covert theism vis-à-vis his Irenaean theodicy—but only at the expense of divesting it of any and all realist implications: "Such a theodicy is mythical in the sense that the language in which it speaks about the Real, as a personal being carrying out intentions through time, cannot apply to the ultimate Reality in itself. But such a theodicy nevertheless constitutes a true myth in so far as the practical attitudes which it tends to evoke amid the evils of human life are appropriate to our present existence in relation to the Real."[33] Thus, theodicy becomes merely a matter of the phenomenal realm of religion—rendering it as mere "myth" vis-à-vis the noumenal Real. In relation to the Real itself, it says nothing, since here, by definition, nothing substantial ever can be said.[34]

Third, during this period, Hick also constructed a response to the lingering charge that the Christian "God of love" remains the true animating force behind his pluralistic enterprise. With the publication of *Interpretation of Religion*, Hick brought a new resource into play—namely, what he identified as the common interreligious notion of "cosmic optimism."[35] Hick explains the importance of this shift when he writes:

> Whilst the Christian concept of a loving personal divine Father
> is indeed, in my view, incompatible with traditional Christian
> exclusivism, when we are concerned with the religious life of
> humanity as a whole we have to look beyond this to the more basic
> affirmation of the ultimate goodness of the universe from our human
> point of view. And so I have used Jewish, Christian, Muslim, Hindu
> and Buddhist sources to establish the 'cosmic optimism' of the great
> post-axial streams of religion. The belief in a sovereign and loving
> Creator is only one of the forms that this belief takes.[36]

Thus, with the adoption of the idea of "cosmic optimism" as a motivating
force, Hick maintains the basic "goodness" of the universe while distancing
his pluralistic philosophy—and especially his conception of the Real—from any
form of theistic, let alone specifically Christian, manifestation of this general
theme.[37]

Fourth and finally, in accordance with the shifts previously noted, Hick
has fine-tuned his conception of the Real so as to further safeguard his model
from the charge of privileging any particular phenomenal manifestation. He
now stresses more strongly than ever that the ineffable Real is beyond *all*
human conceptual-linguistic categories: "We cannot apply to the Real *an sich*
the characteristics encountered in its *personae* and *impersonae*. Thus it cannot
be said to be one or many, person or thing, substance or process, good or
evil, purposive or non-purposive. None of the concrete descriptions that apply
within the realm of human experience can apply literally to the
unexperienceable ground of that realm. . . . We cannot even speak of this as a
thing or an entity."[38] In light of this state of affairs, Hick suggests that a fitting
symbol for the ultimately Real can be found in one particular development of
the Buddhist notion of *sunyata* (emptiness), which can actually signify "an anti-
concept excluding all concepts."[39]

With these adjustments to his model, I would suggest that Hick has
successfully avoided several particular forms of the cryptotheism (and equally
crypto-nontheism) charge previously discussed. Unfortunately, it appears that
a number of Hick's critics either have not noticed these modifications or else
simply have not adequately appraised their effectiveness.[40] In any case, putting
forth now-obsolete forms of the cryptotheism charge can only serve to impede
the critical assessment of Hick's mature model of religious pluralism. Hick is
correct that unless his critics thoroughly shift their focus to his "more fully
developed pluralistic hypothesis" (i.e., as developed in *Interpretation of Religion*
and beyond), significant headway in the discussion will not be made.[41]

CRYPTOMONOTHEISM NONETHELESS

Despite his best efforts, I will now argue that Hick's mature model of religious pluralism remains vulnerable to the charge of cryptomonotheism at a number of points. Several lines of analysis are relevant here.

HICK'S HYPOTHESIS AS CRYPTO-MONO-THEISM

I will begin with the first half of this compound charge: namely, *mono*-theism. Throughout his pluralist project, Hick has unswervingly referred to the noumenal Real in fundamentally *singular* terms and categories. To be fair to Hick, it is important to note that he has recognized this problem and has tried to circumvent the problems associated with this practice. He writes, "If we are going to speak of the Real at all, the exigencies of our language compel us to refer to it either in the singular or the plural. Since there cannot be a plurality of ultimates, we affirm the true ultimacy of the Real by referring to it in the singular. . . . The Real, then, is the ultimate Reality, not one among others; and yet it cannot literally be numbered: it is the unique one without a second."[42] When pressed, Hick admits that something like a poly-Realism is logically possible and cannot be ruled out a priori. However, he argues that the postulation of (in human terms) one, single Real is the "simplest hypothesis" and one that is defensible on several grounds.[43]

HICK'S DEFENSE OF A SINGULAR REAL

Hick begins by noting that, for better or worse, one must speak of the Real in either singular or plural terms. When speaking of the noumenal Real, the problem of using some sort of less-than-literal designation is unavoidable. However, to call it "one" breeds fewer conceptual problems than to call it "many." Second, if one were to refer to it in the plural, the problem arises of how to delineate "the relationship between these different realities."[44] Third, to posit more than one Ultimate religious referent would be to necessarily relativize, and in this way violate, each of the various religions' claims to experiential relationship with the one "ultimate" Reality.[45] Since, for Hick, the essential "truthfulness" of each tradition has already been demonstrated by the fact of their apparent coequal soteriological effectiveness, such a violation is unwarranted. In fact, Hick argues that this common soteriological process "is indeed the main reason for preferring the assumption of a single universal ultimate to that of a plurality of co-penultimates."[46] So Hick offers as the primary basis for his assumption that all the major religions are referring to the same ultimate Reality the "striking similarity of the transformed human state described within the traditions as saved, redeemed, enlightened, wise, awakened, liberated. This similarity strongly suggests a common source of salvific transformation."[47] Finally, Hick argues that, since human language necessitates that we refer to something in either the singular or the plural, and that to refer to the Ultimate in anything but singular terms would, by definition, render it less than ultimate, we are justified in speaking of *one* ultimate Reality. Yet all the while, we must remember that "it cannot literally be numbered." Again, it is, as Indian thought suggests, "the unique One without a second."[48]

From the very beginning of his pluralistic probings, Hick has been challenged as to the problematic nature of what one can now refer to as his "mono-Realist" presumption and the unitive, harmonizing impetus behind it.[49] Interestingly, this charge is leveled at Hick both by those within and by those outside of the pluralist camp.[50] The central question is this: Given the radically divergent, even mutually contradictory religious conceptions of ultimate reality, upon what basis does Hick maintain that each and every one of the conflictive phenomenal manifestations are perceptions of *one and the same* noumenal Reality? Does not a thesis involving multiple noumenal realities better account for the apparent phenomenal evidence?[51] Certainly, this would be the case in the sensory realm. Thus, one would expect that only very compelling arguments to the contrary could allow for Hick's apparently counterintuitive thesis. I will now argue that Hick's arguments, as summarized here, are, in fact, far from compelling.

POLY-REALISM AS PHILOSOPHICAL CONUNDRUM

Hick's resistance to recognizing a plurality of noumenal Realities, due to the fact that such a move would raise thorny philosophical questions regarding how they would be related to each other, is understandable. But such a problem can, itself, hardly be an argument against the attempt to explore such poly-Realist possibilities. After all, Hick's pluralist project itself includes at its core a philosophical attempt to take seriously the diversity among the gods and absolutes within the world's religions. In addition, Hick has strongly argued for years that the various religious traditions of the world should set about revising their own theological visions and philosophical self-understandings in order to acknowledge and accommodate the authenticity of these diverse (to his mind "phenomenal") religious realities. With respect to their doctrines, Hick's suggestion asks the various religions to engage in any number of conceptual gymnastics and theological contortions necessary to recognize what he sees as the pluralist implications of the diversity of human religious experience. So if the evidence of human religious diversity points toward multiple Realities at what Hick considers to be the noumenal level, he can hardly balk at being asked to wrestle with the philosophical difficulties this might raise. And, perhaps, just such considerations will suggest the need for revision of certain elements of his hypothesis—namely, ones that are embedded in an all-too-often unexamined mono-Realist paradigm that tends to drive the modern, Western analytical philosophical tradition. In any case, when it comes to being asked to wrestle with seemingly intractable philosophical difficulties, what is good (on Hick's judgment) for the traditional religious believers the world over is good for the modern liberal pluralist.

MONO-REALISM AND RELIGIOUS ULTIMACY

Furthermore, Hick's justification of mono-Realism based upon an appeal to the various religions' claims to be in touch with the "ultimate" is less than compelling. Ironically, Hick himself provides the tools to undermine just such a claim. He has made a career out of explicating the manner in which traditional religious truth claims can be mythologized—and in this way relativized—without (to his mind) doing violence to their essential nature. When Hick is willing to detach any and all religious doctrines from their traditional realist moorings, such as (to use Christian examples) the incarnation,[52] the atonement, the Trinity, and even the ontological ultimacy of a personal God, what reason is there to recoil from similarly mythologizing the religious claim of experiencing the single ultimate Reality? In fact, given Hick's paradigm, this claim is most easily understood as just one more mythological religious affirmation vis-à-vis ultimate reality. It may be "mythically true," which, for Hick, means attitudinally appropriate. But such claims can in no way be used to support Hick's assertion that ultimate (noumenal) Reality itself is best conceptualized in ontologically singular terms.

SOTERIOCENTRISM AND MONO-REALISM

Finally, Hick's soteriologically based argument for a single noumenal Reality remains unconvincing. His understanding of salvation—defined as the human transformation from self-centeredness to Reality-centeredness—must be highly abstract and generalized in order to accommodate all religions, and so loses any real unitive force. Moreover, when one begins to analyze the supposed common soteriological structure of the various religions, the presumed abstract unity quickly unravels. In the end, then, soteriologically speaking, little remains upon which to base the notion of a single noumenal Real behind a supposed common and universal process.[53]

However, even if Hick were able to make a convincing argument for a common soteriological experience, this would not solve the problem for him. To draw an analogy from the sensory realm: Simply because I share the same type of "self to other-orientedness" experience within the bounds of a loving marriage as do numerous other husbands, there is nothing to suggest that we husbands are all loving the same noumenal wife, experienced in diverse phenomenal ways. Simply put, common experience does not necessarily entail a common object of experience. To claim so, without any further reasons than Hick offers, is to beg the question at hand. Thus, Hick's arguments for the plausibility of a mono-Realism over against a poly-Realism fail to convince, while the radically diverse phenomenological evidence itself counts directly against the idea.

LOCATING HICK'S "MONO-" IMPULSE

If Hick's ostensive reasons for positing an (in some sense) ontologically singular noumenal Real are themselves not compelling, we are left with the question of just what drives him in this direction. Given Hick's philosophical and religious background, several lines of influence seem likely. First, there is the fact that Hick's own sociocultural context in general and his Anglo-Western (i.e., British) philosophical tradition in particular are indebted to a strong drive toward philosophical unification.[54] Hick reveals his penchant for just such conceptual unification when he writes, "That humankind is one, the world one, and the divine reality one is a truth whose time has come."[55] It appears that this philosophical proclivity, in part, has kept Hick from seriously entertaining the truly pluralist implications—at the noumenal level—of his own thesis.

Furthermore—and here we begin to move toward the second half of the compound charge under discussion—there is the issue of vestigial remnants of Hick's liberal Christian monotheism at play within his hypothesis. In this respect, it is worth noting that, while a number of additions and subtractions have occurred throughout the four editions of Hick's well-known book *Philosophy of Religion*, most of them occasioned by his pluralist shift, his opening chapter devoted to a monotheistic presentation of God has remained essentially unchanged. This is an important observation, because it is precisely here, in a work ostensibly done in his philosophical, as opposed to Christian theological, mode, that one would expect to see evidence of a divestment of his prior monotheistic commitments.[56] Given the extensive pluralist reworking Hick has done for this and other more recent editions of his earlier works, this can hardly be accounted for as an accidental oversight on his part.

Intriguingly, Hick's unwillingness seriously to entertain the notion of multiple noumenal Realities behind the radically diverse religious phenomena is paralleled in the Western liberal Christian tradition by the general refusal to take seriously the idea of multiple entities in the spiritual world behind, say, the "polytheism" of many traditional religions. Theologically speaking, this idea has often been resisted in the name of monotheism. This sort of monotheism, what one could term "philosophical" or "absolute" monotheism, holds that the single God is the "only divine being."[57] However, under this type of strict definition, the question of the existence of other spiritual beings, fashioned by the Creator God, who are ontological objects of religious worship is at least ignored, if not flatly denied. But as Peter Hayman has argued, this sort of pure "philosophical" monotheism is probably not seen in the Jewish tradition until the "philosophers of the Middle Ages."[58] In contrast, the "monotheism" of both biblical Testaments and much of Second Temple Judaism acknowledged the existence of lesser spiritual entities beyond and beneath Yahweh-God, whether understood as members of Yahweh's divine council, rebellious created "gods," angels, or demons, some of whom function as real, ontological objects—however unworthy—of human religious worship.[59]

Interestingly, Hick himself acknowledges the possible existence of Satan and other "disembodied minds," whether good or evil.[60] But as soon as Hick entertains this possibility—namely, the existence of a plurality of independently existing entities in a supernatural/spiritual (might one say "noumenal"?) realm—he is faced with the prospect of something like a plurality of noumenal Realities behind the various religions. His refusal to take this possibility more seriously, then, may well reflect the vestigial influence of the philosophical monotheism of his liberal Christian tradition. Thus, in sum, I contend that Hick's unwillingness to seriously countenance the possibility of multiple ontological noumenal ultimates—each of which would correspond to one or more of the distinctive phenomenal religious ultimates—reveals a cryptomonotheism at the heart of his mono-Realist project.[61]

HICK'S HYPOTHESIS AS CRYPTO-MONO-THEISM

This final section will concentrate on the second half of the compound charge—namely, "theism." My main contention here will focus on the inherent discrepancy between Hick's claim that the Real is not personal, intentional, or purposive and the equally solid commitments to his long-standing religious epistemology and his eschatological scenario, both of which, from their inception during his prepluralist days, have been intimately—even necessarily, I shall argue—linked to a theistic understanding of ultimate Reality.[62]

CRYPTOTHEISM AND HICK'S RELIGIOUS EPISTEMOLOGY

First, a brief recap of the nature of Hick's religious epistemology is in order. The essential structure of this epistemology has not changed since its formative days in the 1950s, as explicated in his first book, *Faith and Knowledge*. Early on, Hick embraced the notion that the universe is "religiously ambiguous." That is, one cannot argue convincingly for the probability of—let alone demonstrate—either a religious or a naturalistic interpretation of the world over against the other. Again, this idea is central to his understanding of faith as a free act of interpretation and, thus, the necessity of an "epistemic distance" between God and humanity if the latter are to retain their creaturely freedom as they respond to God's offer of relationship.[63] Fundamental to Hick's original development of this understanding of religious experience and epistemology is the idea of a personal God who creates free creatures and then invites them to freely enter into a personal love relationship. Prior to his pluralist move, Hick was always eminently clear on this point: "The reason why God reveals himself indirectly . . . is that only thus can the conditions exist for a *personal* relationship between God and man."[64]

Interestingly, even after his pluralist shift, Hick explicitly retained this same epistemological framework.[65] In fact, Hick has made it quite clear that his move to a pluralist perspective is linked with the working out of the full and logical implications of his original religious epistemology.[66] Early on, he attempted to state it in terms that were equally applicable to nontheistic systems.[67] As time went on, the explicitly theistic elements of the system were either modified or, often I suggest, simply left implicit. Always, the notions of human "freedom," the fundamental religious ambiguity of the universe, the various religious traditions as functional "filters" that preserve human religious autonomy, etc., were at the fore.[68] In fact, even after his adoption of the neo-Kantian mechanism, Hick is found writing of our need for a high degree of "cognitive freedom and responsibility, without which we should not be personal beings, capable of a free response to the Eternal One."[69] To explicate this idea further, Hick shifts to "explicitly theistic terms." Tellingly, he never does state the matter in terms understandable to a nontheistic tradition.[70]

Within Hick's current model, the "systematic [religious] ambiguity" of the universe continues to retain an important role.[71] And while the term *epistemic distance* is not used per se in *Interpretation of Religion*, Hick has indicated that the idea is still at work, particularly in his understanding of cognitive freedom.[72] Similarly, in an essay written in the mid-1990s and thus from the perspective of his mature pluralist model, one finds Hick explicitly affirming the same general epistemological apparatus when he writes: "But our relationship to the more ultimate environment of which the religions speak is importantly different [than to the sensory realm]. This latter confronts or surrounds or undergirds or envelops us as the bearer of ultimate value, and value differs from matter in leaving us free to recognize and respond to it or not. We are not forced to be aware of the Transcendent as we are forced to be aware of our physical surroundings."[73]

Although Hick has substituted religiously neutral terms like *value* and *Transcendent* for his former idea of "personal God," in fact his general religious epistemology remains essentially unchanged. And such an epistemology, as noted earlier, presupposes a personal Reality in that only such a reality could—and/or would care to—"create" such a state of affairs. A nonpersonal/impersonal noumenal Reality simply could not account for this state of cognitive affairs, nor could it play the role required by ultimate Reality in Hick's epistemological system.[74] It seems that unless Hick is willing to dismantle his long-standing religious epistemology, his thought at this point will implicitly require the presence of a personal or superpersonal Real—but never anything less (i.e., nonpersonal/impersonal). Thus, once again, embedded within his purportedly tradition-neutral pluralist philosophy of religions, one finds an element that can only be explained as a vestigial remain of Hick's cryptomonotheism.[75]

CRYPTOTHEISM AND HICK'S ESCHATOLOGICAL SCENARIO

Finally, I will argue that Hick's current eschatological scenario remains inextricably linked to fundamentally monotheistic presuppositions. To begin, there is the sense that, for Hick, the grand eschatological state of humanity remains under what must be something analogous to "supervision" by the divine Reality. The problem this raises, of course, is that anything like divine supervision demands qualities of the Real that are of a "personal," or "superpersonal" nature, such as purposiveness, foresight, etc. Mark Heim has noted this problem when he writes of "the assumption" in Hick's model that humanity's eschatological destiny is "administered in some way."[76] But this observation only points to a more fundamentally theistic—if subtly implicit—assumption in Hick's theory.

The more basic problem is this. In order for Hick's eschatological scenario to function in his philosophical system as it always has and presumably must—namely, as providing the necessary verificational context for his religious realism—there must, on the other side of death, be some form of personal entity with identity ties to the prior terrestrial religious person.[77] In other words, Hick's theory requires some form of postmortem personal, self-conscious existence that can "verify" its prior realist claims via the eschatological experience. In a relatively recent explanation of how the eschatological state can establish a religious, as opposed to naturalistic, interpretation of religion, Hick writes, "If, then, we find after our bodily death that we still exist, our experience will have falsified the naturalistic hypothesis."[78] That this sort of eschatological experience remains a nonnegotiable part of Hick's mature pluralist conception of religion is clear from the following comment found in a new preface to the 1993 edition of his 1976 work, *Death and Eternal Life*: "Any religious understanding of human existence—not merely of one's own existence but of the life of humanity as a whole—positively requires some kind of immortality belief and would be radically incoherent without it."[79]

The problem here involves the implicit theistic privileging that such a notion entails. The nontheistic religious traditions (e.g., Advaita Vedanta Hinduism or Theravada Buddhism) whose postmortem scenarios clearly do not include the idea of individual conscious existence (whether in terms of a "pareschatological" stage, a "bardo" phase, or any other) find no place in Hick's eschatological verificationist schema and thus run the risk of falling outside of Hick's realist model of religion.

Hick, it seems, is cognizant of this potential problem for his pluralist theory of religion. In response, he has proposed that we imagine Advaita Vedanta Hindu eschatology in terms of a single, eternal eschatological Self composed of all individual human selves, and thus able to verify their past realist claims. But this raises some very real interpretive problems. It seems to me that Hick must posit a number of very questionable assumptions here for his thesis to fly, including the notion that Brahman, though traditionally understood in *impersonal* terms, can actually function very much like a self-conscious, personalistic supermind, and that this personalistic Brahman will serve to "verify" as authentic the past experiences and general religious claims of individual consciousnesses which, according to the Advaitic system, are—and always were—nothing more than deceptive *maya*. Tellingly, when it comes to the question of correlating the postmortem scenario of Theravada Buddhism with his eschatological verificationist schema, Hick essentially skirts the issue. Nirvana, after all, appears to leave little room for a final "consciousness" of any kind, and thus a verificationist reinterpretation is out of the question. So Hick's claim of a possible future verification of a religious, as opposed to a naturalistic, interpretation of religion for "all" the world's religions based upon "their common affirmation of continued personal existence beyond the present life" betrays the presence of a strong theistic presumption at the core of his pluralist enterprise.[80]

But one might wonder: Could Hick not offer the following rebuttal to this line of criticism?[81] It may be true that an eschatological scenario requiring an actual conscious experience of verification on the part of some (quasi) personal entity would privilege a theistic vision. However, viewed merely as a formal category (as opposed to a concrete conscious experience), eschatological verification could equally serve to authenticate a nontheistic, as well as a theistic, religious perspective. For example, it may be that nirvana as understood by a Theravada Buddhist is the final eschatological state. If so, there will be no conscious personal experience of any type that could verify it or falsify, say, the Christian view. However, metaphysically speaking, such a state would, in fact, obtain. Thus, one could say that nirvana could be "verified" in a formal, if not an actual humanly conscious, sense.

In response, it is important to note that Hick himself has not followed this line of thought. Although he raises the question of how Buddhist thought could fit his eschatological requirements, Hick never answers the question—and he certainly does not resort to suggesting that eschatological verification be considered as merely a formal category. Instead, he simply confirms one's natural suspicions that such an explanation is "elusive."[82] I would argue that the reason Hick does not go this route is that to reduce his eschatological verification principle to a formal category alone would be to render it ineffective for the very purpose it was originally designed—namely, to protect his religious realism from the epistemological critique of naturalism. Someone could, of course, propose to Hick that he rethink his eschatologically based epistemology in order to avoid this line of critique. But to do so would be to end up with a religious epistemology quite different from the one Hick has unflinchingly defended for the last six decades. Again, from the very beginning, Hick has made it abundantly clear that his notion of eschatological verification is absolutely dependent upon some form of actual, conscious experience of postmortem existence, thereby falsifying the naturalistic worldview.[83] For this reason, Hick has consistently rejected the temptation to solve the problem at hand by reducing the concept of eschatological verification to a purely formal category. And so must anyone reject this path who desires to remain faithful to the fundamentals of Hick's experience-based, realist religious epistemology.

It is tempting at this point to pursue a detailed archaeological tracing of the roots of Hick's cryptomonotheism. It will suffice to say, as the preceding discussion suggests, that the evidence points to an obvious generative context: namely, Hick's decades-long commitment to the Western liberal intellectual tradition, in terms of both rationality and religion. Hick's fellow British religious thinker Don Cupitt has stated it quite bluntly: "John Hick is the platonic ideal of the liberal theologian who believes in the fatherhood of God and the brotherhood of man. He is sweet reasonableness incarnate."[84] In any case, the observations in this essay serve to elucidate the cryptomonotheism (one is tempted to add the prefix *liberal Christian*) that attaches to—and ultimately undercuts—John Hick's ostensibly tradition-neutral pluralist philosophy of world religions.

Notes

1. John Hick, *An Interpretation of Religion: Human Responses to the Transcendent*, 2nd ed. (New Haven: Yale University Press, 2004 [1989]), 240. This essay is a summarization and development of one of two primary lines of philosophical critique of John Hick's religious pluralism offered in my book, *John Hick's Pluralist Philosophy of World Religions* (Burlington, VT: Ashgate, 2002).

2. See Hick's essay "The Outcome: Dialogue into Truth," originally presented on the eve of his pluralist move at a 1970 conference, in *Truth and Dialogue in World Religions: Conflicting Truth-Claims*, ed. J. Hick, 148–53 (Philadelphia: Westminster, 1974); and even prior to this, *Christianity at the Center* (London: SCM, 1968), 80–81.

3. See the essays that make up the last half of *God and the Universe of Faiths*, 2nd ed. (London: Macmillan, 1973; repr. ed., London: Fontana, 1977).

4. "The New Map of the Universe of Faiths," in *God and the Universe*, 144.

5. Ibid.

6. Ibid.

7. Ibid., 144–45.

8. See Duncan B. Forrester, "Professor Hick and the Universe of Faiths," *Scottish Journal of Theology* 29 (1976): 69; Philip Almond, "John Hick's Copernican Theology," *Theology* 86 (1983): 38–39.

9. See Almond, "John Hick's Copernican Theology," 37–38; J. J. Lipner, "Does Copernicus Help? Reflections for a Christian Theology of Religions," *Religious Studies* 13 (1977): 253–54.

10. See its use in the following works of Hick: "The Reconstruction of Christian Belief for Today and Tomorrow II: Other Religions," *Theology* 73 (1970): 400; "Copernican Revolution," in *God and the Universe*, 122–23; "Philosophy, Religions, and Human Unity," in *Philosophy: Theory and Practice*, ed. T. M. P. Mahadevan (Madras: University of Madras, 1974), 463; "Jesus and World

Religions," in *The Myth of God Incarnate*, ed. John Hick (Philadelphia: Westminster, 1978), 180; *The Center of Christianity*, 2nd ed. (San Francisco: Harper & Row, 1978), 79; *The Second Christianity*, 3rd ed. (London: SCM, 1983), 92; "The Theology of Religious Pluralism," *Theology* 86 (1983): 338.

11. See Gavin D'Costa, *John Hick's Theology of Religions: A Critical Evaluation* (Lanham, MD: University Press of America, 1987), 152.

12. Hick, "Mystical Experience as Cognition," in *Mystics and Scholars: The Calgary Conference on Mysticism 1976*, ed. Harold Coward and Terence Penelhum (Calgary: Canadian Corporation for Studies in Religion, 1977).

13. For a critical examination of Hick's neo-Kantian move, see Paul Rhodes Eddy, "Religious Pluralism and the Divine: Another Look at John Hick's Neo-Kantian Proposal," *Religious Studies* 30 (1994): 467–78; reprinted in Philip L. Quinn and Kevin Meeker, eds., *The Philosophical Challenge of Religious Diversity* (New York: Oxford University Press, 2000), 126–38. Hick has responded to my critique in "Religious Pluralism and the Divine: A Response to Paul Eddy," *Religious Studies* 31 (1995): 417–20, reprinted in Hick, *Dialogues in the Philosophy of Religion* (New York: Palgrave Macmillan, 2001), 90–94. I have offered a rejoinder in Eddy, *John Hick's Pluralist Philosophy*, 175–82.

14. Hick, "Mystical Experience as Cognition," 52.

15. See Hick, *God Has Many Names* (Philadelphia: Westminster, 1982), chs. 3, 5, 6.

16. E.g., see ibid., 91, 110; Hick, *The Philosophy of Religion*, 3rd ed. (Englewood Cliffs, NJ: Prentice-Hall, 1983), 118; *Interpretation of Religion*, 236–37.

17. *God Has Many Names*, 110.

18. Hick, "Theology of Religious Pluralism," 336–37.

19. See ibid., 336; also *Philosophy of Religion* (3rd ed.), 118; "On Conflicting Religious Truth-Claims," *Religious Studies* 19 (1983): 488.

20. See C. Robert Mesle, *John Hick's Theodicy: A Process Humanist Critique* (New York: St. Martin's, 1991), 89. This issue of John Hick the Christian theologian vs. John Hick the (ostensibly) tradition-neutral philosopher of religion is, I believe, critically important to this whole discussion. See Eddy, *John Hick's Pluralist Philosophy*, 100–102.

21. See D'Costa, "John Hick's Copernican Revolution: Ten Years After," *New Blackfriars* 65 (1984): 323–31.

22. See D'Costa, *Theology and Religious Pluralism: The Challenge of Other Religions* (Oxford: Blackwell, 1986), 32.

23. Hick, *Death and Eternal Life* (San Francisco: Harper & Row, 1976), 464.

24. D'Costa, *John Hick's Theology of Religions*, 170.

25. E.g., see D'Costa, "John Hick's Copernican Revolution," 328–29.

26. Hick, *Evil and the God of Love* (London: Macmillan, 1966).

27. E.g., see Hick's "An Irenaean Theodicy," in *Encountering Evil: Live Options in Theodicy*, ed. Stephen Davis, 39–52 (Atlanta: Knox, 1981); *Interpretation of Religion*, 118–22.

28. E.g., see "An Irenaean Theodicy," 52.

29. John Hick, *Problems of Religious Pluralism* (New York: St. Martin's, 1985), 124.

30. *Interpretation of Religion*, 182–83.

31. See Hick's "Straightening the Record: Some Response to Critics," *Modern Theology* 6 (1990): 191, where he forthrightly admits the inherent "contradiction" between his earlier position in *Death and Eternal Life* and his current pluralistic hypothesis, and his repudiation of the former in this regard. See also *Interpretation of Religion*, 177–88.

32. *Interpretation of Religion*, 118–22.

33. Ibid., 359–60.

34. See Hick's discussion on these matters in "Myth, Mystery and the Unanswered Questions," in *Interpretation of Religion*, 343–61.

35. *Interpretation of Religion*, 56–69, 380.

36. "Straightening the Record," 190.

37. For an extended discussion of the "cosmic optimism" theme, see Hick, *The Fifth Dimension: An Exploration of the Spiritual Realm* (Boston: Oneworld, 1999), 51–73.

38. *Interpretation of Religion*, 246.

39. Ibid.

40. E.g., regarding the "God of love" form of the covert theism charge, see Keith Ward, "Divine Ineffability," in Arvind Sharma, ed., *God, Truth and Reality: Essays in Honour of John Hick* (New York: St. Martin's, 1993), 216. Regarding the charge that Hick's pluralism depends upon a nontheistic bias, see William Rowe, "John Hick's Contribution to the Philosophy of Religion," in Sharma, *God, Truth and Reality*, 22. In both cases, if they have noticed Hick's more recent moves to avoid such charges, their arguments do not seem to betray such knowledge.

41. "Straightening the Record," 194.

42. *Interpretation of Religion*, 249.

43. Ibid., 248.

44. John Hick, *A Christian Theology of Religions: The Rainbow of Faiths* (Louisville: Westminster John Knox, 1995), 70.

45. *Interpretation of Religion*, 248.

46. "A Religious Understanding of Religion: A Model of the Relationship between Traditions," in *Many Mansions: Interfaith and Religious Intolerance*, ed. Dan Cohn-Sherbok (London: Bellew, 1992), 132.

47. *Christian Theology of Religions*, 69.

48. *Interpretation of Religion*, 249.

49. E.g., this type of concern is at least hinted at in two responses, by William D. Nietmann and Margaret Chatterjee, to Hick's 1970 paper "Philosophy, Religions, and Human Unity"; see *Philosophy: Theory and Practice*, 473, 477. For two more recent critiques that question Hick's monizing tendency (both from an Asian perspective), see Jung H. Lee, "Problems of Religious Pluralism: A Zen Critique of John Hick's Ontological Monomorphism," *Philosophy East and West* 48 (1998): 453–77; Anri Morimoto, "The (More or Less) Same Light but from Different Lamps: The Post-Pluralist Understanding of Religion from a Japanese Perspective," *International Journal for Philosophy of Religion* 53 (2003): 163–80.

50. This criticism has taken different forms, from pluralists and nonpluralists alike. See, e.g., Harold Netland, "Professor Hick on Religious Pluralism," *Religious Studies* 22 (1986): 261; Raimundo Panikkar, "The Jordan, the Tiber, and the Ganges: Three Kairological Moments of Christic Self-Consciousness," in *The Myth of Christian Uniqueness: Toward a Pluralistic Theology of Religions*, ed. John Hick and Paul Knitter (Maryknoll, NY: Orbis, 1987), 109.

51. Hick's "pluralism" is all about the phenomenal realm. When it comes to the noumenal realm of the Real, he seems to be guilty of something like a widespread "monotheist complacency," on which see A. H. Armstrong, "Some Advantages of Polytheism," *Dionysius* 5 (1981): 181–88.

52. One of the most controversial aspects of Hick's pluralism has been his reinterpretation of the incarnation purely in terms of "myth" or, more recently, "metaphor." See Hick, *The Metaphor of God Incarnate: Christology in a Pluralistic Age*, 2nd ed. (Louisville: Westminster Knox, 2006 [1993]). For an account of Hick's christological development and problems associated with his mature pluralist Christology, see Paul Rhodes Eddy, "John Hick and the Historical Jesus," in *The Convergence of Theology: A Festschrift in Honor of Gerald O'Collins*, ed. Stephen T. Davis and Daniel Kendall, 304–19 (New York: Paulist, 2001).

53. Against the notion that one can easily understand the various religions under any harmonizing soteriological rubric, see J. A. DiNoia, "Varieties of Religious Aims," in *The Diversity of Religions: A Christian Perspective* (Washington, DC: Catholic University of America Press, 1992), 34–64. For similar criticisms (some of which could apply to Hick) of Paul Knitter's "soteriocentric"

model of religious pluralism, see Paul R. Eddy, "Paul Knitter's Theology of Religions: A Survey and Evangelical Response," *Evangelical Quarterly* 65 (1993): 242–43.

54. A related observation is made by John Lyden, "Why Only 'One' Divine Reality? A Critique of Religious Pluralism," *Dialogue and Alliance* 8 (1994): 63.

55. Hick, "On Wilfred Cantwell Smith: His Place in the Study of Religion," *Method and Theory in the Study of Religion* 4 (1992): 20.

56. It is no secret that the concept of monotheism has always been a central category for both Hick the theologian and Hick the philosopher of religion. See *Faith and Knowledge*, 128–29; *Philosophy of Religion* (all four eds.), ch. 1; "A Recent Development within Christian Monotheism."

57. Peter Hayman, "Monotheism—a Misused Word in Jewish Studies?," *Journal of Jewish Studies* 42 (1991): 15.

58. Ibid., 2.

59. In contrast, see N. T. Wright's illuminating discussion of "creational monotheism" in *The New Testament and the People of God* (Minneapolis: Fortress Press, 1992), 248–59.

60. *Interpretation of Religion*, 218.

61. As Joseph Prabhu has pointed out, the radical pluralist sees in Hick a commitment to a form of religious pluralism with an equally strong—and questionable—commitment to "a metaphysical universalism" in the sense of "one, sovereign Ultimate, differently mediated in the religious traditions." Prabhu, "The Road Not Taken: A Story about Religious Pluralism, Part 2" (a reply to Julius Lipner's "At the Bend in the Road: A Story about Religious Pluralism"), in *Problems in the Philosophy of Religion: Critical Studies of the Work of John Hick*, ed. Harold Hewitt (New York: St. Martin's, 1991), 239.

62. This line of criticism, in less developed forms, was first suggested by critics of Hick such as Mesle, *John Hick's Theodicy*, 91–92; Rowe, "John Hick's Contribution," 22.

63. *Faith and Knowledge*, esp. ch. 8.

64. Ibid., 184, also 186. For other relevant statements of the issue by Hick, see *Philosophy of Religion*, 1st ed., 70–73; *Evil and the God of Love*, ix, 17, 308–13; *Christianity at the Center*, 50–57; "God, Evil and Mystery," 540; *Arguments for the Existence of God*, 104–105, 114.

65. Peter Byrne is simply wrong when he claims that Hick has abandoned the idea that ultimate reality must maintain an epistemic distance in order to preserve human freedom. Byrne, "John Hick's Philosophy of World Religions," *Scottish Journal of Theology* 35 (1982): 295. The problem here is that he has identified a (possible) shift in Hick's assessment of theistic proofs in this regard and apparently has falsely assumed that such a shift must also have occurred in Hick's thought concerning religious experience itself.

66. Hick, "Religious Pluralism and the Rationality of Religious Belief," *Faith and Philosophy* 10 (1993): 242–49.

67. See "Mystical Experience as Cognition," 50–51.

68. E.g., see *God Has Many Names*, 50–51, 86, 113; *Philosophy of Religion*, 3rd ed., 68–70; 4th ed., 64–67.

69. *God Has Many Names*, 50.

70. Ibid.

71. *Interpretation of Religion*, 124.

72. As noted by Mesle, *John Hick's Theodicy*, 89.

73. Hick, "Religious Experience: Its Nature and Validity," in *Disputed Questions in Theology*, 31. See also his related statements in Hick, afterword to R. Douglas Geivett, *Evil and the Evidence for God: The Challenge of John Hick's Theodicy* (Philadelphia: Temple University Press, 1993), 234; Hick, "Response to Eddy," 419.

74. For related observations on Hick's epistemology, see Lipner, "At the Bend in the Road," 224; Eliot Deutsch, review of *Interpretation of Religion*, by John Hick, *Philosophy East and West* 40 (1990): 559; Peter Slater, "Lindbeck, Hick, and the Nature of Religious Truth," *Studies in Religion* 24 (1995): 72.

75. It is telling that with an opportunity offered to him to address this specific criticism in published response form, Hick did not broach, let alone answer, the charge. See Hick, "Response to Mesle," in *John Hick's Theodicy*, 115–34. It is important to note here (in response to a question of Lipner, "At the Bend in the Road," 225) that what is being identified here is not merely vestigial traces of theism in Hick's *style* of presentation. Rather, I am suggesting that the problem lies in the very logic and content of his hypothesis itself.

76. Heim, *Salvations*, 29, n. 11.

77. More recently, in his defense of religious realism, Hick has shifted from using the term *verification* to that of *falsification*; see *Christian Theology of Religions*, 71–76. However, in *Interpretation of Religion* (178), he defends the use of the term *verification* with regard to his eschatological thesis, if in a qualified sense.

78. *Christian Theology of Religions*, 73.

79. *Death and Eternal Life*, 15.

80. Hick, "On Religious Experience," in *Faith, Scepticism, and Personal Identity*, ed. J. J. MacIntosh and H. A. Meynell (Calgary: University of Calgary Press, 1994), 29.

81. I am indebted to Paul Griffiths and Paul Reasoner for raising the following question while commenting on an earlier version of this essay.

82. *Interpretation of Religion*, 183.

83. See especially *Faith and Knowledge*, 150–52.

84. Don Cupitt, review of *God Has Many Names*, by John Hick, *Times Literary Supplement*, August 8, 1980, 902.

7

Why the World Is Not Religiously Ambiguous: A Critique of Religious Pluralism

Paul Copan

The Enlightenment's disdain for special revelation and religious particularism is reflected in the story of *Nathan the Wise*, penned by biblical critic Gotthold Ephraim Lessing (1729–1781). In this story, a father "in a far Eastern clime" possesses a priceless magic ring. Yet he rather unwisely promises the ring to each of his three sons. Though not a mathematician, he realizes the authentic ring can be given to only one of his three sons. How can he save face and fulfill the promise made to all the sons? It dawns on him that he can have two replicas made for the other two, and no one will be the wiser. So just before he dies, he separately calls his sons to his side and presents each one with a ring, accompanied by a blessing. Each son leaves his father's presence thinking that he—not the others—has the magic ring; the others have the imitations. The moral of Lessing's story?

> Vainly they search, strive, argue.
> > The true ring was not proved or provable—
> > Almost as hard to prove as to us now
> > What the true creed is.[1]

Using this precious-metal imagery, Peter Byrne believes that underneath the varying religious perspectives and expressions stands one reality. This can be compared to gold. Though its atomic number is necessarily 79, it comes in solid, molten, or ore form. Ultimately, human attempts to express these religious perspectives theologically or philosophically will be metaphorical: "Each set of doctrinal statements is to be understood in metaphorical fashion. They are the workings out of divergent but mutually apt models for understanding a reality which is for the most part beyond all literal, positive statement."[2] (Presumably, Byrne's statement about the nature of religion is intended to be taken literally and not metaphorically.)

The Enlightenment has, of course, opened the floodgates for a diversity-sensitive, multiple-narrative, "post-metaphysical" religious context.[3] This "post-axial" understanding of the world's religions affirms, as the late philosopher of religion John Hick (d. 2012) put it, "different ways of experiencing, conceiving, and living in relation to the ultimate divine Reality which transcends all our varied versions of it."[4]

According to Hick, the universe is religiously ambiguous. That is, it can be experienced and interpreted either religiously or naturalistically (using Lessing's ring analogy, we could say magically or mundanely).[5] In Hick's words,

> [The universe] is capable from our present point of view within it of being consistently thought and experienced in both religious and naturalistic ways. Each aspect of the universe that prima facie supports a religious understanding of it (for example, the fact of moral goodness) can also be incorporated into a naturalistic worldview, and each aspect that prima facie supports a naturalistic understanding (such as the reality of evil) can also be incorporated into a religious worldview. And there is no objective sense of probability in which it can be shown that one of these interpretations is more probable than the other.[6]

In our post-Enlightenment world, humans are apparently coming to realize that the world can evoke religious or nonreligious responses.

Philosopher Terence Penelhum adds that religious ambiguity moves beyond the more parochial Western debates between theists and atheists. Things seem to get even more ambiguous as we look at the bewildering array of religious outlooks throughout the world.[7]

When we say "religiously ambiguous," do we mean that the probability of God's existence dangles at around 0.5? What if we find that God is a better explanation for a certain phenomenon? Hick responds, "A best-available explanation may or may not be the true explanation," and he gives the example of the once commonly held belief that the sun revolves around the earth, but this explanation proved false.[8]

Furthermore, Hick calls for a Copernican revolution of theology that decenters the seemingly arrogant, parochial assertion of religious exclusivism (a

Ptolemaic view);[9] rather, the Real is at the heart of the religious universe. The religious "planets" of Christianity, Buddhism, Islam, and Hinduism are simply culturally conditioned attempts to get at, or approximate, the "sun" of Ultimate Reality. All of the world's great religions, though culturally conditioned, are equally capable of bringing salvation or liberation—which is evident in the moral fruits of their respective adherents. This Ultimate Reality can be experienced and conceived in different ways, but it transcends all our varied versions of it.

If the world is religiously ambiguous, then perhaps the pluralistic interpretation can perhaps gain some traction. On the other hand, if good reasons exist for seeing the world in nonnaturalistic—yea, theistic—terms, perhaps we can discern in the universe and our experience glimmers of transcendence so that we might "seek God . . . grope for Him and find Him, though He is not far from each one of us" (Acts 17:27, NASB).

It is this theme of religious ambiguity or religious/nonreligious epistemic parity that I would like to explore. I shall engage with John Hick's version of pluralism in particular, although what I have to say has a bearing on other versions as well.

In the first section, I shall maintain we have very strong evidence for a personal Creator's existence and for the utter religious uniqueness of Jesus of Nazareth, as evidenced by his authoritative claims and miracles, which are vindicated by his bodily resurrection from the dead.[10] The wide-ranging evidence for these claims undermines Hick's ambiguity thesis.

In the second section, I shall argue that the religious pluralist's claims are fairly religiously *un*ambiguous. That is, the pluralist makes ample exclusivistic truth claims in support of religious pluralism, to the exclusion of traditional Christian, Muslim, Buddhist, and other religionist truth claims. Pluralism not only reveals the same alleged hubris and triumphalism of traditional religious exclusivism. Pluralism exceeds this by homogenizing (and thus distorting) traditional religious doctrines in order to accommodate its own perspective. In the end, we find ourselves examining not religious exclusivism at one end of the spectrum and religious pluralism at the other, but simply two religious exclusivisms.

WHY THE WORLD IS NOT RELIGIOUSLY AMBIGUOUS

Hick acknowledges that his view is not merely a personal preference, but an explanatory theory—a religious explanation rather than a naturalistic one. Hick's gives advice to his detractors: "Critics who don't like it should occupy themselves in trying to produce a better one."[11] By way of response, we should, first, distinguish between *likable* theories, on the one hand, and *explaining* theories, on the other, which (whether we like them or not) possess explanatory scope, explanatory power, and plausibility; are not ad hoc in nature; and explanatorily outstrip rival theories. Thus, a particularistic view, though politically incorrect, may be far more persuasive abductively.

Second, although Hick acknowledges a best-available explanation may or may not be the true explanation (the geocentric model wasn't), we should also seek explanations for a wide range of phenomena, not merely this or that particular consideration. In doing so, we find that certain religious beliefs better approximate reality than others. For example, the beginning of the universe better supports a theistic perspective than a Buddhist perspective. A Christian perspective matches up nicely with the historicity of Jesus' crucifixion—in contrast to Islam, which denies it.

Surely, in search of explanations that best match up with reality, we could ask: Do we have good reasons ab initio for excluding certain worldview options from consideration precisely because they fail to match up with reality? For example, what if we encounter kooky religions complete with charlatan founders and obviously forged or fabricated scriptures, no matter how decent their adherents turn out to be? While we are not claiming that no truth is to be found in these options, perhaps their core metaphysical outlook is so deeply problematic that it becomes self-eliminating.

I would argue that a powerful, good, personal, rational Being's existence makes better sense of features of the universe and human experience than the major alternatives.[12] Indeed, if such a Being exists, then this means that many Eastern philosophical views would be in error on this major point. Buddhism's Dalai Lama concedes this: "Among spiritual faiths, there are many different philosophies, some just opposite to each other on certain points. Buddhists do not accept a creator; Christians base their philosophy on that theory."[13]

British Buddhism scholar Paul Williams became a Christian after thirty years' devotion to Buddhism because it couldn't answer this fundamental question: Why does the contingent universe exist at all? He concluded that only a *necessary* being—something classical Buddhism rejects—could serve as an adequate explanation to that question: "I have come to believe that there is a gap in the Buddhist explanation of things which for me can only be filled by God, the sort of God spoken of in a Christian tradition such as that of St. Thomas Aquinas."[14] Williams kept on bumping up against implications of this question, which would worry him, eventually prodding him to a different understanding. Williams realized that the existence of a personal God answers key *why* questions. As Alvin Plantinga observes, God's nature and existence offer "suggestions for answers to a wide range of otherwise intractable questions."[15]

Phenomena We Observe, Assume, or Recognize	Theistic Context	Naturalistic Context
(Self-)consciousness exists.	God is supremely self-aware/self-conscious.	The universe was produced by mindless, nonconscious processes.
Personal beings exist.	God is a personal being.	The universe was produced by impersonal processes.
We believe we make free personal decisions/choices, assuming humans are accountable for their actions.	God is spirit and a free being, who can freely choose to act (e.g., to create or not).	We have emerged by material, deterministic processes beyond our control.
Secondary qualities (colors, smells, sounds, tastes, textures) exist throughout the world.	God is joyful, and secondary qualities make the world pleasurable and joyful to his creatures.	The universe was produced from colorless, odorless, soundless, tasteless, textureless particles and processes.
We trust our senses and rational faculties as generally reliable in producing true beliefs.	A God of truth and rationality exists.	Because of our impulse to survive and reproduce, our beliefs would only help us survive, but a number of these could be completely false.
Human beings have intrinsic value/dignity and rights.	God is the supremely valuable being.	Human beings were produced by valueless processes.
Objective moral values exist.	God's character is the source of goodness/moral values.	The universe was produced by nonmoral processes.
The universe began to exist a finite time ago—without previously existing matter, energy, space, or time.	A powerful, previously existing God brought the universe into being without any preexisting material. (Here, *something* emerges from *something*.)	The universe came into existence from nothing by nothing—or was, perhaps, self-caused. (Here, *something* comes from *nothing*.)
First life emerged.	God is a living, active being.	Life somehow emerged from nonliving matter.
The universe is finely tuned for human life (known as the Goldilocks effect—the universe is "just right" for life).	God is a wise, intelligent designer.	All the cosmic constants just happened to be right; given enough time and/or many possible worlds, a finely tuned world eventually emerged.
Beauty exists—not only in landscapes and sunsets but also in elegant or beautiful scientific theories.	God is beautiful (Ps. 27:4) and capable of creating beautiful things according to his pleasure.	Beauty in the natural world is superabundant and in many cases superfluous (often not linked to survival).
We (tend to) believe that life has purpose and meaning. For most of us, life is worth living.	God has created/designed us for certain purposes (to love him, others, etc.); when we live them out, our lives find meaning/enrichment.	There is no cosmic purpose, blueprint, or goal for human existence.
Real evils—both moral and natural—exist/take place in the world.	Evil's definition assumes a design plan (how things ought to be but are not) or standard of goodness (a corruption or absence of goodness), by which we judge something to be evil. God is a good designer; his existence supplies the crucial moral context to make sense of evil.	Atrocities, pain, and suffering just happen. This is just how things are—with no "plan" or standard of goodness to which things ought to conform.

Theism vs. Naturalism: Which Is the Better Fit?

If the above chart comparing theism and naturalism suggests the greater likelihood of theism, then it seems that we have good reasons for affirming theism's greater explanatory capacity over nontheistic religions as well, mutatis mutandis.

As we consider these major features in the universe and in human experience, it becomes apparent that theism offers us a remarkable context to account for these phenomena. We are not here denying puzzles, mysteries, and unanswered questions. Later in this paper, I shall briefly address two such questions—frequently raised by the pluralist—concerning the unevangelized as well as the matter of cultural conditioning (religious belief through the accidents of birth). I shall argue, though, that these are secondary questions to God's existence and the uniqueness of Jesus of Nazareth.

For now, I want to argue that a personal God's existence helps us make the best overall sense of these fundamental phenomena. To reinforce the greater explanatory work of the theistic perspective, many naturalists themselves recognize that a wide range of features are difficult to account for, given naturalism or nontheistic religious perspectives. As I have explored these phenomena in greater detail elsewhere,[16] for the sake of space, I limit myself to the following three considerations: (1) the universe's temporal origin, corroborated by empirical evidence for the big bang cosmological model; (2) the fundamental recognition of rationality and objective morality; and (3) the existence of consciousness. Unless otherwise noted, I shall be quoting naturalists who reinforce the point I am making about the universe's theistic indicators.

THE UNIVERSE'S ORIGINS

If we have to choose between naturalism (or various nontheistic religions) and theism, we can (for starters) consider how things were "in the beginning." The origin of the universe is better explained by a theistic view over against naturalism/nontheism. The theistic context makes excellent sense of the universe's dramatic origin a finite time ago, as opposed to the alternatives (popping into existence from nothing or being self-caused). Physicist Paul Davies, who takes a more deistic view of things, sees the clear implications of the question of what caused the big bang: "One might consider some supernatural force, some agency beyond space and time as being responsible for the big bang, or one might prefer to regard the big bang as an event without a cause." But "we don't have too much choice": it's either "something outside of the physical world" or "an event without a cause."[17]

The universe began to exist a finite time ago—a statement affirmed by the nontheist. Physicist Stephen Hawking puts it plainly: "Almost everyone now believes that the universe, and time itself, had a beginning at the Big Bang."[18] Nobel Prize–winning physicist Steven Weinberg acknowledges his dislike of this fact: "[The now-rejected] steady state theory [which views the universe as eternally existent] is philosophically the most attractive theory because it least resembles the account given in Genesis."[19] Indeed, the big bang gives us very good reason for thinking that something independent of the universe brought it into existence. Astrophysicists John Barrow and Joseph Silk point out, "Our new picture is more akin to the traditional metaphysical picture of creation out of nothing, for it predicts a definite beginning to events in time, indeed a definite beginning to time itself." They ask, "What preceded the event called the 'big bang'?" The answer they offer to this question "is simple: nothing."[20] They even admit our universe resembles the "traditional metaphysical picture of creation out of nothing."[21] Agnostic philosopher Anthony Kenny notes, "A proponent of the big bang theory, at least if he is an atheist, must believe that matter came from nothing and by nothing."[22]

Does such a cosmic free lunch make metaphysical sense? No, our universe couldn't be uncaused or self-caused. Philosopher Kai Nielsen puts it this way: "Suppose you hear a loud bang . . . and you ask me, 'What made that bang?' and I reply, 'Nothing, it just happened.' You would not accept that. In fact you would find my reply quite unintelligible."[23] If nothing can begin to exist without a cause when it comes to little bangs, why not the big bang? So if an immensely powerful Being exists, then we have good reason for thinking that the world began to exist by his activity. If something *begins* to exist, then it must come from being, not nonbeing. Something can't come from nothing, since there's no *potential* for anything to begin existing. Even Hick admits, "For myself, I can accept that something cannot come out of nothing. And also that there must be something eternal."[24]

If Hick is correct, then this conclusion would undercut Buddhism and other nontheistic religions. Even when Hick claims that the world's great religions are equally capable of bringing salvation or liberation, and that this is evidenced by saint production in which humans move from self-centeredness toward Reality-centeredness, there still remains the glaringly obvious and more fundamental question, What is real? As it turns out, Hick himself takes a posture that negates a Buddhist metaphysic, with its doctrine of impermanence. So on this particular point, we have commonality between the theist and the Hick-like pluralist, as opposed to, say, the Buddhist.[25]

Something spaceless, immaterial, and very powerful brought the universe into existence. If we have good reason to think the universe is "ontologically haunted,"[26] then we have reason for revising the religious ambiguity thesis at least on this point.

RATIONALITY AND OBJECTIVE MORAL VALUES

Eighth-century Hindu philosopher Shankara adopted the monistic metaphysic known as *nirguna Brahman* (Brahman has no qualities). This entails that all reality is one, no distinctions exist, and any apparent differences are an illusion (*maya*). Brahman is *neti neti* (not this, not that). Such a perspective, though, calls into question the very legitimacy of ratiocination and logic. This resembles religious pluralism. Pluralist Wilfred Cantwell Smith (1916–2000) claimed that "in all ultimate matters, truth lies not in an either-or but in a both-and."[27] Basic laws of logic (e.g., A ≠ non-A) do not reflect ultimate rationality. Of course, in the very denial of laws of logic, Smith affirms them. He chooses *between* either-or and both-and, favoring the latter, rejecting the former.

The story is told of the raja (ruler) of Theri, who was hosting the Hindu philosopher Shankara ("Sankara"). The raja tested his illusion theory by setting against him a rogue elephant: "On seeing it, Sankara immediately climbed a tree to save himself. On reaching the palace, the raja told Sankara that there was no need for him to climb the tree because the elephant was only maya. 'The elephant was no doubt maya,' said Sankara, 'so were my climbing the tree, withdrawal of the beast by the raja, and my climbing down the tree.'"[28]

It seems that, for the most part (unless we're habitually on mind-altering drugs or under alcohol's influence), we humans can differentiate between a dream state and an awareness of a real world outside our minds. This commonsense view quite obvious to us, and the burden of proof would fall to the one who rejects what is so apparent to so many.

Now, we can appreciate the Buddhist emphasis on the transitory nature of earthly existence and the call for some degree of detachment. (As 1 John 2:17 [NIV] expresses it, "The world and its desires pass away.") Yet the question arises why anyone would accept this Eastern view of reality. The best procedure is to believe what is apparently true unless there is some known reason to believe that it is not. For example, despite those who may have taken the earth to be flat because it *seemed* flat, such thinking today can be readily rejected given the overwhelming evidence that it is spherical. Indeed, the best we can do as humans is to believe what seems to be true unless we have good reasons to reject it. But to believe what does not even *seem* to be true when we have no good reason to accept it is counterintuitive.[29] Why think that our senses are regularly deceiving us? It seems that Aristotle was right when he said that the rejection of sense perception is a rejection of common sense: "To disregard sense perception . . . would be an instance of intellectual weakness."[30]

Certain versions of Hinduism and Buddhism propound a two-truth-levels view: the lower illusory (*maya*) level of ignorance (*avidya*) and the higher level of the Ultimate Reality/Truth. Since the Ultimate Reality ("Brahman" or the like) is beyond logic or illogic, then how will these Hindus or Buddhists persuade us to accept their view? After all, logic doesn't even apply to the Ultimate Reality. There's no reason to accept any such arguments. To use logic to persuade us that logic doesn't apply to Brahman is incoherent. What's more, this two-tiered view itself distinguishes between higher and lower levels!

This no-distinctions perspective has a bearing on objective moral values—particularly with regard to distinctions of right and wrong. In *The Lotus and the Robot*, Arthur Koestler recounts an interview in which a Zen Buddhist scholar called Hitler's use of gas chambers "very silly." He refused to call it evil. In his estimation, evil is "a Christian concept. Good and evil exist only on a relative scale."[31]

The theist can readily affirm that a good, rational Creator (who makes creates humans in his image to be thinking, morally responsible agents) affords a more plausible context for rationality and objective moral values.

Regarding the latter view, the presumed value statements made by the United Nations Declaration on Human Rights (1948) that all humans "born free and equal in dignity and rights" and the *Humanist Manifesto III* (2003) that humans have "inherent worth and dignity"[32] lead us to wonder how, if we are the products of mindless and valueless processes, could value emerge. From valuelessness comes valuelessness. Human rights and dignity or moral duties are difficult to justify if a good personal Being (God) doesn't exist.

In light of the existence of objective moral values, a theistic world is much less surprising than a naturalistic world. If God does exist, then we have a readily available basis for affirming these features of the universe. To quote J. L. Mackie, "Moral properties constitute so odd a cluster of properties and relations that they are most unlikely to have arisen in the ordinary course of events without an all-powerful god to create them."[33]

What of the problem of evil? While this is the nontheist's most notable argument against God's existence, objective evil still assumes that things ought not to be a certain way. But why think the world should be any different if it is the result of purposeless, material processes? Some sort of design or plan is being assumed when criticizing theism.

CONSCIOUSNESS

Our first of several philosophers of mind, Ned Block, confesses that we have no idea how consciousness could have emerged from nonconscious matter: "We have nothing—*zilch*—worthy of being called a research programme. . . . Researchers are stumped."[34] Berkeley's John Searle says this is a "leading problem in the biological sciences."[35] Jaegwon Kim notes our inability to understand consciousness in an essentially physical world.[36] Colin McGinn observes that consciousness seems like "a radical novelty in the universe";[37] he wonders how our "technicolour" awareness could "arise from soggy grey matter."[38] David Papineau wonders why consciousness emerges: "To this question physicalists' 'theories of consciousness' seem to provide no answer."[39]

If, however, we have been made by a supremely self-aware Being, then the existence of consciousness has a plausible context.

THE EXPLANATORY POWER OF JESUS' BODILY RESURRECTION

Here I depart from indicators for a powerful, rational, conscious, and good Being, legitimately inferred from broadly observable phenomena, to mention something more particularistic, though still possessing publicly available evidence. The vast majority of historians take for granted four secure historical facts regarding the first Easter, accepted by even the most skeptical:[40]

- Jesus' burial in Joseph of Arimathea's tomb
- The discovery of Jesus' empty tomb
- The postmortem appearances to the disciples
- The origin of the earliest disciples' belief in Jesus' resurrection

For instance, some scholars will interpret these appearances as hallucinations or psychological/guilt projections, but historians acknowledge that the disciples were convinced that the risen Jesus had appeared to them, which inspired the earliest Christian preaching about the resurrection.

Now, in themselves, these four lines of evidence aren't "miraculous facts" that are somehow beyond historical research; they're available to all historians. While historical facts themselves are not miraculous, an explanation certainly may be, and if God exists, such an explanation is legitimate and theologically warranted. The point at issue is this: Which interpretation or explanation—natural or supernatural—makes the best sense of these facts? The careful historian N. T. Wright concludes that the combined historical probability of (a) the empty tomb—something Jesus' enemies assumed (Matt. 28:12-15)—and (b) the postmortem appearances is virtually certain, being on the level of Caesar Augustus's death in C.E. 14 or the fall of Jerusalem in C.E. 70.[41] To have one without the other wouldn't do: just an empty tomb would have been merely a puzzle or a tragedy; Jesus' postmortem appearances alone could have been chalked up to hallucinations. But taken together, these two matters give the origin of the early church its powerful impetus.

Hick considers Saint Paul to be the source (or culprit!) behind an apotheosized Jesus, which was a distortion of the historical Jesus' teaching. A very lofty view of Jesus evolved. However, this flies in the face of the fact the Paul knew the Lord's brother James, who was fully in line with what Paul was proclaiming (Acts 15; Gal. 1–2). If not, James could have corrected any such distortions. The earliest Christian message of the resurrection is found not just in one source, but in an array of sources—the Synoptics, John, the early Christian sermons in Acts, Paul's epistles, and the very early Jerusalem tradition mentioned in 1 Corinthians 15, which itself dates to less than two years after Jesus' death.[42] Historian E. P. Sanders, who is hardly an orthodox Christian, asserts, "That Jesus' followers (and later Paul) had resurrection experiences is, in my judgment, fact. What the reality was that gave rise to these experiences I do not know."[43]

As for a crucified Messiah, we can't imagine how contradictory and even insane this would sound to Jews and Greeks alike (1 Cor. 1:18-23)! Yet Jesus' resurrection helps us make sense of the early church's sudden start, all the while preaching a crucified Messiah, rather than it being another failed messianic movement of the first century. And why start preaching immediately in Jerusalem, where the authorities could readily investigate, rather than Rome or Athens?

Hick seems far too dismissive of the available historical evidence for Jesus' resurrection, not to mention his identity claims mentioned in the Gospels and the incorporation of Jesus into the worship of the fledgling church. The available evidence is more forceful than Hick is willing to admit. In fact, Hick's view ends up distorting the historical evidence, as we shall see. What best accounts for this is something on the scale of a resurrection as a divine imprimatur on Jesus' authoritative role in God's kingdom.

WHY RELIGIOUS PLURALISM IS NOT RELIGIOUSLY AMBIGUOUS

The universe looks much more theistic than naturalistic. What about religious pluralism's unambiguous stance? In this section, I would like to explore certain realms of pluralistic *non*-ambiguity, regarding (a) its affirmations, (b) its revisions of exclusivistic religions, and (c) its self-exemption from cultural conditioning.

THE UNAMBIGUOUS DOGMAS OF RELIGIOUS PLURALISM

Rejecting religious exclusivism, Hick declares that each religion, left to itself, claims its own unique saving access to the Real. As a result, each religion "can only accommodate other traditions by subordinating them to itself, whether as total errors or as partial truths."[44] Yet that is exactly what pluralism does: it subordinates religions to itself, whether as total errors or as partial truths! Hick claims to begin from ground-level observation, assuming that the Christian faith is not simply a projection but a cognitive response to the transcendent. Yet his version of the Christian faith does not remotely resemble orthodox Christianity. He guts the Christian faith of its literal, historical meaning in order to accommodate the quest for a comprehensive understanding of religions.[45]

This seems somewhat analogous to George Orwell's *Animal Farm*, where "all animals are equal, but some are more equal than others"; likewise, the pluralist appears to claim that that all religions are equal, but some religious views—like pluralism—are more equal than others. So if the Christian faith is outrageously exclusivistic and religiously chauvinistic, then so is pluralism. It claims to be true, and where others (like Christians or Muslims) disagree, they would be in error.

Ironically, pluralism is logically no different from the Christian faith's exclusivism. The particularist/exclusivist affirms that if a certain claim is true (say, "Jesus died for the sins of the world"), then those rejecting it are in error. Yet pluralists believe *their* claim to true while exclusivists are in error. The pluralist believes *he* has a virtue the particularist doesn't have. As Gavin D'Costa writes, "The pluralist is, in fact, no different from the exclusivist, except in the criteria employed for what counts as truth."[46]

Here I would like to note how pluralists like Hick are unambiguous exclusivists at several levels.[47]

- *Knowledge (epistemology):* We've already seen that Hick believes he has a virtue that traditional religionists don't have: he "knows" that particularistic religions like Islam or Christianity are false in their literal claims about salvation or uniqueness. He "knows" that no religion is uniquely salvific.
- *Final things (eschatology):* Hick has claimed that in the end, his pluralistic view will be proven right (eschatological verification);[48] so eventually, it will be decisively shown that many religious doctrines

conflicting with pluralism are literally false. In other words, all others—we're talking billions of people—are wrong except the pluralist! Despite Hick's "cosmic optimism" about how everything will turn out,[49] why think that such will be the case? Is the Real going to ensure this happens? If so, does this not suggest that the Real is personal rather than impersonal? And why the optimism? Why not argue for an ultimate personal obliteration for all individuals, as some Eastern religions maintain? Or why not the eventual extinction of the human race—end of story? Why is optimism, rather than pessimism, warranted?

- *Ultimate reality (metaphysics):* Hick claims that the Real doesn't have any characteristics or properties we can truly describe. Even when challenged to affirm that at least "the Real is not a tricycle,"[50] Hick asserted, "I do indeed hold that the Real cannot properly be said to be either a tricycle or a non-tricycle."[51] Yet Hick seems to have access to the Real by asserting this. Hick's approach, of course, resembles that of Kant; we cannot know things in themselves (noumena), but only things as they appear to us (phenomena). One common criticism of Kant is this: How does Kant know that there is a noumenal realm behind the phenomena, and how does he know that the noumenal realm is unknowable?

The same applies to Hick: How does Hick know so much about the unknowable Real and that there *is* a Real at all behind the various religious personae or impersonae? And how one can know that this Ultimate Reality is unknowable? Could we not at least say we know this following about the Real: that it cannot be truly known by humans?[52] Someone, it seems, has been whispering metaphysical secrets into Hick's ear. It seems that Hick's metaphysical confidence parallels that of the Christian, who maintains that the self-existent triune God has broken into our world and uniquely and savingly revealed himself in the person of Jesus of Nazareth. Moreover, we can genuinely know God and that he is love, as is evidenced by the sacrifice of Jesus (1 John 3:16; 4:8-9, 16).

Getting back to Hick's metaphysic, we could ask: Why not say that religion is a completely human idea or projection—that it has nothing to do with the Ultimate Reality? Why not be a religious skeptic instead of a pluralist? After all, lots of people seem to come to understand the Real in times of war, oppression, and desperation. Why think that the Real has anything to do with religion itself?[53] Why think that any Ultimate Reality exists—unless Hick has decent reason or evidence to the contrary? If he does offer any such reasons, then he would be at odds with the various religious conceptions of the Real, which means the traditional religionist is wrong.

- *Ethics:* Hick has written about "grading religions."[54] Some religions, such as Islam or Buddhism (at least in their positive expressions), are more "appropriate" than others (Jim Jones, Bhagwan Shree Rajneesh, David Koresh, the Heaven's Gate group, Satanism).[55] Why? Because of the ethically inferior activities of the latter. Likewise, pluralist Paul Knitter claims we should judge religions to be true because they bring liberation from oppressive societal, psychological, and spiritual structures. If they don't promote justice or show concern for the poor, they're false.[56] Both Hick and Knitter have a moral measuring stick: they exclude certain (un)ethical actions and beliefs that oppose their ideals.[57] It seems that Hick is adopting Paul's stance that all people are ultimately without excuse (Rom. 1:20).

Eastern religious traditions (and Hick's own pluralism)[58] tend to deny or diminish the existence of a personal God/Ultimate Reality. Yet they somehow praise *personal* virtues, which are a plumb line for judging whether salvation or liberation is taking place in the world's religions. Yet some religions do not have the proper metaphysical justification for such affirmations. Why favor *personal* virtues, as Hick does, when the Ultimate Reality is impersonal, inert, and abstract?

By contrast, the doctrine of the essentially relational, mutually indwelling triune God, for instance, would offer us a rich context for affirming such virtues—which furnishes an argument in Christianity's favor. The Christian faith has robust resources for affirming personal virtues such as love, kindness, and compassion—unlike nontheistic traditions.

Hick's own *Evil and the Love of God* takes for granted the existence of—and distinction between—good and evil; here he advocates an Irenaean soul-making theodicy.[59] Elsewhere, he repudiates immoral and oppressive expressions of religion in favor of their saint-producing ones.[60] Eastern philosophies and religions that relativize evil and goodness would be a strong argument in favor of rejecting their outlook on the subject. If we take evil seriously, then it would be difficult to account for evil apart from some kind of design or plan, from which evil is a deviation. As for naturalism, Hick thinks that a naturalistic account of morality as wholly explicable on evolutionary grounds (e.g., Dawkins's version) is "highly implausible."[61] Hick recognizes what the Jewish-Christian scriptures assume—that there a moral law written on human hearts, which renders them accountable.

- *Anthropology:* Related to the previous point (and further reinforcing Hick's belief in general revelation available to all) is that pluralism assumes a certain stance regarding the human condition—namely, that humans are self-centered, that this is wrong, and that they can and ought to recognize this condition in order to alter it. That is, Hick admits to a basic moral outlook that is universal and accessible to all: "So the concrete reality of salvation consists in a spiritual transformation whose natural expression is unrestricted love and compassion. I stress the word *basic*, because what is common to the different faiths is this truly basic principle, not the specific moral codes or ethical applications which have developed within different societies at different times and places and in different circumstances."[62]

Such knowledge is not accessible solely through special revelation (Amos 1-2 and and Rom. 1 suggest this type of knowledge is available to all), nor does this awareness seem to support naturalism (since how humans *ought* to behave suggests some kind of master plan or teleology, to which naturalism is averse). Hick refers to a common moral theme that cuts through the world's civilizations and religions—namely, that of the Golden Rule, of doing to others as you would have them do to you.[63] Caring for weak, sick, helpless humans as religions affirm is strikingly un-Darwinian.

- *Salvation (soteriology):* Hick's assertion that religions are capable of saving or liberating leaves us wondering how he *knows* this. And we're left with a number of questions: Why think that salvation is really going on at all in these religions? Couldn't religion simply be a completely naturalistic or human phenomenon? Why bring an Ultimate Reality into the picture? Furthermore, why is doctrinal content utterly irrelevant to salvation? Will any be excluded from salvation, or will the Real give Satanists and Rajneeshis and Koreshis a pass?

If the Christian faith declares that certain historical events—such as a crucifixion and resurrection—are necessary and foundational for the Christian faith and the very possibility of salvation (1 Cor. 15:17, 32), how can pluralists maintain that Christianity can be sustained without them?

- *History:* Pluralists are exclusivists when it comes to history. They deny that the virgin birth, the dramatic miracles of Jesus, and his resurrection are literal history. They deny that Jesus made the lofty,

> authoritative claims he did. Pluralists say that these events didn't
> literally take place and that they are ultimately historical falsehoods.[64]

Hick makes many confident, exclusivistic assertions in a number of areas, and such assertions strongly resemble those of traditional Christianity. And if Hick is correct about religion being culturally conditioned, then his pluralism is no less culturally conditioned than the Christian or Islamic faiths, as we shall explore later.

UNAMBIGUOUS REVISIONS OF RELIGIONS

But things seem to be even worse for pluralism. It not only promotes a logically exclusivistic view while pretending not to; it also presumptuously revises and distorts the religions of others. How? By imposing an "enlightened" framework on them and standing in judgment over them.[65] Apparently, only the Western liberal academic can understand the world's religions! He has privileged access to the elephant. Traditional religionists are just blind and misguided.[66] They just can't rise above their cultural influences as the pluralist can.

So Hick will reinterpret the doctrine of Jesus as God's incarnate Son as simply a "mythological and poetic way of expressing his significance to us."[67] He wasn't literally divine; he was "wholly human."[68] According to Hick,

> Within Judaism any outstandingly good and pious person could
> be called a son of God. A son of God was someone who was
> close to God, sometimes with a special mission from God. And the
> uniqueness that the church has read into it by restricting it to Jesus as
> the one and only Son of God, came as the gospel went out beyond
> Judaism into the Roman world, under St Paul's leadership, when
> 'son of God' became literalised, so that gradually in the course of
> the first centuries the metaphorical son of God was transformed into
> the metaphysical God the Son, Second Person of a divine Trinity.
> . . . What became the great theological doctrines of Incarnation,
> Atonement and Trinity are just not there [in Scripture].[69]

Thus, when we ourselves love sacrificially, "divine love has become incarnate on earth."[70] Hick claims that Jesus came to be deified by his followers, just as the Buddha was. In asserting this, Hick is telling Christians what they really should think about Jesus—that their essential doctrines centering on him are false. In trying to preserve pluralism and reject Christian exclusivism, Hick takes his own exclusivistic chainsaw to the Christian faith, leaving it an unrecognizable stump. If the apostle Paul is correct in his assertions about Jesus' resurrection in 1 Corinthians 15, then Hick's Christianity is in no wise recognizably Christian. His is a quest for the pluralistic Jesus, so from the outset, his "Christianity" is incarnationless, atonementless, resurrectionless, and unitarian—that is, not recognizably Christian at all.[71] If true, Hick's Christianity prohibits and even condemns the worship of Jesus as idolatry—worshiping and serving the creature rather than the Creator.

Hick is fond of citing C. F. D. Moule in support of his claim that belief in Jesus as divine evolved over time.[72] Ironically, Moule says the very opposite of Hick. Moule asserts that we should speak in terms of the development—not evolution—of the view that Jesus is God. Whereas *evolution* implies mythical ideas being attached to the human Jesus, *development* implies an outworking of something already implicit at the outset.[73] Hick conveniently ignores this point.

Now, in religious dialogue, we just expect the true Muslim to believe—and desire that the world believe—that "there is no God but Allah, and Muhammad is his messenger." If he didn't, then he wouldn't be doing a respectable job representing his faith.[74] The same is true of other religious adherents. But if Hick is right, then you or I can't really be a Christian, since Christianity is literally false. If I become enlightened by Hick to adopt his pluralistic stance, then I'll have to give up core Christian doctrines like Jesus' incarnation, saving uniqueness, and bodily resurrection.

In their strenuous attempt to avoid exclusivistic imperialism, they go beyond traditional religious exclusivisms by telling us what is essential to our faith and what isn't.[75] Equipped with their own dogmas, pluralists desire to assist the religionist by dramatically purging his belief system of perceived errors to better suit pluralistic assumptions. Once all religions have been purged of error, then they'll have a lot more in common with each other because, oddly enough, all these religions will be sounding so pluralistic! Keith Ward writes of this drastic pluralistic revisionism, "If a Buddhist is prepared to regard belief in reincarnation as a myth, a Christian thinks of the Incarnation as a mistaken fourth-century doctrine, and a Muslim agrees that the Koran is a fallible and morally imperfect document, they might well be able to agree much more than they used to."[76]

The same is true of Knitter. He says that Jesus can't be "full, definitive, and unsurpassable." Jesus is indispensable only in the sense that our understanding of religion is enhanced and enriched by Jesus.[77] (To say only this, of course, goes against key texts like John 1:18; 14:6, 9; Col. 1:15-20; and Heb. 1:1-3, and it ends up bringing down Jesus from his worship-worthy status to becoming an equal with the Buddha and Muhammad—topics I cannot address here.[78]) Knitter thinks that traditional Christian language about Jesus prevents genuine religious dialogue. But what is Knitter doing himself? He's setting new ground rules before discussion can make "progress": upon accepting his pluralistic starting points, all religions can engage in real dialogue!

Knitter claims that Jesus' first followers were speaking confessionally, not ontologically. That is, they were not trying to make absolute statements about reality, but were so in love with Jesus that they utilized superlatives, the way husbands and wives do of each other ("You're the best!"). However, Knitter does not seem to appreciate the weighty New Testament claims in the context of the anti-idolatrous mind-set of first-century Judaism: the first followers are calling Jesus creator (1 Cor. 8:5-6), praying to him (Acts 7:59; 1 Cor. 16:22), receiving forgiveness from him (Matt. 9:6).

This is more than just language about being in love with Jesus. Jesus' first followers believed he shared the divine identity and attributed the honors, titles, actions, and prerogatives of Yahweh to Jesus. The New Testament writers affirmed this without dispute. Such a conviction, buttressed by Jesus' own resurrection from the dead and postmortem appearances, vindicated those authoritative claims—that in him the kingdom of God, the new exodus, and the new creation had come. And if their language is literally true but Jesus is just a man, then the earliest Christians were guilty of idolatry. Contrary to Knitter, we don't see Jesus open to other ways; he sees himself as the final revelation. He is *it*. So we shouldn't be surprised when Jesus said that he came to bring not peace, but a sword (Matt. 10:34) and that the one who loves family more than he loves Jesus can't be a disciple (Luke 14:26).

Is the allegedly objective pluralist better positioned to give help to an exclusivist like the orthodox Christian? Not necessarily. Why think those outside a belief system are necessarily in a better position to decide between competing truth claims? Why should we feel obliged to defer to an outsider's judgment?[79] Gavin D'Costa puts it well: "[The pluralist position] has the effect of claiming there are no true religions, for all misunderstand themselves until they embrace the pluralistic hypothesis. They must fundamentally reinterpret their self-understanding in modernity's terms. Thus it can still be argued that pluralists should be called exclusivists."[80]

Furthermore, Hick is incorrect that the innocent Jewish idea of a pious person as a "son of God" is hijacked by Paul to become a doctrine utterly foreign to the historical Jesus. However, Paul's letter to the Galatians offers a counter to Hick: Paul's message to the Gentiles was affirmed by the Jerusalem apostles—including Jesus' brother James—as identical to James' and Peter's gospel to the Jews. The New Testament's high Christology was embedded in the early church's worship. What is more, no hint of controversy exists in the early church about the exalted status of Jesus and the inclusion of Jesus in worship.[81]

Consider the assessment of two notable New Testament historians. Edinburgh's Larry Hurtado writes that devotion to Jesus emerged as "a veritable 'big bang,' an explosively rapid and impressively substantial development in the earliest stage of the Christian movement."[82] The late German scholar Martin Hengel said that in the twenty years between Jesus' death and Paul's earliest epistles, more happened in the developing of Christian beliefs about Jesus "than in the whole subsequent seven hundred years of church history."[83]

Religious pluralism not only *disguises* its exclusivism; it also is unwittingly presumptuous and perhaps even condescending. It claims that billions of people are wrong about religion, and it waters down robust doctrines of the world's religions to accommodate pluralism.

THE UNAMBIGUOUS EXCEPTIONS TO CULTURAL CONDITIONING

To be sure, pluralism—and the diversity of religions itself—raises puzzles and questions that traditional religionists must grapple with. One such question pluralists are fond of raising is that of the unevangelized and the implications for Christian exclusivism. According to Hick, "When *someone* is born to Buddhist parents in a Buddhist culture, that person is very likely to be a Buddhist and to be related to the Real in ways made possible by Buddhist understanding and practice."[84] Hick thinks religious exclusivism is arbitrary in that religious adherence primarily "depends upon the accidents of birth."[85]

While not denying cultural conditioning, we can deny its ultimacy. After all, what happens when we apply this reasoning to the pluralist himself? He is just as culturally conditioned as the Buddhist or Muslim. That being so, why prefer his view over anyone else's culturally conditioned view? Alvin Plantinga comments, "Pluralism isn't and hasn't been widely popular in the world at large; if the pluralist had been born in Madagascar, or medieval France, he probably wouldn't have been a pluralist. Does it follow that he shouldn't be a pluralist or that his pluralistic beliefs are produced in him by an unreliable belief-producing process? I doubt it."[86]

We can even doctor up Hick's quotation a bit: "When someone is born to religiously pluralist parents in a pluralist culture, that person is very likely to be a pluralist." The pluralist's own culturally conditioned position is no more privileged—and no less arbitrary—than anyone else's. Why take that perspective seriously but not the Christian's? Do we detect something of the cultural imperialism of which he accuses orthodox Christianity?

More to the point: Christians can and do acknowledge these difficulties, and they commonly offer responses to them (such as a middle-knowledge/Molinist view or an inclusivist perspective). But the pluralist ought not to allow the tail to wag the dog (or, de-tail to wag the dogma!). If a personal Creator exists, then this fact would undermine a fundamental tenet of various Eastern religions and of naturalism. And if the identity claims made by Jesus of Nazareth to reveal the Father uniquely (e.g., Matt. 11:27) and the strong reasons for his bodily resurrection stand up under scrutiny better than their naturalistic alternatives, then we have good reason to regard the secondary question of the unevangelized as something of a red herring. Pluralism's protests about the apparent "accidents of birth" should not overpower the primary issue. If God exists and has uniquely revealed himself in Jesus, we should begin here and then move to the matter of the unevangelized, not vice versa.

Concluding Remarks

Paul Knitter thinks we should stay away from absolute claims while making universal claims. We should be more concerned with orthopraxy than orthodoxy—with how a religion is lived out and how it inspires rather than with doctrines it affirms. Knitter is known for his warnings against triumphalism—whether to Christians or religionists in general—not to act as though "We're number one!" He rightly reminds us of how easily we can slip into idolatry. Orthodox Christians should return to the great truths of the gospel—that salvation by grace through faith in Christ excludes boasting and smug superiority (Rom. 3:27).

We could add that just as the Torah was a tutor to lead Jews to Christ (Gal. 3:24-25), certain aspects of the world's religions can be stepping-stones to the full revelation of God in Jesus of Nazareth. He is indeed the historical fulfillment of the greatest genuine human ideals and yearnings found in the world's religions, philosophies, fairy stories, epic tales, and inspiring legends (1 Cor. 1:24; Col. 2:3). The historical, incarnate Christ is "myth become fact."[87] God in Christ perfects and fulfills the highest hopes and ultimate aspirations contained within human cultures, philosophies, and religions around the world and across the ages.

Hick's call for a Copernican revolution of theology is misplaced. Indeed, I would proffer C. S. Lewis's statement of the illuminating centrality of the savingly unique Christ: "I believe in Christianity as I believe that the Sun has risen, not only because I see it, but because by it I see everything else."[88] Or, as Heb. 1:3 (NASB) describes Jesus' centrality, "He is the radiance of His glory and the exact representation of His nature, and upholds all things by the word of His power."[89]

Notes

1. Gotthold Ephraim Lessing, *Laocoon, Nathan the Wise, Minna von Barnhelm*, ed. William A. Steel (New York: Dutton, 1967 [repr. ed.]), 166–69.

2. Peter Byrne, *Prolegomena to Religious Pluralism* (London: Macmillan; New York: St. Martin's Press, 1995), 164.

3. Calvin Schrag, "Pluralism," in *The Cambridge Dictionary of Philosophy*, ed. Robert Audi (Cambridge: Cambridge University Press, 1995).

4. John Hick, *Interpretation of Religion* (London: Macmillan, 1989), 235–36.

5. Ibid., xvii. See also Robert McKim, *Religious Ambiguity and Religious Diversity* (Oxford: Oxford University Press, 2003). Philosopher Terence Penelhum writes, " "I am by training and practice a philosopher, who found himself, through a combination of institutional circumstances, in the midst of a department of scholars of religion: that is, a department that included Biblical scholars, Sanskritists, Hindu and Buddhist scholars, and Islamicists. This led to a change in the way in which many questions in the philosophy of religion presented themselves to me. I could no longer conscientiously ask those questions as though the religious tradition most familiar to me were the only one there is in the world. I always knew it was not, of course. We all know that. But I now found that I could no longer proceed as if I did not know it. My colleagues and my students would not let me." See Terence Penelhum, "The Religious Ambiguity of the World," University of Calgary Department of Religious Studies, http://www.ucalgary.ca/rels/files/rels/Penelhum.pdf.

6. John Hick, afterword to R. Douglas Geivett, *Evil and the Evidence for God* (Philadelphia: Temple University Press, 1993), 233.

7. Penelhum, "The Religious Ambiguity of the World."

8. Hick, afterword to Geivett, *Evil and the Evidence for God*, 230.

9. John Hick, "Copernican Revolution of Theology," in *God and the Universe of Faiths: Essays in the Philosophy of Religion* (London: Macmillan, 1973), 120–32.

10. For the definitive treatment of miracles from a philosophical and historical point of view, see Craig S. Keener. *Miracles: The Credibility of the New Testament Accounts* (Grand Rapids: Baker Academic, 2011).

11. John Hick, *A Christian Theology of Religions* (Louisville: Westminster John Knox, 1995), 50.

12. See Paul Copan, *Loving Wisdom: Christian Philosophy of Religion* (St. Louis: Chalice, 2007), ch. 10; Paul Copan, *"How Do You Know You're Not Wrong?"* (Grand Rapids: Baker, 2005), ch. 3.

13. Dalai Lama, *Kindness, Clarity and Insight* (New York: Snow Lion, 1984), 45.

14. Paul Williams, *The Unexpected Way: On Converting from Buddhism to Catholicism* (Edinburgh: T & T Clark, 2002), 27–30. Cf. Harold Netland, "Natural Theology and Religious Diversity," *Faith and Philosophy* 21 (October 2004): 503–18.

15. Alvin Plantinga, "Natural Theology," in *Companion to Metaphysics*, eds. Jaegwon Kim and Ernest Sosa (Oxford: Blackwell, 1995), 347.

16. For example, see Paul Copan, *Loving Wisdom: Christian Philosophy of Religion* (St. Louis: Chalice, 2007).

17. Paul Davies, "The Birth of the Cosmos," in *God, Cosmos, Nature and Creativity*, ed. Jill Gready (Edinburgh: Scottish Academic Press, 1995), 8–9.

18. Stephen Hawking and Roger Penrose, *The Nature of Space and Time* (Princeton, NJ: Princeton University Press, 1996), 20.

19. Cited in John D. Barrow, *The World within the World* (Oxford: Clarendon, 1988), 226.

20. John Barrow and Joseph Silk, *The Left Hand of Creation*, 2nd ed. (New York: Oxford University Press, 1993), 38, 209.

21. Ibid., 227, 26, 227, 38.

22. Anthony Kenny, *The Five Ways* (New York: Schocken, 1969), 66.

23. Kai Nielsen, *Reason and Practice* (New York: Harper & Row, 1971), 48.

24. John Hick, review of *The Clarity of God's Existence: The Ethics of Belief after the Enlightenment*, by Owen Anderson (unpublished).

25. Owen Anderson, "John Hick, Philosophy of Religion, and the Clarity of God's Existence." *Reviews in Religion and Theology* 11, no. 1 (2004): 15–20. Hick offers the oscillating universe model as a possible option, but this option is physically impossible. Hick, afterword to Geivett, *Evil and the Evidence for God*, 232. See Paul Copan and William Lane Craig, *Creation out of Nothing: A Biblical, Philosophical, and Scientific Exploration* (Grand Rapids: Baker Academic, 2004), 226–9.

26. Dallas Willard, "Language, Being, God, and the Three Stages of Theistic Evidence," in *Does God Exist? The Great Debate*, ed. J. P. Moreland and Kai Nielsen (Nashville: Thomas Nelson, 1990), 207.

27. Wilfred Cantwell Smith, *The Faith of Other Men* (New York: Mentor, 1965), 17.

28. S. N. Sadasivan, *A Social History of India* (New Delhi: APH, 2000), 202.

29. Peter van Inwagen, *Metaphysics* (Boulder, CO: Westview, 1993), 31.

30. *Physics* 8.3, 253a33.

31. Arthur Koestler, *The Lotus and the Robot* (New York: Macmillan, 1961), 273–74. (For the sake of clarity, I have laid out the conversation in a more readable format than Koestler's account.) Alternatively, in contrast to Shankara's *monism*, even if we take Ramanuja's pantheistic view, in which differences exist with "God" (*saguna Brahman*), we are left with the acute difficulty of regarding evil as part of the Ultimate Reality.

32. *Humanist Manifesto III*, accessed October 12, 2012, http://redbankhumanists.org/PDF/HumanistManifesto_III.pdf.

33. J. L. Mackie, *The Miracle of Theism* (Oxford: Clarendon, 1982), 115.

34. Ned Block, "Consciousness," in *A Companion to the Philosophy of Mind*, ed. Samuel Guttenplan (Malden, MA: Blackwell, 1994), 211.

35. John Searle, "The Mystery of Consciousness: Part II," *New York Review of Books*, November 16, 1995, 61.

36. Jaegwon Kim, "Mind, Problems of the Philosophy of," s.v. *The Oxford Companion to Philosophy*, ed. Ted Honderich (New York: Oxford University Press, 1995), 578.

37. Colin McGinn, *The Mysterious Flame* (New York: Basic, 1999), 14.

38. Colin McGinn, *The Problem of Consciousness* (Oxford: Basil Blackwell, 1990), 10–11.

39. David Papineau, *Philosophical Naturalism* (Oxford: Blackwell, 1993), 119.

40. Gary R. Habermas, "Resurrection Research from 1975 to the Present: What Are Critical Scholars Saying?," *Journal for the Study of the Historical Jesus* 3, no. 2 (2005): 135–53.

41. N. T. Wright, *The Resurrection of the Son of God* (Minneapolis: Fortress Press, 2003), 710.

42. James Dunn, *Jesus Remembered: Christianity in the Making*, vol. 1 (Grand Rapids: Eerdmans, 1983), 855.

43. E. P. Sanders, *The Historical Figure of Jesus* (New York: Penguin, 1993), 280.

44. John Hick, *A Christian Theology of World Religions* (Louisville: Westminster John Knox, 1995), 47–48.

45. Ibid., 49–50.

46. Gavin D'Costa, "The Impossibility of a Pluralist View of Religions," *Religious Studies* 32 (June 1996): 226.

47. Some observations here taken from Bradley N. Seeman, "Verifying Pluralism," *Philosophia Christi* n.s. 9, no. 1 (2007): 129–43; Owen Anderson, "The Presuppositions of Religious Pluralism and the Need for Natural Theology," *Sophia* 47 (2008): 201–22.

48. John Hick, "Theology and Verification," *Theology Today* 17 (1960): 12–31; John Hick, "On Grading Religions," *Religious Studies* 17 (1981): 451-67.

49. John Hick, "The Religious Meaning of Life," in *The Meaning of Life in the World Religions*, ed. Joseph Runzo and Nancy M. Martin (Oxford: Oneworld, 2000), 277.

50. Alvin Plantinga, *Warranted Christian Belief* (Oxford: Oxford University Press, 2000), 45.

51. Hick, *Interpretation of Religion*, xxi.

52. Brad Seeman, "What if the Elephant Speaks? Kant's *Critique of Judgment* and an *Übergang* Problem in John Hick's Philosophy of Religious Pluralism," *International Journal for Philosophy of Religion* 54 (2003): 157–74.

53. Plantinga, *Warranted Christian Belief*, 56.

54. Hick, "On Grading Religions," 451–67.

55. Hick, *Interpretation of Religion*, 351.

56. Paul Knitter, "Dialogue and Liberation," *Drew Gateway* 58 (1987): 1–53.

57. D'Costa, "Impossibility," 232.

58. John Hick, "Straightening the Record: Some Response to Critics," *Modern Theology* 6 (January 1990): 189.

59. John Hick, *Evil and the Love of God* (New York: Fontana, 1968).

60. Hick, "On Grading Religions."

61. John Hick, "Is There a Global Ethic?," 2007, available at *John Hick: The Official Website*, http://www.johnhick.org.uk/article17.html, accessed March 12, 2009. Hick elsewhere rejects such naturalistic accounts of morality. For example, see John Hick, *Arguments for the Existence of God* (London: Macmillan, 1970), 63.

62. John Hick, "Is Christianity the Only True Religion, or One among Others?," available at *John Hick: The Official Website*, http://www.johnhick.org.uk/article2.html, accessed March 12, 2009.

63. See Hick, "Is There a Global Ethic?"

64. For more discussion of these themes, see Owen Anderson, "The Presuppositions of Religious Pluralism and the Need for Natural Theology," *Sophia* 47 (2008): 201–22.

65. Peter Donovan, "The Intolerance of Religious Pluralism," *Religious Studies* 29 (1993): 218.

66. Alister McGrath, "The Challenge of Pluralism for the Contemporary Church," *Journal for the Evangelical Theological Society* 35 (September 1992): 371–72.

67. John Hick, ed., *The Myth of God Incarnate* (London: SCM, 1977), ix.

68. John Hick, *God Has Many Names* (Philadelphia: Westminster, 1982), 58.

69. John Hick, "What Does the Bible Really Say?" Available at *John Hick: The Official Website*, http://www.johnhick.org.uk/article13.html, accessed March 12, 2009.

70. Hick, *God Has Many Names*, 59.

71. Furthermore, doctrine really mattered to the founders of world religions. The Buddha rejected the key Hindu doctrine of atman (the enduring soul) in favor of its impermanence (*anatman*). Hebrew prophets rejected polytheistic idol worship, pointing Israel back to the Mosaic covenant. Jesus announced that God's kingdom had come and that he was central to God's program on earth. Muhammad preached monotheism and denounced polytheism. These doctrines aren't superficial trappings. Their founders believed that salvation literally depended upon

embracing these doctrines. Harold Netland, *Dissonant Voices: Religious Pluralism and the Question of Truth* (Vancouver: Regent College, 1999), 153. Yet Hick tells us these are ultimately mythological—not literally true. So whom should we believe—Hick or these religious leaders—about whether doctrine matters? See John Hick, *Problems of Religious Pluralism* (New York: St. Martin's, 1985), 43, 96.

72. Hick, "A Pluralist View," in *More Than One Way? Four Views on Salvation in a Pluralistic World*, eds. R. Douglas Geivett and W. Gary Phillips (Grand Rapids: Zondervan, 1995), 53.

73. C. F. D. Moule, *The Origin of Christology* (Cambridge: University Press, 1977), 11–22.

74. Timothy C. Tennent, *Christianity at the Religious Roundtable* (Grand Rapids: Baker, 2002), 240.

75. Plantinga, *Warranted Christian Belief*, 62.

76. Keith Ward, "Truth and the Diversity of Religions," in *The Philosophical Challenge of Religious Diversity*, eds. Philip L. Quinn and Kevin Meeker (Oxford: Oxford University Press, 1999), 124.

77. Paul Knitter, "Five Theses Regarding the Uniqueness of Christ," in *The Uniqueness of Christ: A Dialogue with Paul Knitter*, ed. Leonard Switler and Paul Mojzes (Maryknoll, NY: Orbis, 1997), 10. Knitter rejects that Jesus is "a total container of the divine" (73); the orthodox Christians would agree here: God is triune. So while Jesus is (fully) God, God is not Jesus but also consists in Father and Spirit. See also Knitter's *One Earth Many Religions* (Maryknoll, NY: Orbis, 1995).

78. See part IV in Paul Copan, *"True for You, but Not for Me,"* 2nd ed. (Minneapolis: Bethany House, 2009).

79. George Mavrodes, "The Gods above the Gods: Can the High Gods Survive?," in *Reasoned Faith*, ed. Eleonore Stump (Ithaca: Cornell University Press, 1993), 202.

80. Gavin D'Costa, *The Meeting of Religions and the Trinity* (Maryknoll, NY: Orbis, 2000), 46.

81. Larry W. Hurtado, *Lord Jesus Christ: Devotion to Jesus in Earliest Christianity* (Grand Rapids: Eerdmans, 2003), 135.

82. Ibid.

83. Martin Hengel, *Between Jesus and Paul* (London: SCM, 1983), 39–40.

84. Hick, "On Grading Religions," 454.

85. Correspondence from John Hick cited in Alvin Plantinga, "Ad Hick," *Faith and Philosophy* 14 (July 1997): 295. The critique of Hick in this paragraph is taken from Plantinga's essay, "Pluralism: A Defense of Religious Exclusivism" in *The Philosophical Challenge of Religious Diversity*, eds. Philip L. Quinn and Kevin Meeker (Oxford: Oxford University Press, 1999).

86. Plantinga, "Pluralism," 183–84.

87. The "myth become fact" theme is prominent in the writings of G. K. Chesterton, J. R. R. Tolkein, and C. S. Lewis. For an exploration of this point, see Gerald R. McDermott, *Can Evangelicals Learn from World Religions?* (Downers Grove, IL: InterVarsity, 2000); and idem, *God's Rivals: Why Has God Allowed Different Religions?* (Downers Grove, IL: InterVarsity, 2007).

88. C. S. Lewis, "Is Theology Poetry?," in *The Weight of Glory and Other Addresses* (New York: Macmillan, 1965), 140.

89. Thanks to Owen Anderson for his comments on an earlier draft of this paper.

8

Has Normative Religious Pluralism a Rationale?

Keith E. Yandell

In what follows, I assume that there actually are religions.[1] What we call religions are not simply scholarly artifacts. This assumption is shared by religious pluralism, both descriptive and normative. If there are not, religious pluralism must be at least radically recast. I am not assuming that there is an essence of religion, but merely that there are self-identifying communities that center at least part of their lives around institutions, rites, rituals, and ceremonies that are shaped in terms of beliefs about a certain sort of matter that I will describe in terms of diagnosis and cure. A religion, I suggest, offers a diagnosis of some deep spiritual disease that plagues us all and proposes a cure for that disease. Religions can be differentiated by reference to what pairing of disease and cure their adherents embrace. The diagnoses and cures assume, or are offered from the perspective of, a set of metaphysical, epistemological, and ethical claims—with *ethical* being broadly construed as "concerning values." Thus, each religion, at least implicitly, accepts some view in metaphysics, epistemology, and ethics.[2] These claims are either true or false, and typically adherents of a religion suppose that those accepted as normative in their religion are true. While there have been challenges to this general account of things, I believe that—with sufficient fine-turning that cannot be done here—this account is true.

A religion, we have suggested, gives a diagnosis of a deep spiritual disease that plagues us all and proposes a cure for it. Devotees of a particular religion are those who accept that diagnosis and seek that cure, and that are serious about doing so. For any religion R, there will be people who participate in R's institutions, rite(s), practices, and ceremonies who do so from social, familial, political, cultural, or economic reasons or simply from habit. These are not devotees, but they belong to *R*dom (e.g., Christendom), *R*ism (e.g., Hinduism, Buddhism, or Jainism), or the like. Our focus will be on that to which the devotees are devoted—that to which the adherents adhere. Since the diagnoses and cures differ, and the status of something as cure depends on its providing healing from the disease, religions differ in ways that are significant to their adherents.[3] Conversion to another religion, or abandoning a religion for some secularism, is a major change. It is like switching to a different treatment for a different illness or stopping going to doctors altogether when one's major prior focus had been on the success of the treatment—only more so.

There are theories of meaning and justification on which what seem, and purport to be, religious claims, actually express nothing either true or false. These, I take it, are utter failures.[4] The view that all of our concepts are abstracted from sensory experience and can only be applied to the sort of things that were experienced in the process of our abstracting them cannot even explain what the view is intended to be—namely, a theory of meaning. This is so for Hume's less formal and logical positivism's more formal attempts. Thus, again, I take it that there really are religious views of the world, and—like any other sort—they are either true of false. Strictly speaking, the propositions that make up such views are either true or false, and in any religion, there may be some of each.

That said, my concern is with normative religious pluralism, which rides piggyback on descriptive religious pluralism. Descriptive religious pluralism simply reports that the different world religions teach different, and logically incompatible, things; their teachings are either logically contradictory or logically contrary to other teachings. Normative religious pluralism proscribes what we are to do with the facts that its distinct descriptive cousin reports. I take it that no one without a large ax to grind will deny the truth of descriptive religious pluralism. For the remainder of this essay, by *pluralism* I mean normative religious pluralism.

THE CONTROVERSIAL CONTENT OF NORMATIVE RELIGIOUS PLURALISM

Since it seems often to be supposed that pluralism is simply a reaction to the comparatively recent detailed knowledge of other religions we now possess, it seems to me proper to remember some other features of pluralism's conceptual environment. Pluralism arose in a context in which controversy concerning the reliability of historical reports regarding what Jesus did and said plays its roles. The idea of the worship of Jesus taking considerable time to develop, and being analyzable in the same manner as other slow deifications, aids and abets pluralism. The standard line that Paul invented Christianity while Jesus was a simple moral teacher with no pretensions to deity, atonement, or resurrection, and that Christian doctrine was read back into the history of the early church, helps pluralism along. These issues and the views taken on them are highly relevant to whatever inroads pluralism has made in Christian circles. When the ground has been softened by radical rain, the seeds of normative religious pluralism can be planted with a greater chance to grow. Religious pluralism arises from, and lives on in, the context of various controversial claims to which it has no distinctive contribution to make, but on which it relies. The degree to which such varied claims are controversial is properly measured, not by checking to see how much they are controverted in the secular academy, including many seminaries, but by the strength of the arguments actually offered on their behalf. It seems to me that, like physicalism, religious pluralism more floats on the sea of various sentiments than it rests on the firm basis of solid argument.

Limiting myself to the topics to which my field has most relevance, the arguments that the doctrines of the incarnation and Trinity are logically inconsistent are weak and can be answered.[5] Given naturalism, resurrections typically are nonstarters, but they are not on a theistic view of things. The doctrine of the atonement, in my view at least, is the most complex of the tightly knit theological claims of which it is an essential member. But there, too, the criticisms, when they are of more substance than the sorry quip about child abuse, are nothing like decisive. Recent works by Bauckham, Wright, Hurtado, Dunn, Witherington, and many others challenge academic orthodoxy on the major bases of historical skepticism and the lateness of high Christology.[6] These issues are highly relevant to the overall plausibility of pluralism, and if they are false, the loss is a loss for pluralism, not its critics.

This is not the place to engage firsthand in these controversies. I can only point out their relevance to whether or not pluralism has a justifying rationale. Our concern will be with pluralism directly, not with its conceptual background.

Definitions and Distinctions

Something at least much like the following is true: the view that, in philosophy, one must define all of one's terms and prove all of one's points is as sophomoric as it is self-defeating. When examined, the definition idea is that, in order to know what term A means, I must define A by using term B, and I must define B by using C, and then I must go on forever, unless my definition is circular. The proof idea is that, in order to prove that *P*, I must derive it from *P1*, and derive *P1* from *P2*, and so on forever, unless my proof is circular. But if my definition or proof is circular and I am to know the meaning of any term or the truth of any proposition, I must be able to start somewhere or other in the circle with some term whose meaning I know or some proposition whose truth is available to me.

Nonetheless, in a discussion, it is good that, if possible, the key terms be clearly defined, and this is possible regarding pluralism. There is a relatively uncontroversial brand that I accept. As we have noted, descriptive religious pluralism is the view that different religions teach different things. Since their teaching different things is an important part of what makes religions different, this is hardly surprising. I take descriptive religious pluralism to be true, and anyone who bothers to look at the relevant data can see it to be so. It, as they say, simply states a fact. But the fact raises two questions. First, does any, do some, or do all of the religions lead to salvation or enlightenment? This is the religious question. Second, is any of these religious views, taken literally as its proponents typically take it, true (or closer to true than other religious views)? Indeed, are there any truths in the religions at all, or are they simply collocations of falsehoods, cognitive disasters along the road to a glorious secularism? The second question I take to be the central philosophical question concerning religion, leading to such further questions as "How can you tell whether a religious claim is true?" and so on. The questions are distinct, but it seems clear that, insofar as pluralists enter the lists regarding the second question, they do so with a specific (and affirmative)[7] answer to the first question in mind, so long as "salvation" and "enlightenment" are understood as meaning something like "leads to increase in the sort of moral behavior approved by Pluralists"—that is, given a particular at least quasi-secularist reduction.

THE ELEMENTS OF NORMATIVE RELIGIOUS PLURALISM

While making no claim to cover all of the relevant ground,[8] it seems right that pluralism contains at least these elements. There is the *epistemic parity thesis*—world religions are approximately even regarding relevant supporting evidential and argumentative support. There is a *"No one is wrong" rule*. There is also a *criterion for dialogical engagement*—a condition that participants in such high occasions as meetings for religious dialogue must meet, namely accepting the rule just specified.

Connected closely with these, there is the interpretive principle: Never interpret doctrinal sentences literally. This obviously raises the question as to what to do with these sentences, and this topic is worth immediate pursuit. Arguments in favor of pluralism are conspicuous by their absence. The reason in John Hick's case is that we are supposedly simply offered a hypothesis to the effect that the "Real" is the ground of the experiences central to all the world religions. But when one asks what the hypothesis amounts to, we find there is no hypothesis. The reason is that it is utterly against Hick's rules to ascribe to this supposed Real any property in virtue of which it might fill this grounding or causing role. Were there to be some such property ascribed, then one religion or another might be able far better to accommodate within its worldview a being having that property, and of course we can't have that. Argument is replaced by a vacuous hypothesis. Another fatal flaw looms.

Religion is said to be all about turning from being self-centered to being, as the phrase goes, reality-centered. The phrase *reality-centered* is loaded with unadmitted danger for the pluralist. Someone might ask what "reality" in reality-centered means—what features does this alleged reality possess? Why would anyone want to be centered on it?

Symbolic logic requires the notion of a variable. In the sentence frame "Every X is red," X is a variable, and when it is replaced by some appropriate specific word, a statement results. The result is true or false. "Stoplights are red" is true, and "Elephants are red" is false. "Being reality-centered" is a variable. To become reality-centered is to be "X-centered," and of course there is no such thing as being X-centered. So the variable X needs to be replaced by some actual description, proposed as true of reality. But no such account of reality can be given, consistent with Hick's pluralism. The supposed "Real" cannot be the subject of any nonformal predicate, and whatever exactly "nonformal" means here, it does not include any properties the possession of which would make their owner worthy of being the center around which anything was placed. The removal of all religious particularity is shown to be illusory, or else becoming "centered on the Real" or "reality-centered" is as vacuous as "X-centered." It sounds more impressive but means no more.

The best that can be made of all this seems to be a weak replacement. "Being reality-centered" turns out to be vacuous. The obvious replacement for "going from being self-centered to being reality-centered" (nothing actually seems to justify the capital R for "reality") is "going from being self-centered to not being self-centered." But then a positive replacement is needed, and there is no single replacement to be found.

A common answer to such objections is to offer an old but still radical way of treating doctrinal claims. It is to propose that such claims are given either translation into, or replacement by, moral sentences, declarative or imperative—something along the lines of Paul Knitter's "action language" (see below). The notion of action language is used to assert the old, oft-refuted claim that religion reduces to morality—more carefully, that what for all the world seem to be doctrinal claims reduce to moral principles and/or imperatives. There may be some qualifying clause, such as "mainly" or "are best understood as" or "most significantly," but they serve no more purpose than adding a blue light on top of a Chevy and claiming that this makes it a Cadillac: they are window dressing that will be appealed to only if, in the light of criticism, it is said that reduction is not *really* being claimed. The issue is not whether the doctrinal claims have moral entailments for which they actually provide some sound basis. If the doctrinal claims really just *are* moral claims, there is no possibility of their providing such a basis. Here is a sample reduction attempt.

> Recognition of the primacy of orthopraxis over orthodoxy can also be used pastorally to enable Christian believers to understand the nature of New Testament language and what it means to be faithful to this language. . . . The christological language and titles of the New Testament had as their primary purpose not to offer definitive, ontological statements about the person or work of Jesus but to enable men and women to feel the power of Jesus' vision. . . . It would be more accurate and pastorally effective, I think, to call the New Testament claims about Jesus as "action language."[9]

So far as I can see, from the perspective of traditional Christianity and put in plain English, this would come out as something like this:

> I prefer to read the claims that the New Testament makes concerning God, Jesus Christ, the forgiveness of sins, the resurrection, and the like as meaning moral claims with which I feel comfortable. At most, they are ways of repeating moral principles and/or imperatives that one finds stated as such in the same document, and at worst, they are a sadly misleading shell placed around the moral kernel of the text. And I will preach this as asserting the Christian message, thereby replacing the Gospel by moral assertion and exhortation.

The apostles did not preach "the vision of Jesus." They preached "Jesus, and Him crucified" (1 Corinthians 2:2 NIV); they preached that Christ died for our sins, according to the Scriptures, was buried, and rose again the third day. The sermons in Acts are no more about "the vision of Jesus" than was the preaching of Paul. J. Gresham Machen, now sadly neglected, was right to call this "liberal Christianity," as it was called in his time, a new religion. This is one way in which the context of pluralism, noted earlier, is relevant to its content. It can claim to be dealing with Christianity only given that a variety of controversial views are accepted as what constituted the early Christian message, or provides its "real meaning." Traditional Christians will see this "interpretation" as a thick and warping filter. Pluralism takes the small-*o* orthodoxy shared by the typical varieties of historical Christianity to be false, whether or not orthodoxy is guilty of having grossly misunderstood its own texts. The relevance of the conceptual context of pluralism here becomes patently obvious.[10]

As a philosophical or theological proposal, the reduction of Christian doctrine to moral claim is perhaps classically represented and best exemplified by a proposal made in the heyday of logical positivism that went something to this effect: the doctrine that God created the world really means simply that every material thing can be used for some human purpose. Perhaps the best response to this sort of thing is to say that the person who proposes it really means to say that the possible good uses of material things are among the good things that come from God's hands. Sometimes two wrong turns put you back on the right track.

OTHER PLURALISM ELEMENTS EXAMINED

In addition to the just-discussed interpretive principle, "Never interpret doctrinal sentences literally," there remain the epistemic parity thesis (roughly equal evidential and argumentative support for every approved religion – curiously the question of whether there is epistemic parity relative to evidence and arguments against various religions), the "No one is wrong" rule, and a criterion for dialogical engagement. These other elements merit discussion. Their discussion endeavors to answer the query: has Religious Pluralism, defined in terms of a perspective that includes the above elements, a justifying rationale? Are we offered any good reason to think that pluralism, so defined, gives the proper reaction to de facto religious diversity?

EPISTEMIC PARITY THESIS

Having discussed the notion of becoming "reality-centered," we turn to the epistemic parity thesis. Part of what lies behind it seems to be the idea that every religion contains some truth. What does *contains* mean? Perhaps it means "entails," where "P entails Q" is defined as follows: where P and Q are propositions (items true or false), P entails Q if and only if it is logically impossible that P be true and Q be false. Thus, that there are eight books on the shelf entails that there are at least seven. On this account, consider any religious doctrine R. The proposition R entails all necessary truths, so R contains lots of truths. Being true of each proposition that expresses a religious doctrine, and indeed every proposition, this gives none an advantage over any other. Further, the contents of the necessary truths will not themselves provide any diagnosis or cure. The next thing to note is that falsehoods can entail truths. The false premises "Every elephant is green" and "Everything green thing is a mammal" entail "Every elephant is a mammal"; the premises are false, but the conclusion is true. So a religion can contain nothing but vacuous truths and otherwise only falsehoods among its doctrines, and —in the entailment sense of *contains*—contain lots of truths. This sense of *contains* does not capture, in any interesting way, the idea that a religious tradition may contain truths. The thing to do seems to be to offer some more restricted sense of *contains*.

Something closer, perhaps, to what is wanted can be derived in this fashion. Leave aside necessary truths that lack distinctly religious content. Consider some particular religion R, and let the set of its doctrines be RS. Then consider the diagnosis it gives (RD) and the cure it offers (RC). Then consider this set of propositions: Proposition P is a member of the proposed relevant set RS of truths that R contains if and only if the falsehood of P entails the incorrectness of RD or the inefficacy of RC. In English, the doctrinally relevant set RS of a religion is simply the set of propositions that must be true if religion R's diagnosis is correct and its cure is efficacious. Even if, however, this gives us a way of identifying the propositions of most interest to a given religion, it places us no further ahead concerning the idea that all religions contain some truth.

Perhaps one can identify some propositions that are included in the doctrinally relevant set of at least many religions, thus finding some propositional common ground. To be more concrete, I suppose that at least many religions contain such claims as "Life in this world is not satisfactory," "A person's life does not consist in the abundance of possessions she owns," "People have some deep spiritual problem," "Physicalism is false," "Physical death is not the end of one's existence," and the like. If these are common ground then we can identify some general religious claims whose falsehood will falsify the relevant religions and whose truth will substantiate a part of various religions. But this does not, by itself, do anything to give belief in any or all of these claims salvific or enlightenment power. Perhaps the idea that all religions contain some truth is not so religiously important after all.

It is easy to see how one might reason as follows:

> God loves everyone and is just.
>> Thus, God gives everyone a chance to be saved.
>> The chance to be saved will be given through a religious tradition.
>> So religious traditions, diverse though they are, are salvific.
> But then the view that religious traditions are salvific is based on religious monotheism being true.

There are various problems with this line of argument, and pluralism inherits them. One that seems to be seldom mentioned is expressed by this simple question: Why suppose that salvific opportunity always, or only, comes via religion? Perhaps a sense of power, majesty, and order in nature, and a resultant belief in an intelligence that this power, majesty, and order expresses, elicits a search for God that does not have a route within a religion. Perhaps a moral law "written on the heart," to use St. Paul's phrase, provides the beginning of a search for its writer without a religion being involved. Perhaps these can work together. In none of these cases would a religion play its role. Further, none of these cases fit within a pluralist model; in each case, properties are ascribed to the possessor of power and the giver of the moral law, and there being such a person as the possessor and giver is no common ground among religions.

In any case, we return to the epistemic parity thesis,[11] which tells us the following: Take each of the religions said to be in parity—say, $R1$, $R2$, and $R3$. One source of the claim is that, so far as we can tell, the following is true: take any two religions from among the group of which the thesis is said to be true—say, $R1$ and $R2$. The evidence and arguments in favor of $R1$ and the evidence and arguments in favor of $R2$ are equally strong, the arguments against $R1$ and the arguments against $R2$ are equally strong, the evidence in favor of $R1$ is just as strong as the evidence in favor of $R2$, and the evidence against $R1$ is just as strong as the evidence against $R2$. It seems to me incredibly unlikely that this be true. For example, the monotheistic Vedanta arguments against Advaita Vedanta views and some of the critiques given by some Buddhist traditions against the views of other Buddhist traditions are very powerful. Asserting the epistemic parity thesis smacks much more, to me at least, of failure of nerve than it does of a sober, justified conclusion from the data. It seems to be based on some such thought as this: apparently equally intelligent, rational, and relevantly informed people hold to quite different religious perspectives, and were there a clear lack of epistemic parity they would recognize this, and respond by embracing (or continuing in) the winner in the epistemic race. Another, probably more influential, source is the idea that religion is separated from reason, argument, and evidence by an impassible gulf, and the epistemic tie comes from religions being stuck at zero. Either of these is a strong epistemological claim. The former strikes me as impressionistic, and, while the story is complex, I think it is false. The same goes for the second; but both claims are controversial and arguing for them would take us far afield. Suffice it to say that the assumptions are far from being clearly true, and merit close examination.

"NO ONE IS WRONG" RULE AND CRITERION FOR DIALOGICAL ENGAGEMENT

The assertion that no one ever is wrong (in his or her religious beliefs) is flagrantly contradictory, given the logical relations that descriptive religious pluralism correctly reports, and that seems to be enough said about it unless one follows the non-literal reading rule. The third element is intended to speak to this issue. If we take every religion's diagnosis and cure and its accompanying *RS* nonliterally, in the manner that pluralism requires, then there is no such thing as being wrong—as having false religious belief. Then no one can be wrong, just as no one can be right; the supposed benefit of making error impossible comes at the price of never being right. How this is supposed to be, as is often claimed, a sign of great respect to the religions — or is even compatible with such respect—has always escaped me. Further, Religious Pluralism seems consistent with moral principles being true, and in spite of its optimism about religions embracing the same morality, they do not (see below).

What we offered as compensation for the losses described is a supposed redefinition of truth: a religious metaphor (or whatever modality of being nonliteral is involved) is true if and only if participating in what is left of the relevant religious lifestyle moves one toward greater conformity to the moral beliefs and practices of which the pluralist approves—the ones that she favors. The task of actually assessing competing moral principles, rules, practices, or the like— far as I know—is not within the pluralist horizon. Perhaps a reason for this is that, if such appraisal is possible in ethics, it raises the question of why the same thing cannot be done in philosophy of religion. In fact, there exists a variety of efforts at assessment in both ethics and philosophy of religion, whereas Pluralism assumes its favorite ethic and asserts epistemic parity. The Pluralist seems to be very well stocked with views as to what is right and wrong, and what it rationally possible regarding rational assessment of religions. The Pluralist, like its competitors, requires careful defense. It is also an interesting question as to whether, even assuming epistemic parity among however many religions, accepting any of those religions (which would be incompatible with embracing Pluralism) versus accepting Religious Pluralism is not another case of epistemic parity. In this case, there is no evidence that favors Religious Pluralism over the religious traditions that people have actually embraced. Then why take the pluralist road?

What seems to be the proffered justification of this is the dubious assumption that all religions share the same morality. There is a level of conduct, hard to describe but easier to recognize, required for survival—perhaps not killing or maiming one another, working together to some degree, manifesting some degree of trust, and avoiding chronic theft, or at least something like this list. Acting in these ways is a condition of there continuing to be a community, and we can tell that typically communities share these features, since they would not be around if they did not. That religions share such values is hardly surprising or especially significant for present purposes . If it is true that the world religions share a common morality, this fact will be reflected in the motives and intentions from which it is regarded right to act. Further, to the degree that religious values are taken to be the most important values, moral values will tend to be influenced and constrained by them. The view that all religions—or at least all the nice ones—share a common morality seems to me to be false. It seems to be held more out of necessity if assessment of moral perspectives is to be avoided than from careful analysis of actual religious moralities.

We can look at only one sample case. Comparing the moral theory and practice of one religious tradition with that of another is a complex affair. Nonetheless, something should be said about some deep differences between one type of religious tradition and another type. One relevant example concerns the so-called Vedantic qualified nondualism a and a widely shared Buddhist no-self doctrine.

Two passages from the Buddhist tradition and two from the Hindu may be helpful, particularly if they are properly paired. The first pair of passages, one Buddhist and one Hindu, are as follows, starting with the Buddhist:

> Misery only doth exist, none miserable
> No doer there is; naught but the deed is found
> Nirvana is, but not the man who seeks it.
> The Path exists, but not the traveler.[12]

Then the Hindu:

> [Consciousness is not unowned], as appears from ordinary judgments such as "I understand this matter," "I am conscious of this piece of cloth".[13]

Misery exists, but no one is miserable. There are actions but no agents. What can this mean? The idea behind the passage is the Buddhist no-self doctrine. For simplicity, we will put the doctrine in terms of Buddhist idealism. What we call a person is, at a time, only a causally related collection of conscious states—the so-called person is said to be composed of, to consist in, unowned conscious states—states that are no one's states. Over time, a person is a sequence of these collections. For what seems to be the majority view, namely Buddhist reductionism, the collections are nothing over and above the states that compose them, and the sequences are nothing over and above the collections. On this view, the locus of ultimate value cannot be found in subjects of conscious states; there aren't any such things. This view is cut from a metaphysical cloth at the Utilitarian Tailor Factory. The technical term for this view in contemporary philosophy is perdurantism. It, or something much like it, was held by David Hume in his *Treatise Concerning Human Nature* and assumed in John Stuart Mill's *Utilitarianism*. It is explicitly expressed by Mill in his 1865 *Examination of Sir William Hamilton's Philosophy*,[14] where he candidly admitted that his view entails "accepting the paradox that something which *ex hypothesi* is but a series of feelings can be aware of itself as a series." In this comment, I suggest, Mill is both too harsh and too kind to on view. The supposed sequence, on his view, contains more than feelings; it contains conscious states that have propositional and volitional, as well as affective, content. Thus, his view is richer than his description of it. But a sequence that is "aware of itself" is more than simply the conscious states that allegedly entirely compose it. At the very least, it is composed of second-order states that are aware of first-order states, and if a second-order state actually manages to observe the sequence, it lasts throughout the sequence rather than being momentary. A fundamental motivation of this sort of theory, as is strongly emphasized in its Buddhist context, is to avoid commitment to anything enduring, anything that lasts over times, and any subject of experience. Yet Mill seems to introduce both. This is more than just a paradox; it gives away the theory.

Ramanuja asserts that consciousness is not unowned. Conscious states cannot exist on their own. This view, strongly asserted by Jainism, by Descartes in his *Meditations on First Philosophy*, and by Locke in different ways in books 2 and 4 of the *Essay Concerning Human Understanding*, in contemporary philosophy is called endurantism. Here, the locus of intrinsic value can be (and typically is) found in enduring persons, as in virtue ethics and ethics grounded in respect. In short, much of Buddhist metaphysics pairs conceptually with perdurantism, and much of Hindu metaphysics conceptually pairs with virtue and respect-based ethics. One would have to be unaware of much of contemporary ethics in order to suppose that it would not be highly controversial to think there are no significant differences, theoretical and practical, between these ethical perspectives.

The second pair of passages are these (staying with the line setting in the noted text):

> As many beings as there are in the universe of beings, comprehended
> under the term beings . . . all these I must lead to Nirvana, into that
> Realm of Nirvana which leaves nothing behind. And yet, although
> innumerable beings have thus been led to Nirvana, in fact no being
> at all has been led to Nirvana. And why? If in a Bodhisattva the
> notion of a being should take place, he could not be called a Bodhi-being.
> And why? He is not to be called a Bodhi-being, in whom the notion of a self or of a being should take place, or the notion of a living soul or a person.[15]

Again, from Ramajuna:

> To maintain that the consciousness of the 'I' does not persist in the state of final release is again altogether inappropriate. It, in fact, amounts to the doctrine—only expressed in somewhat different words—that final release is the annihilation of the self . . . moreover, a man who, suffering pain, mental or of some other kind . . . puts himself in relation to pain—'I am suffering pain'—naturally begins to reflect how he may once for all free himself from all these manifold afflictions and enjoy a state of untroubled ease; the desire of final release thus having arisen in him he at once sets to work to accomplish it. No sensible person exerts himself under the influence

of the idea that when he himself has perished there will remain some entity called 'pure light'.

These ultimate religious values differ deeply. What the quoted Buddhist perspective prizes, the quoted Hindu perspective abhors, and conversely. Deep difference concerning what is ultimately valuable ramifies broadly and deeply. Obviously, we cannot develop this here. But the idea that all religions share the same morality, once one looks with care at their metaphysical and corresponding ethical divergence, quickly loses is plausibility. This is especially so when one turns from overt behavior to intentions, motives, and goals.

It is time to turn again to the question as to whether Religious Pluralism has a justifying rationale. Without any claim to have demonstrated that these alternatives are exhaustive, four sorts of rationales come to mind: metaphysical, epistemological, moral, and practical. The policy of taking the diagnoses and cures, and their RS settings, as nonliteral stops the metaphysical alternative cold. The epistemic parity thesis raises an interesting question that we can here put in different terms than those used above. Pluralism has its own notion of what our deep spiritual problem is and how it may be cured. Religion can foster violence—though the centrality of this claim to pluralism would be more persuasive if some effort were made to show that it is religions rather than motivations of an economic, social, political, or cultural nature, or sheer lust for power, and the like, that lead to the evils ascribed to religion. Then there are the manifold uses of religion for justifying violence that violate the very tenets to which the religion is committed. Given the removal of religious doctrines actually viewed as true in a straightforward sense, these doctrines cannot provide any barrier to immoral behavior. The situation is vastly more complex than the "New Atheists" make it and the religious pluralists need it to be, as to whether religions are justifiably accused of causing violence as opposed to religions having prevented violence or been misinterpreted and misused to justify it. The 'it is morally better to buy into Religious Pluralism that to accept one of the world religions or to be a secularist' argument must reckon with the complexities of historical causes of violence and the effect of removing religious sanctions against violence, as well as questions as to the degree in which a world of Religious Pluralists would be nicer, by their own standards, than the present world. I see little reason to think it would, and less chance that Religious Pluralism become widely accepted.

Regarding pragmatic rationale, we should note again that pluralism has its own diagnosis and cure to offer. The problem is suffering and injustice done in the name, or under the auspices, of religion, and its cure is to accept a pluralist account of religion. It is a sort of highly secularized religion on its own. But why should we accept the pluralist account of our disease and cure as fortunately having escaped the epistemic parity that allegedly plagues first-order religions? Why not work within one's own religious tradition, taking advantage of its antiviolent resources, while taking the doctrines of one's religion to be true? And why suppose the pluralist diagnosis and cure, which looks very much like atheist humanism plus incense, gives a deep account of either diagnosis or cure to be adequate to the world as we encounter it?

I want to emphasize the importance of the epistemic parity thesis and Religious Pluralism itself. It is worth emphasizing that defending the set of moral values to which the pluralists appeal, as opposed to alternatives embraced by equally intelligent and astute ethicists, does not seem to be part of the pluralist program. That would require doing careful moral philosophy. Again, if rational assessment is possible in moral philosophy, why be sure that it cannot be in philosophy of religion. If rational assessment is not possible in moral philosophy, why are we not in a situation of epistemic parity between ethical theories, including the ones furthest from Pluralist tastes? .

Finally, what about a practical rationale? It seems to me very unlikely indeed that anything like the majority of religious believers ever adopt the pluralist perspective or program.

Nor is it clear that, minus all the literal basis of religious barriers to violence that such a conversion would include, things would be better regarding violence than they are now.

This is relevant to the final element of pluralism: the criterion for dialogical engagement. The core idea here is that those who engage in pluralist dialogue must be prepared to find that the others in the dialogue may in fact be correct about what our disease is and what serves as the cure. They must actually be prepared to convert or at least admit that converting would be as rational, justified, and proper a thing to do as not to convert. (Does this apply to the Religious Pluralist as well—that she must be prepared to reject her pluralism and join one of the religious traditions that the descriptive religious pluralist notes are logically incompatible?) This just isn't going to happen. If we are going to have religious people working together to promote justice and reduce suffering, we will need people who know perfectly well that they disagree about the deepest things in life, do not intend to change their views, and nonetheless respect each other enough to cooperate—all without becoming pluralists. It this can be based on religious or moral agreement about some things, so much the better, but Religious Pluralism would rob each religion of what is distinctive of it, and thus no common metaphysical view or literally understood religious doctrine could serve as even potential common ground.

My conclusion is that religious pluralism lacks a justifying rationale. This is not a comment on the motives or intentions of anyone. Appeal to motives or intentions for being a religious pluralist will neither refute nor justify it. My claim is that the elements of pluralism are themselves unjustified and indeed are mistaken. They form an unhappy system that requires their truth and thus is debilitated by their falsehood.

Notes

1. At various points in this essay, I make assumptions that I cannot defend here but which I have argued for elsewhere. I hope I may refer to those places as I argue from these assumptions here.

2. This perspective on religion is articulated and defended in Keith E. Yandell, *Philosophy of Religion: A Contemporary Introduction* (London: Routledge, 1999).

3. See Keith E. Yandell, "On the Alleged Unity of All Religions," *Christian Scholars Review* 6, nos. 2–3 (1976): 140–55.

4. This claim is defended in Keith Yandell, "David Hume on Meaning, Verification, and Natural Theology," in *In Defense of Natural Theology*, ed. James Sennett and Douglas Groothuis (Downers Grove, IL: InterVarsity, 2005).

5. See Keith E. Yandell, "The Most Brutal and Inconsistent Error in Counting? The Doctrine of the Trinity," *Religious Studies* 30 (1994): 201–217; idem, "A Gross and Palpable Contradiction? Incarnation and Consistency," *Sophia* 33, no. 3 (1994): 30–45; idem, "Ontological Arguments, Metaphysical Identity, and the Trinity," *Philosophia Christi* 1, no. 1 (1999): 83–101; idem, "How Many Times Does Three Go into One?" in Philosophical and Theological Essays on the Trinity, ed. Michael Rea and Thomas McCall (Oxford: Oxford University Press, 2009), 151–70.

6. A short list of relevant writings follows: Richard Bauckham, *Jesus and the Eyewitnesses* (Grand Rapids: Eerdmans, 2008); Larry Hurtado, *Lord Jesus Christ* (Grand Rapids: Eerdmans, 2005); N. T. Wright, *The New Testament and the People of God* (Minneapolis: Fortress Press, 1992); idem, *Jesus and the Victory of God* (Minneapolis: Fortress Press, 1997); Ben Witherington III, *The Jesus Quest* (Downers Grove: InterVarsity, 1997); James D. G. Dunn, *The Evidence for Jesus* (Philadelphia: Westminster, 1985). These provide a beginning to reflection on the issues relevant to the context of religious pluralism and lead to further sources.

7. Perhaps with some nonfavored exceptions.

8. For exposition, discussion, and defense, see Keith E. Yandell, "Some Varieties of Religious Pluralism," in *Inter-Religious Models and Criteria*, ed. James Kellenberger, 187–211 (New York: St. Martin's, 1993); idem, "Revisiting Religious Pluralism," *Christian Scholar's Review* 31, no. 3 (2002): 319–37; idem, "How to Sink in Cognitive Quicksand: Nuancing Religious Pluralism," in *Contemporary Debates in Philosophy of Religion*, ed. Michael L. Peterson and Raymond J. Vanarragon, 191–201 (London: Blackwell, 2003); idem, "Reply to Byrne," in Peterson and Vanarragon, *Contemporary Debates in Philosophy of Religion*, 211–14; "Religious Pluralism and Epistemic Humility," in *Religious Tolerance through Humility: Thinking with Philip Quinn*, ed. James Kraft and David Basinger, 111–24 (Burlington, VT: Ashgate, 2008).

9. Paul Knitter, "Toward a Liberation Theology of Religions," in *The Myth of Christian Uniqueness: Toward a Pluralistic Theology of Religions*, ed. John Hick and Paul Knitter (Maryknoll, NY: Orbis, 1987), 196.

10. Having earlier cited more recent sources, here I note some classic Christian discussions of relevant matters: Leon Morris, *The Apostolic Preaching of the Cross*, 3rd ed. (Grand Rapids: Eerdmans, 1965); C. H. Dodd, *According to the Scriptures* (New York: Scribner's, 1953); J. G. Machen, *Christianity and Liberalism* (Grand Rapids: Eerdmans, 2001; repr. of 1923 text).

11. Considerations relevant to the truth of the epistemic parity thesis and the proposal that doctrinal statements are to be taken to be nonliteral are discussed in Keith E. Yandell, "On Windowless Experiences," *Christian Scholar's Review* 6, no. 4 (1975): 311–18; idem, "Some Varieties of Ineffability," *International Journal for Philosophy of Religion* 6, no. 3 (Fall 1975): 167–79; idem, "Self-Authenticating Religious Experiences," *Sophia* 6, no. 3 (October 1977): 8–18; idem, "The Ineffability Theme," *International Journal for Philosophy of Religion* 10, no. 4 (1979): 209–31; idem, "Hume's Explanation of Religious Belief," *Hume Studies* 5, no. 2 (November 1979): 94–109; idem, "Some Prolegomena to the Epistemology of Religion," *International Journal for the Philosophy of Religion* 12 (1981): 193–215; idem, "Sensory Experience and Numinous Experience," *International Journal for Philosophy of Religion* 31 (1991): 1–29; idem, "Religious Experience," in *Blackwells Companion to the Philosophy of Religion*, 367–75 (London: Blackwells, 1998); idem, "Is Numinous Experience Evidence that God Exists?," in *God Matters*, ed. Raymond Martin and Christopher Bernard, 361–75 (New York: Longman, 2003); idem, "Religious Traditions and Rational Assessments," in *Routledge Companion to the Philosophy of Religion* (New York: Routledge, 2007), 204–15; "The Epistemology of Religious Experience," in *The Handbook of Epistemology*, ed. Ilkka Niiniluoto, Matti Sintonen, and Jan Wolenski, 676–706 (Dordrecht: Kluwer Academic, 2004); "Some Reflections on Religious Knowledge," *Sophia* 44, no. 1 (May 2005): 25–52.

12. Cited in *A Sourcebook in Indian Philosophy*, ed. Sarvapalli Rhadakrishnan and Charles A. Moore (Princeton: Princeton University Press, 1957), 289.

13. Ramanuja, *Sri-bhasya* 1.1.1.

14. Rhadakrishnan and Moore, Ch. 12, p. 194.

15. *A Sourcebook in Asian Philosophy*, ed. John M. Koller and Patricia Koller (New York: Macmillan, 1991), 258.

9

Religious Diversity and the Futility of Neutrality

R. Douglas Geivett

INTRODUCTION: WHAT IS RELIGION?

Any attempt to define religion is certainly hazardous and probably misguided. But acknowledging this does not satisfy our ambition to understand what is broadly characteristic of religion. Many students of religion seeking a family resemblance among religions employ two devices, both of which are conceptual. These two concepts are particularly useful if we suppose that the human species is *Homo religiosis*—that religiosity is nearly universal, perhaps even inescapable. Neither concept requires this assumption, so they are useful in any case.

TRANSCENDENCE

The first concept is that of "the Transcendent." Whereas it used to be common for philosophers of religion to distinguish alternative religions in terms of their differing conceptions of "deity," and many even used the word *God* as a surrogate for whatever enjoys the status of the "sacred," it is now closer to standard practice to substitute the term *the Transcendent* for making the right sort of reference. To speak of the Transcendent appears less parochial than to speak of "God," since there are manifestly religious traditions which make no explicit reference to God and even deny the reality of God (for example, some forms of Buddhism). To speak of such traditions as religious, we must dispense with the term *God*.

What is needed is a suitably general term for picking out whatever is deemed supremely important, i.e., ontologically ultimate, within any religious tradition. For this purpose, some favor the phrase *the sacred*. Others prefer *the Transcendent*.

Despite its virtues, "the sacred" seems to exclude any religious outlook that is fundamentally secular. What if, for example, we think of Marxism as a "religio-political" system, as some have? Is there anything the Marxist deems sacred? It would seem not. Yet Marxists envision a future condition that transcends the alienated individual.[1]

"The Transcendent" will serve if (among other things) it is in the nature of religious consciousness to regard something as "supremely important."[2] What is transcendent is, of course, variously construed by the different religions. Though particularized differently across traditions, the Transcendent captures what is, in very general terms, common to all traditions properly called religious. The Transcendent is denoted by whatever is conceived as most important within this or that tradition. It is the aspect of supreme *importance* that accounts for the "family resemblance" among religious traditions.[3] The Transcendent as what is supremely important is best regarded as such in relation to the next conceptual earmark for any religious outlook—soteriology.

SOTERIOLOGY

The second concept is that of "the soteriological." John Hick writes that "a clear soteriological pattern is visible both in the Indian religions of Hinduism, Buddhism and Jainism, and in the Semitic religions of Judaism, Christianity and Islam, as well as in their modern secular offspring, Marxism."[4] Others have noticed this feature of the religious outlook.[5] Keith Yandell's expression of this idea is especially helpful and clear in its conciseness: "A religion offers a diagnosis of what it tells us is our deep and paralyzing problem. It also offers a solution."[6]

SUMMARY

We have, then, an operational definition of religion captured in terms of salvific transcendence of one sort or another. This coincides with John Kekes's description of five key characteristics of a worldview: (1) a metaphysics, or an account of the nature of reality, specifying what sorts of things (objects or persons) exist and how they are related to each other; (2) an anthropology, or a theory of human nature that delineates what it is to be a human person, individually and in community with other persons; (3) a value system or ideal culture, with an inventory and orderly arrangement of all that constitutes or contributes to the good of human existence; (4) a diagnosis of the human condition, or detailed description of fundamental obstacles to human flourishing and an analysis of the causes of these obstacles; and, (5) a remedy—some policy or protocol according to which the obstacles to human flourishing are or may be overcome.[7] A worldview is multidimensional, its components integrally related to each other logically, conceptually, and pragmatically. The religious notion of the Transcendent maps onto elements (1) and (2) of this account of a worldview. Elements (4) and (5) parallel the broadly soteriological emphasis of religion.

It is plausible to suppose that the concepts of religion and worldview are coterminous or overlapping, and therefore that religiosity really is a (nearly) universal phenomenon. Those who remain skeptical about the value of construing secular paradigms as religious may acquire some sympathy for the suggestion if they attempt to understand the fundamental nature of religion through close examination of paradigm cases of religion. They might then seek to identify those patterns and elements of each that may be described in very broad terms as shared among the religions and seem intuitively to be essential to the religious outlook of each. From this delineation of patterns and elements that indicate a family resemblance among paradigm cases of religion, they might then extrapolate to any other system of belief and practice that incorporates the same general patterns and elements to determine whether that system is religious or quasi-religious. Five good candidates for sorting out the nature of religion in this way include the three dominant forms of monotheism (viz., Judaism, Christianity, and Islam), and the great nontheistic Asian religions (viz., Hinduism and Buddhism) in all of their variants.[8]

THE DIVERSITY THESIS AND THE PLURALIST THESIS

A critical discussion of religious pluralism might begin with a distinction between the diversity thesis and the pluralist thesis. The diversity thesis is descriptive and rooted in observation. It simply acknowledges the diversity of religious perspectives in the world today. This observation may be tightened into a substantive thesis if we note that, for some, such diversity reflects normatively on the value of religions collectively and individually. As a sociological or anthropological thesis, it need not pronounce upon the specific truth value of any particular religion, though it might reflect a general recommendation to religious people and students of religion to exhibit sensitivity toward other faiths, to act with tolerance toward proponents of alternative perspectives, and to reflect with humility on the nature of one's own religious commitments in light of religious diversity.

The pluralist thesis is more like a normative or evaluative response to religious diversity. It is a thesis about how one ought to understand relations among the various faith traditions and the content and practice of one's own faith in relation to others. The pluralist thesis stipulates that religions within a certain range, at least, are on equal terms alethically, epistemically, and soteriologically. These terms need clarification.

ALETHIC PARITY

Two apparently different religious traditions are on equal footing alethically if (a) their respective doctrines are true, or (b) truth plays no role within these traditions. If a tradition is defined in whole or in part by its doctrinal commitments, which represent truth claims, then belief of those doctrines (i.e., truth claims) is regarded as an important feature of the tradition. Belief being what it is, these truth *claims* are judged to be real verities. And votaries of any such tradition are expected to believe their respective truth claims.

If a religious tradition makes no truth claims whatsoever, then there is no sense in which they conflict *doctrinally* with others that do not, or even with others that do. The idea that some religious traditions are doctrinally empty—though apparently accepted by some—strikes me as implausible. The attraction of the idea may just be that it makes any difference among the religions alethically nugatory and therefore trivial. If "rival" traditions do not differ in making truth claims, or in the truth claims they make, then they do not differ alethically, which trivializes critical comparison. Non-alethic comparisons can hardly be taken seriously as criteria for adopting the pluralist thesis.

EPISTEMOLOGICAL PARITY

Two alternative religious traditions differ epistemically, let us say, if the grounds which justify belief in their respective doctrines (i.e., their truth claims) differ in some significant respect. This is a difference in what makes it likely that what is believed is true. Different traditions may be equally committed to the value of evidence in judging that their respective traditions are true. But they may differ in their respective judgments about what counts as relevant evidence. Even if they agree about salient kinds of evidence, they may differ in their judgments about what is indicated (i.e., made likely to be true) by the evidence. For example, Christians who embrace the practice of natural theology may judge that God exists and has a certain nature, and Muslims may, following the *kalam* tradition (which resembles some forms of Christian natural theology) may judge that God exists and has a nature of a different sort.

SOTERIOLOGICAL PARITY

Religions differ soteriologically if they conceptualize their distinctively religious orientations toward life in the world in fundamentally different ways. To clarify this suggestion, we need to amplify this notion of a religious orientation toward life in the world. Note well: this phenomenon of shared concern about such things may be taken by some as an invitation to reduce all of the enduring religions to their generic common ground. They may, for example, regard the distinctives of "competing" traditions as socially conditioned responses to the same Transcendent reality. Another thesis is required in tandem with this: that truth is concerned with the general points that religions seem to have in common and not with "surface differences," which are to be explained some other way (culturally, for example). But one serious problem with this proposal is that the alleged common ground doesn't exist. What the religions have in common is that they each complete the schema in their distinct ways. The elements of the schema are placeholders for specific content. As such, they are neither true nor false, for they have no specific content. The content is provided by the peculiar doctrinal commitments of the alternative religions.

A kind of "soteriological" obsession informs the whole of this schema. One caveat: the etymology of the term *soteriology* derives from the Latin noun *soter*, meaning "savior." Since some religions do not conceive of the proper remedy for what ails humanity in terms of an agent who saves—that is, in terms of a savior's acts—it can be misleading to use the term *soteriology* for those religions. So "soteriology" must be understood broadly, as is implied in the characterization of religion in diagnostic terms of a solution to humanity's "deep and paralyzing problem."

Soteriological perspectives fill out the content of the schema. These are the fundamental doctrinal commitments of the different religions. Their specifications for the (open) elements in the schema are what make the traditions most significantly different from each other. In other words, differences among traditions are most basic at the level of doctrine (that is, in terms of their respective truth claims). The schema expressly calls for specifying the peculiar shape of one's religious tradition in doctrinal terms—i.e., as truth claims. The schema does include reference to practices and the like, but in subordination to hints provided by the doctrines themselves.

SUMMARY

If this picture of the religious life in general and of what distinguishes religious traditions more specifically is correct, then comparison of religions at the levels of truth, epistemic justification, and soteriology is indispensible. The instinct for neutrality that lies behind the pluralist thesis is futile. It is futile because it seeks to escape the inescapable: a reckoning with doctrinal distinctives as bona fide truth claims that either are or are not epistemically justified.

If the picture I've painted is mistaken, then the pluralist is invited to demonstrate where it goes wrong and how any mistake I've made clears the path toward reinstatement of the pluralist thesis.

WORSHIP-WORTHINESS: AN ALTERNATIVE STARTING POINT

So far, I've described what is distinctly religious in terms of two notions, the Transcendent and soteriology. But to this point, the analysis is truncated and dangerously neglects another vital consideration—that of the worship-worthiness of the Transcendent and of the soteriological significance of worship-worthiness inherent in paradigm cases of religious life.

Paul Moser adopts the term *God* as an honorific title for that being, should it exist, that is "authoritatively and morally perfect who is inherently worthy of worship as wholehearted adoration, love, and trust."[9] This is not a stipulative definition of God, but a conceptual truth that holds whether or not such a being actually exists. As Moser says, "the term 'God' can be fully intelligible to us even if there no is titleholder, that is, even if God does not exist."[10]

This proposal is fruitful for navigating the eddies of religious diversity. We should consider whether a more conceptually ultimate being can be conceived than "God" as understood in this way. The essential concept here is worship-worthiness.

To begin our brief analysis along these lines, I make three observations: First, the aspect of worship is widely believed to be intrinsic to the religious way of life.[11] Second, though we may distinguish between worship as typically conceived in the religious context and an analogue of worship in what are thought to be more secular contexts, we should also recognize the parallels.[12] Third, insofar as worship is intrinsic to the religious way of life, any effort to compare and evaluate religions, or to specify alternative theologies of religion, or even to make sense of so-called "authentic responses" to divine reality (or "the Real," as John Hick puts it—seeking to be nonsectarian), we must get clear about the nature of worship and what this implies about the proper object of worship as the possibly existing Transcendent.

So what is worship? It includes actions as well as dispositions of the heart. Adoration acknowledges the worthiness of the object of worship. Love is affection for the object of worship, an affection that issues in a desire to act with unqualified obedience in accordance with the will of the one who is worshipped. Trust places confidence in the one who is worshipped.

To be worship-worthy, then, is to be a being with whom interpersonal relationship with human subjects is possible and who is deserving of the adoration, love, and trust inherent in acts and attitudes of worship by human subjects. Candidates for this status are few. Indeed, this explains why the honorific title adopted in reference to the worship-worthy being is "God." God within the theistic tradition has at least the "omni-attributes" of limitless power and knowledge, omnipresence, and perfect goodness. Apart from titles, however, the important point is that, to be worthy of worship, "God" must be perfectly loving. Sensations of awe or feelings of horror, though characteristic of certain religious forms of life, are but pale substitutes for worship. The same could be said for other responses to the Transcendent. This is because the object of these responses is perceived to be apt, given the nature of the Transcendent. Thus, the responses reflect concrete perceptions of the Transcendent, and to the extent that they fall short of worship, properly conceived, they are responses to a being that is not worthy of worship. Any such being is, conceptually, inferior in nature to a being truly worthy of worship.

For worship to be the proper response to what is regarded as the Transcendent, the Transcendent to which it is the proper response must be worship-worthy. And it is a fact—however lamentable or seemingly "intolerant"—that on some conceptions, the alleged Transcendent simply is not worthy.

We turn now to the crucial distinction between what is conceptually ultimate, and hence worship-worthy, and what is in fact ultimate, the ultimate *existent*. Worship-worthiness provides a meaningful gauge for determining, at the conceptual level, what would be *absolutely* ultimate. Worship-worthiness depends essentially on a being's having certain properties. There may or may not be some actually existent being that has these properties. If there is not, then the conceptually ultimate does not exist, and nothing that does not exist is worthy of worship. Still there might be something among existing entities that is comparatively ultimate or (relatively) superior. However, being the metaphysically greatest being in existence would not be sufficient to warrant *worship* of it. Some other attitude toward it may be appropriate: awe, fear, fascination, or what have you.[13] But worship would be out of place for any being that lacks the requisite properties for worship-worthiness, however superior it may be among existing things.

What then must be true of a genuinely worship-worthy being? What properties must it have? When we have sketched, at least in outline, the answer to this question, then we might be better able to sort out the conditions under which we could ascertain its existence or nonexistence.[14]

Since we are considering the possible existence of that which is worthy of worship, we should naturally care to know whether there actually is such a being. For if some being that exists is worship-worthy, then it stands in *relation* to us in a way that makes worship both possible and fitting. More important, the existence of a worship-worthy being places a call on our lives. For to be worthy of worship is to be entitled to our worship. It is to be great in that sense that makes any other response than worship an onerous affront, a violation of the deepest (or most basic) moral principle.

Withholding worship is itself a response. One may be more or less aware of the character of the being whose worship is refused; the refusal may be more or less deliberate or self-conscious. But refusal is a response to that being worthy of worship, and given the propriety of worship owed to this being, refusal of worship is an inauthentic response to the Transcendent.

There is a secondary sense in which a response of overt or inadvertent refusal may be regarded as authentic. It would be authentic insofar as it is made possible by the respect paid by God himself to the autonomy of the individual and that person's free decision to worship or not. For worship is a form of self-giving, and this must be a free act. In addition, to be worthy of worship, God must engage the free individual's affections with respect for the person's freedom. The exercise of such freedom is radically self-determining, not only because it is of the libertarian sort, but because the exercise of freedom in response to a worship-worthy being very much determines what sort of person one is and may go on to become. And this is germane to the question of evidence for the existence of God as worship-worthy. For if God exists and is as described, then worship is a natural condition of fellowship between the worshipper and God, and the fruits of fellowship are powerful indicators of the reality of God.

So not everything can be God. Even what is ultimate among existing things (and for that reason considered by some to be "Transcendent") may not be God. To be ultimate is not, as such, to be worthy of worship.

Of course, this does not mean that nothing else could be *deemed* worthy of worship, or in fact *be* worshipped, within this or that religious community. But to deem an unworthy object worship-worthy would simply be misplaced. And this is possible—the worship of an unworthy being—even if God exists. The familiar word for such a posture is *idolatry*. The very real prospect of idolatry further attests to the futility of neutrality in the realm of religious belief and practice.

So idolatry may issue from the worship of what is unworthy when what is worthy exists, but I see no reason why it should be any different if one worships what is unworthy when what would be worthy if it did exist does not exist. So the worship of anything that is not God, whether or not God exists, is idolatry.

But what if God exists and one refuses the worship of God without making something else an object of worship? This would be an evil of omission. And though this sort of omission is seldom thought of as idolatry per se, it should not be construed as somehow less morally onerous or transgressive. What matters is that what is worthy of worship is not worshipped. Call it what you will, the depravity of this posture is as bad when nothing is worshipped as it is when something other than God is worshipped.

This analysis is foreshortened without two important points of qualification. First, on the one hand, "withholding" worship of God in the event that God does not exist would not be idolatrous or otherwise morally reprehensible, *unless* something else that does exist becomes an object of worship. There is no moral failure in refusing to worship what would be worship-worthy if it did exist but does not in fact exist.

On the other hand, refusing worship of any kind may be easier said than done. We may be "hardwired" for worship, and we may find ourselves with worshipful dispositions despite ourselves. (Indeed, this in its own way may attest to the existence of what is worthy of worship—that is, to the existence of God. But the point cannot be developed here.)

THE RELIGIOUS IMPERATIVE: THE QUESTION OF GOD'S EXISTENCE AND OF OUR RELATION TO GOD

The conclusions of the previous section have three important implications. The question whether God, understood theistically, exists is urgent if we are to orient our religious lives in accord with reality, rather than in accord with our predilections or cultural biases. Further, we must acknowledge that if God does exist, this will have a significant bearing on both the kind of evidence that God exists and the attitude one should have if one would discover that God exists. Finally, we should like to know what constitutes fellowship with God and whatever God has done to make way for meaningful fellowship.

What is the evidence that there is a God, a being utterly worthy of worship, deserving of our unqualified adoration, love, and trust?[15] The following reflections are offered in support of the existence of the Transcendent who is uniquely properly worthy of worship, namely, the Christian God.

COSMOLOGICAL EVIDENCE

Scientific and philosophical evidences converge in support of the conclusion that the universe had a beginning.[16] The effort to make intelligible sense of this phenomenon leads to the inference that the universe was caused to exist by a personal being of great power and intelligence. For the beginning of the universe is an event, and as such it has a cause. But the cause of the beginning of the universe could not be some previously occurring event, since the beginning of the universe is the first event in the series of events making up the total history of the universe. If the beginning of the universe has a cause but that cause was not an event, then the cause must be an agent. And this agent must have sufficient power, intelligence, and motive for bringing into existence a universe such as ours.

At any rate, the agent described in the conclusion here is a candidate for deity and, so far as we can tell, has properties compatible with being the God of theism and no properties incompatible with being the God of theism. Admittedly, this is a more modest conclusion than the conclusion normally associated with a cosmological argument for the existence of God. But this is a virtue of a cumulative case for theism.

DESIGN EVIDENCE

Since the universe owes its existence to an extranatural personal agent of great power and intelligence, we proceed naturally to contemplate what is often called "the evidence of design" in the universe. Our initial evidence is merely that the universe had a beginning, that it has the property of being temporally finite. But a fuller description of salient features of the universe will sooner or later refer to a multitude of complexities manifest at every level of observation, whether with the naked eye or with the aid of the telescope, the microscope, or some other device to assist empirical observation. These other properties of the universe redound to the credit of the originator of the universe and bespeak an intelligence and a purpose stretching beyond the limits drawn by the initial cosmological evidence.

It would be a remarkable stroke of good luck—for us, at least—if the creator, intent on creating a different sort of thing or just experimenting wildly with the possibilities, accidentally caused a physical environment like ours to exist. It is especially remarkable that our universe is so conducive to the physical flourishing of human persons and other living organisms. This is indicated by the fine-tuning of the universe and the earth's biosphere, as well as the complexity-linked-to-function of physical organisms. All this suggests that if our sort of universe was brought into existence by a being of sufficient power and intelligence to do so, it must have been for a reason. Presumably, our creator has a plan and is good at what he does.

Naturalists, of course, firmly believe that design features of the universe can be explained in terms of the laws of nature. Never mind that these laws are themselves in need of explanation, since they behave in such an orderly way. The naturalist thesis is dubious, to be sure. So perhaps the design argument, as a stand-alone argument for the existence of God, can be defended against the reductive efforts of naturalists to explain away the impressive appearance of design.[17]

But the present cumulative case argument suggests a different sort of response. Notice how we are led to contemplate the evidence of design, and recall what we already have good reason to believe when we behold the spectacular grandeur of the universe. With apologies to the resolute naturalist, toiling away with his reductive project, we find our universe to be "ontologically haunted" by the fact that it was caused to exist by an extranatural agent.[18] This alone gives us every reason we could realistically require for thinking that what looks like design is design. Gone is the motive to demand a naturalistic account of apparent design that forbids acknowledgment of actual design. In its place is a powerful incentive to acknowledge that there is design and to attribute this design to the very agent who brought the universe into existence in the first place.

The evidence of design goes beyond the data of the physical universe. It includes the data of human consciousness and of human moral experience. Consciousness has a structure. Morality has an order. The psycho-physical unity of moral agents involves the interaction of physical and nonphysical states for ends that have moral significance. This also attests to the realization of a purpose-driven design plan that is never utilized as a datum in traditional moral arguments for the existence of God or standard ways of arguing for the existence of God from consciousness.

The manifestations of design referred to in this step cannot be fully described here. But it should be clear that the evidence of design is extensive and multifaceted. The thing to notice especially is that, at this stage, we have more evidence for the existence of a being of great power and intelligence, and at the same time the basis for making additional inferences about this agent. If causing the universe to begin to exist suggested intelligent purpose, how much more so the arrangement of the physical structure of the universe into a fit habitat for humanity and other living organisms? At the very least, the creator seems to have had a reason to arrange for the existence of creatures such as ourselves. We should wonder why.

We now have a working hypothesis, with strong initial support, that there is purpose to human existence that is linked to the creator's own intentions. As it happens, we also have the wherewithal to test this hypothesis against other data to be considered in subsequent steps.

THE HUMAN CONDITION

Reflection on apparent design presents us with evidence pertaining to the human situation. Now that it has come to that, it is appropriate to develop a realistic description of the human condition and to get into focus those aspects that are most relevant to the question of God's existence. An honest description, it must be admitted, is a mixed bag of positive and negative aspects. At this stage, we pay special attention to the negative aspects of the human situation ("our deep and paralyzing problem"), since these, in combination with the results of cosmological and design evidence, lead us directly to the next inference.

A full description of the human condition will refer to such things as moral failure and moral confusion, undeserved physical and mental suffering, mortality, uncertainty about an afterlife, the quest for personal meaning, alienation (from self, others, and our creator), dashed hopes and dreams, and so forth. These features of human experience must be set alongside the impressive dimensions of human life that indicate an incredibly intricate design plan. This can't be done without feeling a certain tension, genuine perplexity about what this design plan might be if the world of human experience is such a mixed bag of goods and evils. The whole point at this stage is to get this tension into focus, so that we are prepared to ask a question of pivotal significance in the cumulative case for theism.

THE NEED FOR REVELATION

What exactly does the creator have in mind? Is the downside of human existence an indication that the theistic conclusion so far developed is a sham? Or does it suggest that the creator's purposes are sinister? Is our creator a "cosmic killjoy"? Has the creator purposefully set us up for disappointment, despair, and resentment? These are possibilities. But they aren't the only possibilities. Nor are they the most desirable possibilities. Thankfully, they aren't the most reasonable possibilities, either.

One might say that if the foregoing evidence (evidence about the creator and designer of the universe on the one hand, and evidence concerning the human predicament on the other hand) is all the evidence we have, then we should conclude that our creator is unworthy of our faith, loyalty, and affection. That alone would disqualify the creator's claim to be God, for he would not be worthy of worship.[19] In a more charitable mood, we might exonerate the creator by attributing less power to the creator than we first thought appropriate. In that case, we might suppose that the creator is remote or aloof, not so much unconcerned as unaware of our plight. Still, he would not be worship-worthy.

But the evidence does not really justify any of these conclusions. If the evidences of earlier steps are all that we have, then perhaps we should remain agnostic about whether the creator is ultimately worthy of our commitment and worship. After all, it's *possible* that the creator has some ultimate purpose that is both good and consistent with the downside of human experience, but that we simply don't know what that purpose is. It's possible that the creator has provided a remedy for the human predicament, a remedy that has not turned up as such in any of the evidence so far considered.

Come to think of it, how could we perceive a remedy without first recognizing the need for one? But for most people, recognizing the need for a remedy is not going to be enough to support the conviction that there must be one. On the other hand, we might hope for one. And the ingenuity of the creator displayed in various ways set forth at earlier stages of our case should give us some hope that a remedy has been devised. Or perhaps we should say that the attributes of the creator surfaced at earlier stages do encourage in us the expectation that a remedy exists.

It is at least as reasonable to suppose that the creator does have a plan for solving the problems of humanity as it is to suppose that the creator does not have such a plan. And it may turn out to be more reasonable to believe that the creator has a plan if we can devise a way to confirm the existence of such a plan. A revelation from God would be a helpful aid in our quest. Is that too much to ask?

Is the creator on our side or even aware of our predicament and able to do something about it? With this question explicitly before our minds, we already have some basis for expecting the creator to intervene on our behalf, to set things straight. This expectation awaits confirmation by means that would lead on to other stages in a cumulative case for God's existence. So now we must ask: How would the availability of a remedy be confirmed to us?

THE ARENA OF RELIGIOUS TRADITIONS

If the human situation, just described, indicates our need for a remedy prescribed by our creator, and if, as we are led to expect by the evidence concerning the creator at earlier stages in the argument, the creator has produced a remedy, then it is to be expected that this would be manifest within the arena of human experience in some way. This is the arena of religious belief and practice. So the hypothesis that our creator has arranged for the human situation to be healed may well be tested by examining appropriate religious perspectives. By "appropriate," I mean perspectives consistent with what we have already understood to be the creator's nature and relation to the universe.

Suppose the creator has all the properties needed to explain all the phenomena so far considered. This supposition is grounded in evidence developed at earlier stages. And suppose the creator has prescribed a remedy for the human predicament. This supposition is our hypothesis, which we seek to confirm or disconfirm. We have the basis by now for supposing that confirmation of our expectation, generated earlier, will be found in one of the great theistic traditions of the world.

It happens, perhaps not so coincidentally, that these three religious traditions—Judaism, Christianity, and Islam—all maintain that God has produced a revelation. We should wonder whether any such revelation claim addresses precisely the expectation that showed up in the previous section. Our cumulative strategy has yielded a convenient means of narrowing the field of religious options to those that are theistic. The framework of each theistic tradition presents us with the means of conducting our search for confirmation. In the next step, we conduct this search. What do we find?

THE EVIDENCE OF MIRACLES

Each of the theistic religions endorses a particular revelation claim. Jews historically affirm the divine authority of the Hebrew Scriptures. Christians claim that the Bible (Old and New Testaments) is inspired by God. Muslims assert that the Qur'an is the word of God. It is within their respective revelation claims that we are most likely to discover confirming evidence for the hypothesis of a divine remedy generated by earlier considerations. Or if not that, then clues to confirming evidence. These distinct revelation claims might be compared, then, to see whether any one of them emerges as the one that most adequately fulfills our expectation. We should also want to know whether a particular theistic tradition enjoys superior evidential support.

It would be possible to examine each tradition simultaneously, one alongside the others. This exercise is rendered more realistic now than ever before by the proximity of these religions to one another in our day, and by the comparatively greater availability of sacred texts and orthodox statements for each tradition.

There is good reason for conducting our inquiry chronologically, as it were. If humanity is in need of a word from God (our hypothesis being that our creator is God and has produced a revelation), then it is reasonable to expect some fairly strong evidence of God's provision to meet the needs of the human condition. Since this condition has been characteristic of the human situation as far back as our collective consciousness can reach, we should also expect God's revelation to go very far back in human history. The tradition with the longest history is Judaism, followed by Christianity as more recent, and then by Islam as most recent. Not only is the tradition of Judaism the oldest, but it goes back, as documented in its scriptures, to Abraham. In fact, its Scriptures indicate a lineage going as far back as the beginning of time and the creation of humanity.

Whatever one makes of Judaism on its own terms, one would do well to suspend judgment about its successful confirmation of our hypothesis until after examining the claims of Christianity and Islam. There isn't space here for a full investigation along these lines. But the present cumulative case is a case for *Christian* theism. So I'll restrict my remarks to the fortunes of Christianity on this point. It will soon become obvious that Christianity sets a very high standard for evidence needed at this stage in the case.

Christianity claims to be continuous with Judaism. Judaism, as rooted in the Hebrew Scriptures, is very much a religion of anticipation, of unfilled expectation. Christianity is a religion of fulfilled expectation, with the prospect of more and better things to come. The arrangements for healing the human condition, as described in the Hebrew Scriptures, appear to be provisional and temporary, proleptic of something more ultimate and satisfactory. Christianity maintains that this Jewish expectation is fulfilled in the person and work of Jesus Christ, the long-awaited Messiah.

At any rate, sooner or later, however one regards the relationship between Christianity and Judaism, Christianity will come under direct examination. And when it does, something remarkable and unique in the world of religions is presented as a means of testing the truth of its claims. Christianity purports to be evidentially grounded in a historical event, the resurrection of Jesus Christ.

Such an event would, if it happened, be about the best candidate for a miracle one could imagine.

Historical support for the resurrection of Jesus would go a long way toward corroborating the claims of Christianity. For if it really happened, then it would seem that God—who alone may produce such an event, given the laws of nature—had something to do with it. And if God caused the miracle of the resurrection of Jesus, this would be evidence of God's endorsement of Jesus and his teaching.

In examination of Christianity, several things come together at once. First, at the heart of Christianity, there is a clear account of God's provision of a remedy. The Christian story, rooted in the New Testament and in express connection with the Old Testament tradition, is a story of restoration of humanity by means of re-creation.

Second, this remedy is tied to events leading up to and including the death of Jesus Christ, which in turn is directly associated with the most dramatic confirmation of Jesus' message—namely, his resurrection. The background evidence presented earlier in the argument will prove relevant in our evaluation of the available evidence for the resurrection.[20]

Third, the occurrence of a miracle of this sort—supernatural if anything is, and so closely linked with the heart of the Christian message about human restoration—is new evidence for the existence of God. While this evidence may not be sufficient by itself to justify belief in God, it is new evidence that tends to confirm the hypothesis of God's existence.[21]

Fourth, earlier evidence for the existence of a creator led to our expectation that some remedy for the human condition would turn up under this creator's initiative. If this expectation is fulfilled, then that, too, is an independent form of confirmation of the existence of just such a creator. The hypothesis of a creator was already strongly confirmed by cosmological and design evidence. That evidence supported the expectation of a remedy for the human condition. This expectation translated into a novel hypothesis: that the creator would provide a much-needed remedy and thus be worthy of human loyalty, affection, and worship. The confirmation of this hypothesis would enrich our conception of the creator and at the same time increase the confirmation that had already emerged at earlier stages. The idea here is that the hypothesis of God's existence is initially confirmed to a strong degree by cosmological and design evidence, that this hypothesis generated something tantamount to a prediction, and that the fulfillment of this prediction counts as new confirmation of the original hypothesis.

Of course, the availability of a revelation claim—in this case, the Old and New Testaments—could very well enrich our knowledge of the creator's nature and purposes. Such a revelation could thus be a source of evidence for theism.

Now, none of this would be any more than a pipe dream if there was not sufficient evidence that the resurrection of Jesus actually happened. So whatever evidence there is must be collected and assessed. Such evidence consists especially in the fact that the early Christians came to believe with great conviction that Jesus was raised bodily from the dead. They believed this to be so on the basis of evidence they had: Jesus' tomb was found empty on the third day following his crucifixion, and he was seen alive again by numerous sane individuals who would have no difficulty recognizing Jesus.

How strong must this evidence be? It should be strong enough by historical standards to justify the conviction that the alleged historical events did take place. This does not mean that the case for the resurrection stands or falls on the historical evidence alone. Again, the theism indicated by the evidence that brought us to this point plays a valuable role. First, the conclusion reached on the basis of cosmological and design evidence underwrites the *possibility* of miracles.[22] But now our hypothesis makes it *probable* that a miracle would take place as the most decisive corroboration that God's own remedy is truly his own and not a counterfeit.

Under normal conditions, historians can ignore these sorts of background considerations. Much of their work (but certainly not all of it[23]) is reliable whether they are naturalists or not. Metaphysical commitments make a difference to historical results. But I don't need a theist to tell me when and where Lincoln delivered the Gettysburg Address. In the case of the resurrection, though, conditions are not "normal." In this sort of case, one should not investigate the evidence within a metaphysical vacuum. A historian working from a position of metaphysical neutrality may get skewed results. A historian operating from a naturalistic commitment most certainly will.[24]

Nevertheless, the evidence for the resurrection depends on conditions—an empty tomb, Jesus sightings, and the remarkably uniform convictions of the earliest Christians—that can in principle be confirmed by historical investigation. Unfortunately, skeptical historians, theologians, and philosophers stipulate standards of evidence here that are not required for comparable events or physical states. That is, after all, what we are talking about in the case of the empty tomb of Jesus and his postresurrection appearances to others. The only wrinkle is that the actual occurrence of these events, given the occurrence of certain other events—for example, the crucifixion of Jesus, equally well attested historically—implies that a miracle occurred. But the earlier evidence of steps one and two in support of the theistic hypothesis greatly reduces the burden placed on historical evidence. On the evidence, the God of our theistic hypothesis has the power, ingenuity, and motive to produce a miracle, both as the guarantee of the success of his intended remedy for the human condition and as evidence that this was his own remedy and not some counterfeit.[25]

One might think that the cumulative case for God's existence has come to a fitting conclusion with the sort of confirmation we now have. But it turns out there's more.

MAKING THE TRUTH BELIEVABLE

Anyone who has reviewed the sort of case presented so far and found it to be cogent may still find it difficult to believe. This difficulty, as Blaise Pascal suggested in the *Pensées*,[26] has less to do with evidence and more to do with one's passional state in relation to evidence and the conclusion to which it points. Belief and disbelief have the aspect of habit. Coming to believe that Christian theism is true when one did not believe it for a prolonged period of time is tantamount to overcoming a long-established habit—call it a habit of disbelief. This reality produces a certain amount of inertia that evidence alone cannot cure.

The evidence developed to this point can alert one to the need to "kick the habit" of disbelief. As with any habit one wishes to overcome, simple actions practiced on a regular basis can be an invaluable aid. And so it is with belief in God for anyone who has been in the habit of not believing in God.

The habit of disbelief may be overcome by what may be called a "devotional experiment." Armed with the hypothesis of Christian theism and all the weighty accumulated evidence in its favor, the would-be believer engages in an experiment. This person considers what it would mean, in terms of practical decisions and activities, for him to be a true believer. The person then seeks to orient his life in that way. The example and assistance of true believers will be a great aid at this stage.[27]

There's much to say in favor of this notion and about how to conduct such an experiment. The main point is that such a practice often leads to bona fide belief in God. Sometimes it does so without fanfare. Sometimes the experiment culminates in a belief that is attended by a dramatic religious experience of some sort. In any case, there is often an experiential component that signals the achievement of reconciliation with God. It is within the laboratory of one's own life at this stage that one may discover that our souls are so large that finite goods cannot fulfill our deepest aspirations for happiness and peace.

RELIGIOUS EXPERIENCE

Experience of God deserves separate consideration in the final stage of this cumulative case for theism. While religious experience is sometimes offered as one of several supports for the claim that God exists, I believe an appeal to religious experience is often more persuasive within a context that has been prepared by earlier steps in this cumulative case. A person without the benefit of a thoroughly developed systematic case for the existence of God might well come to believe in God on the basis of a direct awareness of God. But for many Westerners today, both the opportunity and the need for prior preparation is very real.

For one thing, many are skeptical about the value of religious experience because they suppose that an experience of this type is conditioned by beliefs a person already has when the experience takes place. If a person has beliefs that are consistent with the idea of direct experience of God, then that person will tend naturally to frame his or her experiences in terms of those beliefs. An experience will be judged to be a genuine experience of God by those who have beliefs that enable them to make sense of their experience in those terms.

The cumulative case sketched here addresses this concern by exhibiting the rationality of such framework beliefs in advance of presenting the data of religious experience. Suppose it's true that an individual's experience is often interpreted in terms of that individual's conceptual framework. It may still be legitimate to regard that experience as an experience of God if the conceptual framework of theism is judged on independent grounds to be reasonable. A cumulative case for theism is sensitive to this when it introduces the "evidence" of religious experience as the culmination of the case for theism.[28]

Also, the earlier stages in the cumulative case may be needed to prepare a person for a religious experience. It may be that there is only a very low probability that a person will ever "experience God"—such that the person can recognize it as such—so long as that person adopts the attitude and behavioral stance of a resolute skeptic. But if this person can be persuaded to practice the sort of devotional experiment recommended here, then this will likely lead to a new passional state that is more open and less skeptical. Such openness would likely increase the probability of an experience that the person could recognize as an experience of God. A devotional experiment places a person in a more auspicious position to experience God. And conducting this sort of experiment is intellectually responsible if the conceptual framework of theism is itself well supported by the evidence. At any rate, with any such experience, there is an increase in the confirmation of theism.[29]

CONCLUSION

In her brief essay "The Dogma Is the Drama," Dorothy Sayers passed along a witticism that is a fitting résumé of my proposal: "Any stigma will do to beat a dogma."[30] Dogma is not all bad, if it's true. But the very idea of dogma has been stigmatized, so that word on the street has it that nothing good can come of it. I should say it needs rescuing. One move in the right direction is to acknowledge that the pluralist thesis is a dogma and not the convenient erasure of dogma it purports to be. Pluralism may pretend to a kind of neutrality about the dogmatic content of any religious tradition. But this is futile, since no serious interaction with a tradition can dismiss the truth claims of that tradition or neglect the evidence for and against any tradition. The pluralist may sincerely wish to advocate for pluralistic conceptions of and responses to the "Transcendent." But then she does not take seriously the idea of the Transcendent as that being that is uniquely worthy of worship. Failure in this risks idolatry as well as futility.

Notes

1. See John Hick, *An Interpretation of Religion: Human Responses to the Transcendent* (New Haven: Yale University Press, 1989), 5, 22, and 33. In this connection, Hick cites Robert N. Bellah, *Beyond Belief: Essays on Religion in a Post-Traditional World* (New York: Harper & Row, 1970), xix. See also Charles Taliaferro, *Contemporary Philosophy of Religion: An Introduction* (Oxford: Blackwell, 1998), 21–24, 30.

2. Hick, *An Interpretation of Religion.*

3. Hick says, "All authentic as opposed to merely nominal religiousness seems to involve *a sense of profound importance.*" Ibid., 4 (italics added).

4. Ibid., 32.

5. Roger Scruton, *The Face of God: The Gifford Lectures* (New York: Bloomsbury, 2012), 15–21.

6. Keith A. Yandell, *Philosophy of Religion: A Contemporary Introduction* (New York: Routledge, 1999), 4.

7. John Kekes, *The Nature of Philosophy* (Oxford: Blackwell, 1980), 58–65.

8. This approximates Charles Taliaferro's strategy for "defining religion by example," in chapter 1 of his book *Contemporary Philosophy of Religion.*

9. Paul K. Moser, *The Elusive God: Reorienting Religious Epistemology* (Cambridge: Cambridge University Press, 2009), 1; cf. 18 and 32.

10. Ibid., 32.

11. See the description of religion by atheist Howard Sobel in *Logic and Theism: Arguments for and against Beliefs in God* (Cambridge: Cambridge University Press, 2004), 9–11.

12. Moser, *The Elusive God*, 30–32, 86.

13. Rudolf Otto and William James have catalogued varieties of religious experience in, respectively, *The Idea of the Holy* (Oxford: Oxford University Press, 1958), and *The Varieties of Religious Experience: A Study in Human Nature* (New York: Longmans, Green, and Co., 1905).

14. This is the burden of Moser's book, which describes the kind of evidence that God himself would provide the would-be *worshipper* (as opposed to the would-be believer), the

conditions under which God would provide such evidence, and the epistemic force such evidence would have.

15. The balance of this chapter is adapted from a portion of my essay, "David Hume and a Cumulative Case Argument," in *In Defense of Natural Theology: A Post-Humean Assessment* (Downers Grove, IL: InterVarsity, 2005), 302–15.

16. This claim has been developed and supported by a number of Christian philosophers. For my own elaboration of the argument, see *Evil and the Evidence for God* (Philadelphia: Temple University Press, 1993), 99–122; "The *Kalam* Cosmological Argument," in *To Everyone an Answer* (Downers Grove, IL: InterVarsity, 2004); and "Reflections on the Explanatory Power of Theism," in *Does God Exist? The Craig-Flew Debate*, ed. Stan W. Wallace (London: Ashgate, 2003), 51–52.

17. See Richard Swinburne's approach in his essay "The Argument from Design," reprinted in *Contemporary Perspectives on Religious Epistemology*, ed. R. Douglas Geivett and Brendan Sweetman, 201–11 (New York: Oxford University Press, 1992).

18. The universe was first described as "ontologically haunted" by my teacher and friend Dallas Willard in "The Three-Stage Argument for the Existence of God," in Geivett and Sweetman, *Contemporary Perspectives on Religious Epistemology*, 216.

19. For a helpful discussion of this point, see Sobel, *Logic and Theism*, 9–11.

20. See R. Douglas Geivett, "The Evidential Value of Miracles," in *In Defense of Miracles*, ed. R. Douglas Geivett and Gary R. Habermas (Downers Grove, IL: InterVarsity, 1997), 178–95.

21. I'm not here passing judgment on the claim that an argument for theism from miracles goes through on its own. I've explored that question elsewhere. See "The Evidential Value of Miracles," referenced in note 20 above; "Reflections on the Explanatory Power of Theism," 56–59; and especially, "The Epistemology of Resurrection Belief," in *The Resurrection of Jesus: John Dominic Crossan and N. T. Wright in Dialogue*, ed. Robert B. Stewart (Minneapolis: Fortress Press, 2006), 93–105.

22. For my extended discussion of the possibility of miracles, see "Why I Believe in the Possibility of Miracles," in *Why I Am a Christian*, ed. Norman L. Geisler and Paul K. Hoffman (Grand Rapids: Baker, 2001), 97–110.

23. If the theism of our cumulative case is true, then a personal God who is actively interested in the human condition—as indicated by the resurrection, no less!—may well be much more of an agent in the historical process than most historians (naturalists and supernaturalists) have yet contemplated. Just to ensure the timely occurrence of the life of Jesus and his resurrection would take quite a lot of hands-on engagement with the historical process. But God's hand in the process may be discernible in any number of unexpected places, once historians have worked out a suitable "providentialist" conception of their discipline.

24. See Geivett, "The Epistemology of Resurrection Belief."

25. Again, see Geivett, "The Evidential Value of Miracles."

26. See the famous Wager passage §233 in Blaise Pascal, *Pensées*, trans. John Warrington (London: J. M. Dent, 1973), 92–96. See also Thomas V. Morris, "Pascalian Wagering," in Geivett and Sweetman, *Contemporary Perspectives on Religious Epistemology*, 257–69.

27. See Carolyn Franks Davis, "The Devotional Experiment," *Religious Studies* 22 (March 1986): 15–28; Franks Davis, *The Evidential Force of Religious Experience* (Oxford: Clarendon, 1989); and, my related article, "A Pascalian Rejoinder to the Presumption of Atheism," in *God Matters: Readings in the Philosophy of Religion*, ed. Raymond Martin and Christopher Bernard (New York: Longman, 2003), 162–75.

28. Contrarian approaches to the data of religious experience have an equal opportunity to ground their assessments of that data in an independently supported conceptual framework. For example, one who favors a naturalistic explanation for the data of religious experience should have strong independent grounds for believing that naturalism is true. For a more developed account of the evidence of religious experience, see my chapter "The Evidential Value of Religious Experience," in *The Rationality of Theism*, ed. Paul Copan and Paul K. Moser (London: Routledge,

2003), 175–203, and the more abbreviated comments in Geivett, "Reflections on the Explanatory Power of Theism."

29. See Geivett, "The Evidential Value of Religious Experience."

30. Dorothy L. Sayers, *Letters to a Diminished Church: Passionate Arguments for the Relevance of Christian Doctrine* (Nashville: Thomas Nelson, 2004), 20.

10

Can the Jews Be the Chosen People of God?

Nancy Fuchs Kreimer

Can the Jews be the chosen people of God? The honest answer to that question is simple. As my teacher Father Gerard Sloyan taught, "in the strict theological sense, God alone knows."[1] So it is with some trepidation and a good dose of humility that I enter this conversation. Having established that I am in no position to answer the question of Truth, I propose to investigate some questions upon which I can shed some light. What has chosenness meant to Jews over time? What has it meant in my own life? What is gained or lost by different formulations of this idea? What are the challenges facing the (perhaps) "chosen people" at this moment in history?

Although the contemporary Jewish philosopher David Novak has written an entire book on what he calls the "classical biblical-rabbinic doctrine of the election of Israel,"[2] my own training has taught me to eschew words like *doctrine* or *tenet* and replace them with ones such as *myth, story*, and *tradition*. I have learned to see the ancestors' testimony as information about their experience, in this case of being part of the Jewish people. Over the centuries, the narrative of election has meant different things to different Jews. It has been experienced as both obligation and privilege, burden and blessing, sometimes both at once.

At key moments in the liturgy—when a Jew ushers in the Sabbath over wine or blesses its departure, upon rising to read from the Torah, at the close of every prayer service—the distinction between Jews and others is iterated and reiterated. As Gerard Sloyan notes in general and, I would argue, correctly, certainly for Jews, "Religious peoplehood is close to the heart of religious reality."[3] Or as Abraham Joshua Heschel put it, "For us Jews, there can be no fellowship with God without fellowship with [the people] Israel. . . . Judaism is

. . . primarily the living in the spiritual order of the Jewish people. . . . Our share of holiness we acquire by living in the Jewish community."[4] The other side of that claim is that the Jewish community itself partakes of holiness.

This is not the contemporary, secular version of Jewish chosenness, often confused with the idea under discussion. Some Jews (and non-Jews) believe, rightly or wrongly, that Jews are simply smarter, more moral, or in some other way better than other people—divinity (should it exist) having nothing to do with it. This idea is known affectionately as "counting Nobel Prize winners."[5] As I understand it, chosenness was never a claim about the merits of people who happen to be Jewish, although it is sometimes misunderstood that way. It is about a quality that permeates the life of Jews in the aggregate. As a group, they are connected to the transcendent. In Heschel's words, "[The people] Israel is a spiritual order in which the human and the ultimate, the natural and the holy, enter a covenant."[6]

It is tempting to dodge the problem of the universal and the particular at the outset by saying that the Jews are holy as a community, but so is everybody else. Contemporary apologists like to say that the idea of chosenness does not trail in its wake any politically incorrect notions—no value judgment about others, no need to define our own boundaries with care, no claim to specialness. "Being chosen does not preclude anyone else from being chosen." Such a maneuver misses the point. A quick look at the traditional prayers should suffice. At the Havdalah service at the close of the Sabbath, we praise God for the act of separating. We thank God for distinguishing "the holy from the profane, light from dark, Israel from the nations, the seventh day from the six workdays." Whether or not Jews say those words—and many Jews do not participate in a Havdalah service at all—they carry their message into Jewish communal life in the twenty-first century. Whether the issue is the survival of the state of Israel, the uniqueness of the Nazi Holocaust, the attitude toward intermarriage, our sense of our people as "set apart, a holy nation" continues to resonate.

Whatever else it has meant, the idea of the chosen people suggests that while every group is different, Jews are different in a special way, in a way that makes it matter who is in and who is out, that puts obligations on those who are in, that makes our survival important, not only to us, but to God. Such an idea is completely outrageous, and we have known it for a long time. And yet we continue to wrestle with it.

To anticipate my conclusion, I will mirror Paul Knitter, who in the historical context in which he finds himself, says (with trademark Knitter humility as a "struggling servant") that he "can and must affirm that Christianity is *not* the only true religion." Similarly, I will conclude that today we can and must affirm that Jews are *not* "the chosen people of God." Except sometimes. I understand Knitter's "different contexts" more broadly than he. It seems to me that even in the same historical moment, we may need more than one way of telling our people's story.

In other words, it's complicated.

MY JOURNEY

The first time I ever encountered the idea that Jews were a "chosen people," my teacher explained that this was a mistaken and even pernicious belief that was held by other Jews. When I memorized the Reconstructionist Torah blessings for my bat mitzvah, I knew that I would have heard a different blessing in most other Jewish settings in the world. (In 1965, there were fewer than a dozen Reconstructionist congregations.) Other Jews, my teacher explained, recite an ancient idea of being chosen from among all the other peoples of the earth. We, however, knew better.

Mordecai Kaplan, the founder of Reconstructionism, developed his naturalistic understanding of the people Israel to be synergistic with his naturalistic understanding of the other two pillars of Jewish thought, God and Torah. But in the liturgy that I grew up with in a "classical" Reconstructionist community, the traditional prayers were altered only moderately in their God and Torah references. The idea that God had chosen the people Israel from all the other peoples of the earth, however, was dramatically and very obviously expunged.

The rejection of the traditional wording made sense to me over the years. I appreciated the forthrightness of the claim of my particular tradition, Reconstructionist Judaism, that my ancestors indeed believed themselves to be in a special relationship to God, his most beloved child, and that other Jews shared that sense, but that I did not. In my experience, changing the wording at key liturgical moments offered a pedagogical payoff. It highlighted the gap between the traditional liturgy's worldview and our own. That gap created the daylight in which I could see the value of other faith traditions.

Strangely, while my early indoctrination in "non-chosenness" contributed to my professional commitment to interfaith work, it is that work itself that has led me to engage the idea of the chosen people more fully than I had ever imagined. In my personal prayer life, as a Jew teaching and leading other Jews, I can and do choose what strands of our rich heritage I want to bring into play at this moment in history. But as a participant in dialogue with those of other faiths, I have a different relationship to the tradition and hence to the traditional understanding of the special role of the Jews.

Entering the world of Christian-Jewish theological dialogue in the heyday of the post-Holocaust conversation, I was surprised when my Christian partners, far from lauding me for rejecting the idea of the divine election of the Jews, were dismayed. Their entire tradition was based on being the "new Israel." These particular Christians were striving to rid Christian doctrine of the negative implications for Jews that idea had historically carried. They did not, however, want to give up the concept that God's work in history had taken a special turn with the call of Abraham. I interact often with Christians who see their own relationship with God to depend upon my people's relationship with God, the very relationship I was taught to deny. I realized that to insist on that denial was, paradoxically, to dishonor their belief, not what I aspire to in dialogue. My very pluralism forced me to at least take their faith seriously.

Later, I found that Muslims, too, built their community's sacred mission on the special role of Abraham and his favored son Ishmael in God's plans for humanity. The Qur'an shares with the Midrash the story of Abraham breaking the idols in his father's shop, and traditional Islam sees any faith other than pure monotheism as sinful. Muslims are often shocked to hear the unorthodox way in which I, a member of one of the "peoples of the Book," relate to some of the teachings in it. The "Abrahamic Tradition," a concept that has grown in popularity in the last decade, reminds us of the post–World War II idea of the "Jewish-Christian tradition." Like any good myth, it reflects a truth. Although we disagree over which of us is now the special people of God, our three traditions share a common thread: elective monotheism. In rejecting chosenness, I am rejecting one of the strong bonds that unite us with our two major faith partners.

However Jews may choose to accept, reject, or reinterpret it, the idea of elective monotheism is one that is fundamental to the self-understanding of over half the people on the globe—that is, Jews, Christians, and Muslims. Neither the New Testament nor the Qur'an doubts the primacy of Jewish election. They merely add to the story. The fact that, as a Reconstructionist, I can elide a piece of our tradition is really not the point. That piece has not gone away, and as a Jew, I still own it, even if I do not speak of it in my prayers.

In the interfaith encounter, I have to resist the temptation to claim only the parts of Judaism I love. I prefer to skip over the Jewish ideas I find objectionable or, more often, to explain that they belong to someone else—"the mistaken Jews." Yet this feels both arrogant and untrue to real pluralism. My inability to inhabit empathetically a belief held by my co-religionists leaves me without sufficient understanding of or compassion for the manifestations of that belief. Even if I deplore certain behaviors, it behooves me to try to understand them. That is also part of the ethos of dialogue.

When I engage in "splitting" Jews into the good ones who share my enlightened faith and the bad ones who do not, I also project the problematic aspects of Judaism on someone else, as if those problems exist only in those "other" Jews—settlers on the West Bank, for example—rather than noticing when they occur closer to my own world. I discovered this from listening to Christians condemn other Christians for their anti-Semitism. After renouncing the theology those "others" believe, they would then reveal, in much subtler form, the same prejudices. As dialogue has forced me to engage sympathetically with more of Judaism, including chosenness, I have also been able to see the residue of chosenness when it appears in my own Jewish subculture. In my experience, the best dialogues turn out to be with people who remain self-critically but lovingly engaged with the breadth of their tradition and community.

A rich conversation emerges when we each confront with honesty our thick and complicated religious heritages. Over the years, I have seen Christians, then Jews, and more recently Muslims grow increasingly frank with each other about these issues—admitting to one another that their sacred texts include texts of terror or, at the very least, texts that lend themselves to being misread in terrible ways. We talk of our traditions' light and shadows. I am inspired by the work of religious thinkers like the Swedish-American Lutheran Krister Stendahl or the South African Muslim Farid Esack, who hold on to their belief in the unique truths of their community while finding ways to tell their story without disparaging others. I have seen Jews, Christians, and Muslims attempt that with integrity.

Unpacking the Past

We begin, of course, with Genesis 12, a call that seems to happen out of the blue, set in the context of eleven chapters tracing the Ur history of the human race. "YHWH said to Abram: Go out from your country, from your family and from your father's house to the land that I will show you. I will make you into a great nation and I will bless you and make your name great. And you will be a blessing. I will bless those who bless you, and curse those who curse you. And through you, all the families of the earth will be blessed" (Gen. 12:1–3, author's translation).

God gives no reason for this call, no explanation for choosing Abraham over anyone else. At the same time, from the start, the call is not just about Abraham and his family. The other families of the earth are involved in the story, too, but the plot revolves around him. In Deuteronomy, as the people are about to enter the land, they learn of their obligations and also of their specialness: "When YHWH your God brings you into the land that you are entering, to take possession of it, and casts out many nations before you . . . {you will destroy them, you will not make marriages with them, you will tear down their alters} . . . For you are a holy people to YHWH your God; YHWH your God has chosen you to be His treasured people from amongst all the peoples of the earth" (Deut. 7:1-6, author's translation).

It is through the prophets of Israel that this holiness takes on the form of obligation. In Second Isaiah, we return to the idea in Genesis 12 that this people's fate in the world includes bringing something to other people, a light to the nations: "I am the Lord, I have called you in righteousness, I have taken you by the hand and kept you; I have given you as a covenant to the people, a light to the nations, to open the eyes that are blind" (Isa. 42:6-7, author's translation).

The Talmudic rabbis enjoy playing with words. In one passage, they explore the question of God's phylacteries (tefillin). One rabbi wonders what might be written inside God's tefillin. His friend surmises that in God's tefillin it says, "Who is like your people Israel, a nation unique on the earth?"

"Could it be," the first rabbi asks, that "the Holy Blessed One sings the praises of Israel?" His friend responds in the affirmative.[7]

There is a grandiosity that can be seen in the self-understanding of Jews that sometimes seems almost inversely related to how grand their lives actually were.

Perhaps the most well-known character from the literature of Eastern European Jewry is the dairyman Tevye, a far more complicated individual than his twentieth-century Broadway musical avatar. In the stories, Sholom Aleichem creates in Tevye a Jew whom the author both mocks and honors. As literary critic Dan Miron understands it, Tevye is to be admired for his pluck, even as he disparaged his creator for his narrowness and his narcissism.

As you may recall from the show *Fiddler on the Roof*, Tevye's daughters become increasingly less willing to go along with the program. The crushing moment comes when the third daughter, Chava, marries outside the tribe. This far Tevye cannot bend, although he suffers terribly in missing his daughter. According to his author, Sholom Aleichem, when he sees Chava in the road, he is tempted to turn his wagon around and make up with her:

"All sorts of strange thoughts came to my mind. What did it mean to be a Jew, and what did it mean to be a non-Jew? And why did God create Jews and non-Jews, and why were they so set apart from one another, unable to get along, as if one had been created by God and the other not? To my regret, not being as learned as others in books and religious texts, I could not find an answer to these questions. To drive away my thoughts, I began to chant the evening prayer, the ashrei: Blessed are they who dwell in Thy house, and they shall continue to praise Thee."[8]

As Tevye's trials reflect, the traditional shtetl life was beginning to crack, questions were emerging well before the Nazi Holocaust. Tevye attempts to find solace in the prayer book's claim that the Jews ("they who dwell in Thy house") are blessed or, as *ashrei* is often translated, happy. But Sholom Aleichem lets us know that this both works and does not work. It is not simple.

Anti-Semitism was intimately connected to chosenness. Sigmund Freud blamed the Jews, at least in part, for having earned the hatred of the anti-Semites:

> There is no doubt that they [the Jews] have a very good opinion of themselves, think themselves nobler, on a higher level, superior. . . . They really believe themselves to be God's chosen people; they hold themselves to be specially near to him, and this is what makes them proud and confident. According to trustworthy accounts, they behaved in Hellenistic times as they do today. The Jewish character, therefore, even then was what it is now, and the Greeks, among whom and alongside whom they lived, reacted to the Jewish qualities in the same way as their "hosts" do today.[9]

And in 1945, the Yiddish poet, Kadya Molodovsky wrote, "O God of Mercy . . . We are tired of death and corpses. . . . For the time being, Choose another people."[10]

The Zionist movement involves a particularly complicated relationship to this idea. Ironically, the movement emerged in part from a desire on the part of its founders for Jews to become "normal" people, to cease all this talk of God and mission and get on with life like other nations. Yet it was not that simple. One strand of Zionism reflects the idea of chosenness, in its most triumphalist version, as the title song for the film *Exodus* put it: "This land is mine, God gave this land to me." The first chief rabbi of Palestine, Rabbi Abraham Kook, exemplified this thinking. But there is also a version of Zionism that embraces the chosen people in a prophetic mode, stressing the ethical obligation involved in returning to the land. Martin Buber, an exemplar of the latter path, chose the latter path:

> We must not forget, however, that in the thousand years of its exile, Jewry yearned for the Land of Israel, not as a nation like other nations, but as Judaism (*res sui generis*). . . . Here the question may arise as to what the idea of the election of Israel has to do with all this. . . . The prophets formulated [our] task and never ceased uttering their warning: If you boast of being chosen instead of living up to it, if you turn election into a static object instead of obeying it as a command, you forfeit it![11]

I am struck by Knitter's point that "exclusive claims foster violence between religious groups or civilizations. They do not necessarily cause such violence; but they can condone it, encourage it, and strengthen it."[12] Yes, but in this case, they can also do the reverse. Compare Buber's comment to one recently made by the novelist Michael Chabon in the *New York Times*: "Let us shed our illusions, starting with ourselves, whoever we are and however august our inheritance of stupidity. . . . Let us not, henceforward, judge Israel or seek to have it judged for its intelligence, for its prowess, for its righteousness or for its moral authority, by any standard other than the pathetic, debased and rickety one that we apply, so inconsistently and self-servingly, to ourselves and to everybody else."[13]

Mordecai Kaplan, the greatest American Jewish thinker of the last century, insisted on this issue above all else: "The idea of Israel as a Chosen People must . . . be understood as belonging to a thought-world which we no longer inhabit. . . . It can no longer help us to understand relations, or to orient ourselves to conditions, as they exist today. . . . The assumption by any individual or group that it is the chosen and indispensable vehicle of God's grace to others is arrogance, no matter how euphemistically one phrases the claim,"[14] and, "By no kind of dialectics is it possible to remove the odium of comparison from any reinterpretation of an idea which makes invidious distinctions between one people and another."[15]

On the other hand, critics have pointed out that Kaplan would have been the first to decry Michael Chabon's manifesto. His last book was entitled *The Religion of Ethical Nationhood*. In the end, chosenness returns. Even Kaplan could not let it go completely.

BEYOND KAPLAN: THE JEWISH PEOPLE IN A POST-ETHNIC AMERICA

As a pragmatist, Kaplan believed that a major concern for any theology is its ability to support the flourishing of the community. Kaplan was ahead of his time in imagining and promoting, before it became a buzzword, multiculturalism. But today we are dealing, arguably, with a different situation. Horace Kallen famously observed, "Men may change their clothes, their politics, their wives [sic], their religions, their philosophies, to a greater or lesser extent; they cannot change their grandfathers."[16] David Hollinger does not agree. In his 1995 book, *Post-Ethnic America: Beyond Multiculturalism*, he developed the idea that we are moving from communities of fate, to community of choice. He calls our relationship to the latter "solidarity." In a time and place where pressures from outside are lessened, solidarity becomes a choice.

He writes, "A post-ethnic social order would encourage individuals to devote as much—or as little—of their energies as they wished to their community of descent, and would discourage public and private agencies from implicitly telling every citizen that the most important thing about them was their descent community. Hence to be post-ethnic is not to be anti-ethnic, or even color-blind, but to reject the idea that descent is destiny."[17]

Jews, for most of our history, have been a community of fate, if not always faith. If Hollinger is right, I wonder: What is the meaning of jettisoning the idea of the special holy nature of our community of descent at the very moment when solidarity is becoming increasingly optional?

Shaul Magid is one Jewish thinker who sees this problem quite clearly. In an article that reviews responses to Arthur Green's most recent theological formulation, *Radical Judaism*, Magid notes that Green earns the title "radical" perhaps more for his view of the Jewish people than for anything else. Clearly, Green's idea of God, while radical, has roots in kabbalah and *hasidut*, and his relaxed views of Jewish law have been around in various forms since the Enlightenment. But his position on Jewish peoplehood comes in for serious criticism.

Green writes, "Who is my Israel? . . . You indeed, are my Israel. You for whom I write, you whom I teach, you with whom I share a deep kinship of shared human values and love for this Jewish language. Are you all Jews in the formal sense? I'm not much worried about that question."[18] Green goes on to explain that he feels more in common with seekers of other faiths than with secular, materialistic Jews.

Magid, noting the criticism Green has invited by this kind of comment, analyses the reasons why: "It is precisely because the differences are becoming ever-more subtle and ethnic Jewishness ever more precarious, that rabbis are adamant about stressing separation whenever possible. . . . The 'radicality' of Green's theology is the way he openly erases or at least attenuates the very distinctions that insure Jewish distinctiveness in a society of acceptance."[19] I think Magid is exactly right. As he notices, Green's consciousness is global, more so than Buber's or Heschel's. He goes on to note of Green's thought, "It is a theology that does not have sufficient room for national survival. . . . While Green is not oblivious to these concerns, for him they are not central."[20]

Throughout this paper, I speak of "Jewish peoplehood" as if I were speaking of something known, with clear boundaries. We know what citizens of a state are, and we know (or at least once thought we did) what a race or ethnicity is. But what is a Jewish people? I see two opposite trends developing within the Jewish world. On the one hand, some Jews are becoming more insular, ignorant of others not like themselves, the results increasingly toxic. At the same time, we see among Jews, mostly younger ones, that identities are becoming more fluid. People belong to multiple groups; they belong for short periods of time. Spirituality, not religion, is a source of meaning.

Arnold Eisen wrote, "Chosenness grips us . . . through the power of the pictures it presents to our innermost vision, the images it conjures before us, the way it thereby makes sense of things. . . . Consider only its most obvious resonances. The love of a parent. A place at the center of things. Work which needs doing and awaits us and no one else. Uniqueness. Blessing."[21]

Eisen's recognition of the psychological power of chosenness opens up the possibility of alternative resonances that are not as appealing. For example, a young woman recently told me of how uncomfortable she felt walking across her college campus with a Palestinian friend whose family left in 1948 and seeing a table to sign up for "Birthright Israel," a program that would give her, an unaffiliated Jew, an all-expenses-paid trip to Israel, based on nothing but her proof that her parents were Jewish.

Concluding Thoughts

My admittedly selective romp through Jewish history followed by my idiosyncratic exploration of the present moment leads me to two conclusions. On one level, and for many situations, I affirm Mordecai Kaplan's position that we boldly dismiss rather than try to recuperate an idea that, when honestly confronted, fits poorly with our contemporary understanding of ourselves in relationship to the rest of the world. I think we need to teach and preach that message with clarity. Ignoring the whole matter does not make it go away.[22] But we also should push ourselves to engage the problematics. The idea that human beings were created in God's image is not a scientific fact. Its claim on me as truth, one I accept on faith, comes with no more or less authority than the teaching about the chosen people.

We should not give up the struggle with the traditional words, as if performing surgery on the prayer book can somehow solve an issue that is still with us. Our humanity feels at once both universal and tribal. Is there a way to affirm the spiritual value of the tribal that fully recognizes those outside the tribe? Can we base that recognition from within the tradition itself, rather than treat it as a modern import? Can a commitment to deep pluralism be combined with a Jewishly authentic reinterpretation of chosenness?

That is precisely the project embarked upon by Rabbi Lord Jonathan Sacks, chief rabbi of the United Hebrew Congregations of the Commonwealth since 1991. In the first edition of his 2002 book, *The Dignity of Difference,* he offered a theology that critiqued chauvinism from within Jewish teaching and made important pluralistic claims about the relationship of Jews to other peoples, particularly in chapter 3. Within one year, Sacks published a second edition of that book with major changes to the problematic chapter.

In his preface the second edition, Sacks explained that the changes were the result of feedback from his community. People thought he was abandoning the idea of Jews as the chosen people, which he had no intention of doing. According to him, in this new edition, he simply makes his points more clearly. I read the changes differently. It seems that the 2002 theology was simply too radical for the Jews to whom Sacks owed allegiance; in the revised edition, he dials back.

For example, in the first edition Sacks wrote, "[God] is a particularist, loving each of his children for what they are, Isaac and Ishmael, Jacob and Esau, Israel and the nations."[23] The revised version reads, "He is a particulatist . . . favouring Jacob but also commanding his children not to hate those of Esau."[24]

In another place, he writes, "The truth at the beating heart of monotheism is that God is greater than religion; that He is only partially comprehended by any faith. He is my God, but also your God. He is on my side, but also on your side. He exists not only in my faith, but also in yours." In the revision, this passage becomes, "The truth at the beating heart of monotheism is that God transcends the particularities of culture and the limits of human understanding.

He is my God but also the God of all mankind, even of those whose customs and way of life are unlike mine."

Finally, the original text reads, "We encounter God in the face of the stranger. That, I believe, is the Hebrew Bible's single greatest and most counterintuitive contribution to ethics. God creates difference; therefore it is in one-who-is-different that we meet God. Abraham encounters God when he invites three strangers into his tent."[25] In the revision, this becomes, "God cares about the stranger and so must we. Abraham invites three strangers into his house and discovers that they are angels. . . . Welcoming the stranger, said the sages, is even greater than 'receiving the divine presence.'"[26]

It is in the changes that Sacks felt compelled by his community to make that we find the crux of the question of this essay. In the original version, Sacks is pushing Jewish particularism to its very edge. The three strangers in the tent go from being God to being angels, even "greater than the divine presence" but, we are assured, not precisely God.

"The God of all mankind" is a comfortable idea. "He is my God, but also your God" is just too much. Of course, God loves all humankind, but when we speak about anyone in particular, it is the Jews he loves. We are not to hate the others; we are to welcome them. We are to see them as angels. But "He is on my side but also on your side" is too much.

I do not know if Sack's critics are correct in claiming that the original version of his book abandons chosenness. That, of course, is the ongoing question of this essay. What I do know is that Sacks is in conversation with his people and I with him. I love that it still matters to all of us to argue about chosenness—as it is said—"for the sake of heaven." Jewish tradition challenges us to grapple with a claim that may not easily fit into our postmodern worldview. Yet, like Jacob wrestling with the angel, we will not let it go until it blesses us.

Notes

1. Gerard S. Sloyan, "Who Are the People of God?," in *Standing before God: Studies on Prayer in Scriptures and in Tradition with Essays: In Honor of John M. Oesterreicher*, ed. A. Finkel and L. Frizzel (New York: KTAV, 1980), 103.

2. David Novak, *The Election of Israel: The Idea of the Chosen People* (Cambridge: Cambridge University Press, 1995).

3. Sloyan, "Who Are the People of God?," 104.

4. A. J. Heschel, "To Be a Jew, What Is It?," in *Moral Grandeur and Spiritual Audacity*, ed. Susannah Heschedl (New York: Farrar, Straus and Giroux, 1996), 7.

5. Steven L. Pease, *The Golden Age of Jewish Achievement: The Compendium of a Culture, a People, and Their Stunning Performance* (Mevagissey, Cornwall: Deucalion, 2009).

6. Ibid.

7. Babylonian Talmud, *Berakhot* 6a.

8. Sholem Aleichem, *Tevye the Dairyman and Motl the Cantor's Son*, trans. Aliza Shevrin (New York: Penguin, 2009), 81.

9. Sigmund Freud, *Moses and Monotheism* (New York: Vintage, 1939), 134–35.

10. Kadya Molodovsky, "God of Mercy," in *Truth and Lamentation: Stories and Poems on the Holocaust*, ed. Milton Teichman and Sharon Leder (Urbana: University of Illinois Press, 1993), 428.

11. Martin Buber, "Nationalism," in *A Land of Two Peoples: Buber on Jews and Arabs,* ed. Paul Mendes-Flohr (New York: Oxford University Press, 1983), 55–56.

12. See Paul Knitter's essay in this book.

13. Michael Chabon, "Chosen, but Not Special," *New York Times*, June 6, 2010.

14. Mordecai Kaplan, *The Future of the American Jew* (New York: Reconstructionist Press, 1948).

15. Ibid.

16. Horace Kallen, "Democracy versus the Melting-Pot: A Study of American Nationality," *The Nation*, February 25, 1915.

17. "Communalist and Dispersionist Approaches to American Jewish History in an Increasingly Post-Jewish Era," *American Jewish History*, March 1, 2009, 22.

18. Arthur Green, *Radical Judaism: Rethinking God and Tradition* (New Haven: Yale University Press, 2010), 132.

19. Shaul Magid, "(Re)Reading Radicalism: Reading Reviews of Arthur Green's Radical Judaism," *Zeek*, March 10, 2011.

20. Shaul Magid, "(Re)Reading Radicalism: Reading Reviews of Arthur Green's *Radical Judaism*," *Zeek*, March 2011, zeek.forward.com/articles/117106.

21. Arnold Eisen, "Kaplan and Chosenness: A Historical View," *The Reconstructionist*, September 1984, 11–14.

22. Interestingly, Elliot Cosgrove notes that few of the contributors from across the denominational spectrum even mention chosenness, and if they do, it is to dismiss it. *Jewish Theology in Our Time: A New Generation Explores the Foundations and Future of Jewish Belief* (Woodstock, VT: Jewish Lights, 2010).

23. Jonathan Sacks, *The Dignity of Difference: How to Avoid the Clash of Civilizations* (London: Continuum, 2002), 56.

24. Jonathan Sacks, *The Dignity of Difference: How to Avoid the Clash of Civilizations*, rev. ed. (London: Continuum, 2003), 56.

25. Sacks, *The Dignity of Difference*, 59.

26. Sacks, *The Dignity of Difference*, rev. ed., 59.